DANCING WITH THE VOID

S unyata, all through his simple and natural life in the world, danced blissfully in the Void, the No-thing-ness, the Silence in the invisible Real. Out of the Void, the fullness of the universe has paradoxically evolved. Empty of all personalities and all forms, the Void is paradoxically the root of all personalities and all forms. There is no movement or change in it, yet it contains the endless possibility of all movements and all changes. From Void arises everything, from Silence come all sounds, from unconsciousness emanates consciousness, from intangibility arises all tangible things.

DANCING WITH THE VOID

The Innerstandings
of a Rare-born Mystic

SUNYATA

Edited by
BETTY CAMHI AND GURUBAKSH RAI

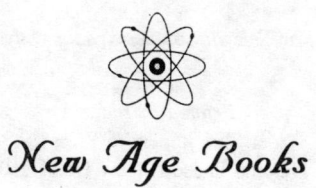

New Age Books

ISBN: 81-7822-134-9

First Indian Edition: Delhi, 2004

First Edition: 2001, USA

(Published by arrangement with Blue Dove Press, USA)

Published by
NEW AGE BOOKS
A-44 Naraina Phase-I
New Delhi-110 028 (INDIA)
Email: nab@vsnl.in
Website: www.newagebooksindia.com

For Sale in Southeast Asia Only

Printed in India
at Shri Jainendra Press
A-45 Naraina Phase-I, New Delhi-110 028

"In this life play I have not been in quest of Guru, God, Truth, Grace, Salvation, Nirvana, or power lust. I had no ambition to be different from what I am. Blessedly, I had escaped headucation, and I was free of any imposed knowledge. I had no property. I did not marry, I did not belong to any cliques or creed. I felt all is within our Self. I had nothing to assert or resent. Nor had I anything to boast about or regret. I was fully contented. I had joy in 'that which is'."

—*Sunyata*

Table of Contents

Preface   ix

A Short Biography   xv

1   Who am I?   3

2   Spiritual Practices   7

3   Pilgrimage to India   11

4   Snow Maiden   19

5   Meeting with Rabindranath Tagore   23

6   In the Light of Tagore's Radiance   27

7   Meeting with Mahatma Gandhi   33

8   Jawaharlal Nehru   43

9   Ramana Maharshi   49

10   Peer A. Wertin (Ramana Giri)   59

11   John Blofeld   65

12   Grecian Lila   77

13   Rudolph Ray   83

14   Passings   89

15   Albert Schweitzer   95

16	Milarepa–Tibet's Great Yogi	101
17	Kabir	111
18	Carl G. Jung	125
19	Mysticism	131
20	Towards the Mysteries	139
21	Sunyata Ever Is	151
22	A Whole Man	157
23	Wholeness	171
24	Gautama Buddha	181
25	Dhammapada	185
26	Suffering	189
27	Awakening	197
28	All is Divine Play	203
29	Eternal Silence	207
30	The One Remains	211
31	There is Only the One	215
32	That Thou Art	217
33	Awareness is All	221
34	Beethoven's Four Quartets	225
35	Who is Wuji?	231
36	The Wisdom of Sunyata	235
	Glossary	265

Preface

How This Book Came to Be

How this book came to be is an amazing story. It is a testimony to the power of grace.

I attended Sunyata's weekly satsang aboard the late Allan Watt's houseboat for the first time in 1978. Instantly I liked this elderly, gentle and wise man. At the end of the meeting I went up to him and asked, "Is there anything you need?" He thought for a moment and then said, "I could use someone to type my scribbles." So I became his typist and he became my Friend.

Sunyata's weekly satsangas became the highlight of my week. I enjoyed listening to the questions and Sunyata's responses to them. A few questions that stand out in my memory are:

> **Question:** *Should we try to relieve suffering in the world by joining organizations set up to help?*
> **Sunyata:** Only if you feel the push or urge from within to do so.
>
> **Q:** *Should we meditate?*
> **S:** Yes, but never force it if you don't feel like it.

> **Q:** *Have you ever had sex?*
> **S:** Only once in my life, as there was no need for it on my part. I did it for the woman's sake, as her fiancé had been killed in the war.
>
> **Q:** *Are your teeth your own?*
> **S:** Who else's would they be?

After listening over a period of several years to these questions and answers, I found myself becoming less interested in the verbal exchange and more interested in the silence and radiance that was emanating from this "rare born mystic." He had a healing Presence. It wasn't until I began to edit the writings in this book that I realized that one of Sunyata's many gifts was the power of healing, described in the chapter "Spiritual Practices." I realized that all of my bodies, physical, mental and emotional, were being healed and for this I am most grateful.

Whatever spare time I had I would spend with Sunyata and with whomever else he happened to be with. It became not only easy, but very pleasant to be with people when Sunyata was there, especially since there was never any disharmony. I would often wish that I could experience this genuine harmony with people more often in everyday life. This harmony never seemed to be anything unusual or extraordinary. What seems extraordinary to me is that the natural joy of being together with people is not present more often. Is it because most of us have what is commonly called a "shadow side," the place where our little demons and unresolved ego issues reside?

Sunyata had no such "shadow side." He simply radiated. Here was someone, "Mr. Nobody," as he was often called, who could walk so lightly as to leave "no footprints in the sand." He was childlike and innocent without being childish.

After Sunyata left his body I felt certain that someone would publish his writing. When one year passed and no one had done it, I felt a prompting from within to do it myself. I approached a friend of Sunyata's and asked for his assistance. He gladly agreed to help. In 1990, in celebration of what would have been Sunyata's 100th birthday, the book, *Sunyata-The Life and Sayings of a Rare Born Mystic*, was published. It was well received. An Indian friend of Sunyata's was visiting family in the United States. He wrote me a letter and later phoned to express appreciation for the book. We had a long conversation and an unusually good rapport. He told me that when Sunyata left India to come to the United States in 1979 he'd entrusted many of his writings with him. After Sunyata's passing, this man began editing these writing for eventual publication, but he needed assistance. Would I help him? Since I had just completed one book and needed a rest, I regretfully declined. I told him that if he wanted to publish a book, he would have to do it himself.

I had been seeing Amritanandamayi Ma, Ammachi or the Holy Mother as she is often called, on her annual trip to her ashram in California, for several years. I would get my hug but never asked any questions. I wondered, after so many years of seeing her, if she even remembered me from year to year. Because I wanted to have some additional contact with her I thought it a good idea to ask her a personal question. All I could think of to ask was about a very small desire I had to go to India. I wrote the question down on a piece of paper and after waiting in the long line of devotees I gave this question to her translator. I received my hug and her translator told me to wait on the sidelines for her response. She looked at me for a moment and then told him, which he translated into English, "Yes, yes, you come to India. Your destiny is to be with Mother." Years later I approached Mother's translator for clarification of the word "destiny." I had taken mother's meaning to be that I would be destined to live for the rest of my life in India. The translator said, "No, Mother's meaning was that it was your destiny only at that time to come to India to be with her." I felt somewhat relieved.

I would never have gone to India if not for this clear indication by Mother. So in December, 1993 I traveled to Mother's ashram in South India. After spending almost one month there, I felt it was time to return to the U. S. Then the thought arose that since my health was good and I still had some money, I could visit Ramana Maharshi's Ashram at the foot of Arunachala Hill. The necessary travel arrangements were made and I arrived there via train in January, 1994. About one day after I arrived I noticed a small group of Indian people talking. I heard the man say that he could read palms. I was instantly drawn to him, hoping that he would read mine. However, when I approached him, he changed from the subject of palm reading and was more interested in learning about me, and what had brought a single woman, a Westerner, to this ashram.

I told him, "I had a guru who spoke very highly of Ramana Maharshi." He replied. "Who was your guru?" (For me, Sunyata was a guru but he never declared himself as one). I was sure he had never heard of him and said, "He was quite unknown." The Indian gentleman insisted on knowing his name. I told him. Upon hearing the name "Sunyata" he said, "But I knew him, he stayed at my house several times." We exchanged names and only then did I realize that this was Gurubaksh Rai, the gentleman who had contacted me to help him edit

Sunyata's writings three years earlier when he was living in the USA.

This was a miraculous moment. Both of us were visiting the ashram for the very first time, me from the USA, and him from his home in Delhi. We had both been entrusted by Sunyata with his writings. We had arrived at Ramanashram almost at the same time. Of all of the guests staying there, I had singled him out. From this unlikely meeting, this book, *Dancing with the Void*, was born.

Betty Camhi, Editor
March 2000

A Short Biography

Sunyata was born on October 27, 1890, on a farm in Arhus, in the north of Denmark. His Danish parents christened him Alfred Julius Emmanuel Sorensen. He was called Emmanuel—an unusual name for a Dane that means "God within." He was their third child, born to them after two daughters—Jensine and Mary—who were 10 and 12 years older. Sunyata's father, Soren Sorensen, was a farmer, fully competent in his profession but simple, quiet and unassuming. He did not interfere in the household affairs. "Although my father was very active in running the farm," wrote Sunyata, "he was singularly quiet and still. He didn't assert himself or fuss in any way. In fact, he rarely spoke except when others approached. So, unconsciously and without effort, he taught silence. And so also did nature and God, around and within me."

Emmanuel's mother, Maren Sorensen, was sociable, friendly and assertive. She managed the household with love and efficiency. Emmanuel grew up in a peaceful, happy home in the quiet environs of the farm. The family lived harmoniously, surrounded by the sprawling farm with its green fields, crops, animals and birds. "Servants and helpers were hired at harvest time, and all lived in harmony, naturalness, and joyous ease."

He completed his early education up to the 8th grade, at the village school. He felt that traditional education caused "mental conditioning," which was for him a hindrance to the flowering of Truth. Sunyata writes, "I consider myself lucky to have escaped all that 'headucation.' I certainly did not wish to suffer it longer than I had to." Emmanuel would add humorously, "But there was then in the last century no sports mania, no technical craze, no rat race, no film stars, no schizophrenia, no psychosis and no world record for suicides like nowadays in the little welfare States."

"From infancy, I was ego-free, desire-free, plan-free and carefree," says Sunyata adding, "intuitively I felt and awared the indwelling Christ consciousness as dimly alive. Neither mind nor ego was developed to be of any trouble during seven or even the first fourteen years of my solitary childhood. In rich solitude, I was on good terms with my "Self"—in nature and everywhere. I experienced harmony, contentment and calm grace awareness all the eternal while."

"The mystic Silence was the satisfying medium. It was the Silence of desire and thought. In the freedom of solitude, God was clearly immanent. God simply was, and it contented me that it was unhidden by ideas, unblurred by words. I did not think of or to God. All was real and simple. In this mystic clarity, there was no effort to explain or to understand the mystery of Being and Becoming, the strange (but utterly harmonious) urges to live and to die. In that childhood unitive mode of experiencing God, the one Life was awared as comprising all the changing forms—in that mode of being."

When Emmanuel was 14, the world he had been living in crashed. His father sold the farm to strangers. The incident made Emmanuel feel uprooted and yet made him feel more deeply at home. "I discovered both my wings and my roots. Later on, although I loved my various homes, I was able to make myself at home everywhere. It was easy for me to be a traveler as I was unattached to any special place or to a particular home. Life was a pilgrimage...."

He successfully completed a four year course in horticulture, a specialized study of growing fruits, vegetables, flowers, shrubs and trees. He served his apprenticeship in Denmark, France and Italy. In 1911, when he was 21, he found a job as a gardener in England, earning his livelihood by working on large estates like Forty Hall, Sunbury Court, Hampton Court and Dartington Hall. He settled down in England and managed nurseries for nearly 20 years. He often worked five days a week, from 6 to 6, as he would say with a chuckle, not from 9 to 5.

Emmanuel used to read books that would resonate with his own inner experiences. He was fond of reading "biographies of saints, mystic poetry and the literary works of well-known authors." He went through Danish classics—Hans Christian Andersen, Henrik Ibsen, Gustav Fridring and Anker Larson. In England, he read the literary works of D.H. Lawrence, Murry, Aldous Huxley, Shelley, Shakespeare, Keats, Wordsworth, Tennyson and Goethe. He also read the Russians: Chekhov, Dostoevsky, Tolstoy, Gorky and Pasternak. All this reading was what Emmanuel called "a process of natural maturing and self experiencing." He never felt any need to attend classes nor to seek out any teacher.

Later in life he was to come into contact with the Eastern writers. His first introduction was to the Theosophists—Colonel Olcott, Annie Besant, Madame Blavatsky and J. Krishnamurti. In the bookshops and the libraries of London, Sunyata found a large number of books on Eastern mysticism including the *Bhagavad Gita*, the *Tao Teh Ching*, and the *I Ching*. By the time Emmanuel was 39, he was fairly familiar with Sufi lore, Theosophy, Buddhism, the *Vedas*, the *Upanishads*, and the Egyptian and the Tibetan Books of the Dead.

Emmanuel developed a special interest in reading the books of India's poet laureate, Rabindranath Tagore. He read the books—*Gitanjali*, *Fruit Gathering* and *The Gardener* and recognized in them "an awareness of kindred values, intuitive insight and integral experience."

Emmanuel actually met the famous poet in the summer of 1929. Tagore came to Dartington Hall in Devonshire to stay for three months. He needed rest and solitude to rejuvenate his energies after a strenuous lecture tour abroad. The Nobel Laureate was finally alone, able to recuperate his health in the calm and quiet environs of majestic Dartington Hall.

Tagore had time to himself in this quiet place. Here he painted, went for walks and conversed with the young gardener. Emmanuel recorded in his notes, "The poet had a charming wistfulness, joy of longing and a pathetic beauty.... He had there the time that, in Europe, is money. He had also the leisure which, in India, is wealth."

The poet often called the simple gardener to his suite, where he would recite some of his favorite poems. "It was a momentous meeting with a living embodiment of Indian tradition and Vedantic wisdom, which I already loved dearly," said Sunyata adding, "The poet had eternity in his eyes and in his Being's rhythm." Emmanuel responded to Tagore's request one day to play Beethoven's last quartet on his gramophone. The poet, a lover of music, was appreciative of Emmanuel's kind gesture to play Beethoven's last quartet for him. He later presented his set of Beethoven's records to Tagore and the mystic poet graciously accepted.

Tagore saw quite a bit of Emmanuel, who was about 40 then. Tagore was so impresssed by Emmanuel's deep, natural silence that he invited him to come to his university, "Shantiniketan," in India to teach Silence to the students there. This invitation from Tagore was destined to become a turning point in Emmanuel's charmed life.

EMMANUEL GOES TO INDIA

In 1930, Emmanuel left England for India in response to Tagore's invitation. During the journey, he carried with him only one book—the *Bhagavad Gita*. He says,"In *Gita*, there is clear consistency of awareness that goes beyond mere intellect and ego. This volume of poetical and philosophical discourses between the soul and the Self has become my constant companion. It is, to me, the grandest and most satisfying of all books."

This was Emmanuel's first world pilgrimage. During his overland trip, he dallied on the way, visiting France, Italy, Greece, Egypt, Palestine, Syria and again Egypt. "It was rejuvenating for me to wander new places and to be among strange faces until they were no longer strange. I was greeted and accepted by total strangers wherever I stayed. What direct recognition I received from lovable common folks and fellow workers in Greece, Arab and Ceylon! They seem to come out, you know, shining through their forms. There was a spontaneous recognition and free acceptance of my love. Words or lack of words did not matter."

Sunyata writes, "The Sphinx of Giza is the earliest object that Egypt has created by the Red Race. It has become her centuries' most important symbol and emblem. It was created by the ancient wisdom religion as a picture of the seemingly calm and coordinated nature, its paradoxes and its dangerous secret—a bull torso with a human head, lion feet and eagle wings. In

this unity of the four parts are hidden the four elements—water, earth, air and fire—which are the basis of
occult science. Before Oedipus, Solon and Socrates, the
Red Race knew that the riddle of Sphinx is *man*: Man,
know thyself in conscious awareness, in intuitive fullness
and grace. The Red Race has left no proof of its existence other than the Sphinx of Giza, but it has in it
proved that a great problem had been stated and, in a
way, solved."

From Port Said in Egypt, he traveled by boat to
Colombo, Ceylon (now Sri Lanka), later arriving in India.

SHANTINIKETAN

After a long journey by train and seeing the sights
of Rameshwaram, Madurai, Madras and Calcutta,
Emmanuel arrived in Shantiniketan—Tagore's "abode of
peace"—a new university established by him in accordance with his own ideals. It was a surprise to Tagore to
see Emmanuel, as he had not sent any prior notice of his
arrival. Tagore then recalled meeting him in Dartington
Hall and immediately issued instructions to put him up
as his personal guest in the spacious guest house. There
were many other distinguished persons already staying
there: Lama Govinda, Mrs. Haberman, Charles F.
Andrew, Elizabeth Bruner and Ma Bruner (Hungarian
artists), Arya Nikam, Asha Devi, Amiya Chakravarty
and Anna Ornshort. Lama Govinda was to become a
lifelong friend. Another strong friendship was formed
with Anna Ornshort, who came from his own country,
Denmark. She had been working for 10 years as secretary to Sir Jagdish Bose (1858–1937), India's scientist of
international renown.

He lived with Tagore at Shantiniketan. During the
summer, when the heat was unbearable, he stayed at
Tagore's summer residence in Darjeeling up in the

Himalayas. He said, "I am profoundly grateful for Gurudev's [Tagore's] recognition, inspiration and evocative *karuna* (compassionate) love. This empathy in karuna experiencing gives a new dimension to my conscious self awareness in integral living."

When it was cool in October, Emmanuel left on a month's tour to Burma. He journeyed to Bamo by the Chinese border on the river Irrawadi. Returning to Shantiniketan after his trip to Burma, the poet asked him to stay on as his personal guest for an indefinite period. Emmanuel accepted. He could now see Tagore daily in his own setting. He wrote, "It feels good to be close to the poet's radiance.... Our poet looks a regal, ripe and cultured soul.... There is eternity in his eyes and the dignity of Man in his inner, integral rhythm." Emmanuel was also free to travel around the country visiting ashrams and meeting *sadhus* (wandering monks), swamis and saints adept in Hindu and Buddhist culture.

SUNYATA'S INITIATIONS

In the summer of 1932, Emmanuel was a guest of the famous plant physiologist and physicist Sir Jagdish Chandra Bose (1858–1937) in Darjeeling, where he was initiated into Dhyan Buddhism (like Zen and Chan, the principle practice is meditation). The new name given to him was Mani Dharma. In fact, during the course of his life, he experienced a number of initiations. He writes, "A very salutary initiation occurred in 1904. A still more mature one at Dartington Hall in 1929–30 in the august presence of Dorothy and Rabindranath Tagore. It had a certain inner validity or authenticity, which set a Viking free to move homeward to the Sun in Sun-ya-ta and to be richly at Home." Nothing further is known about these initiations. Wise Sri Yashoda Ma once said to him, "I would give you *diksha* (initiation), Suren (Sorensen), if you were to ask. I know you will never need to ask."

"In Beas and Baghdad, Bethlehem and Ballyganj," says Sunyata,"I was pushed into initiations by terrible, well meaning *chelas* (disciples). It was in 1932 in Sir Jagdish and Lady Bose's home that I was first initiated into Dhyan Buddhism and named Mani Dharma. In 1936, Sri Ramana Maharshi superimposed Sri Sunyata."

In the same year, Emmanuel visited Mathura and Brindavan, the home of Krishna, the avatar of the Bhagavad Gita. Said Sunyata, "I have visited Mathura and Brindaban—places so intimately associated with Krishna, the eternal child, Krishna, the youth, who throughout the centuries has played the children of men into the bliss of pure love, the rhythmic joy of creativeness and of spiritual awareness. Krishna, the charioteer, has been the constant companion of my pilgrimage, and so I have never felt lonely or poor."

Emmanuel remained in India for two years instead of adhering to the original plan of three months. He went back to England in 1933 only to wind up his affairs, and returned in October of 1933 to live there for another 45 years. He was then a mature 43.

"India is a continent embracing all climes and religions, almost all physical features of the larger world," he said, adding,"describe or try to reveal India in one term or in one truth and lo! the exact opposite may also be true. We have the highest peaks and the lowest depths within and around. Somehow we have also, in intuitive synthesis, all the manifestations, paradoxes and contrasts which they encompass. One meaningful and perfect Life informs them all. The mature ego-free soul naturally learns to accept and to enjoy the changeless Life in all phenomena and to livingly know the Self in the endless *Lila* (play of the universe)."

Discarding European dress altogether, Emmanuel now completely switched to the traditional clothing of an

Indian *sadhu*. In the very first meeting with Anandamayee Ma (a highly respected saint made famous by Paramahansa Yogananda in *Autobiography of a Yogi*), she recognized Sunyata and gave him ochre clothes to wear. Yashoda Ma (guru of Krishna Prem a.k.a Richard Nixon) also gave him robes in ochre and Buddhist hues.

Says Emmanuel, "With her pure unpossessive love, Sri Yashoda Ma gave me robes in saffron and Buddhist hues. Sri Anandamayee Ma has also given her *Bhaiji* (brother) yellow robes. Other holinesses have sent me the real garments of orange and gold from Burma and Nepal." He visited with Anandamayi Ma and Yashoda Ma many times.

CLOSENESS TO NEHRU FAMILY

It was through Tagore that Emmanuel came to meet with Jawaharlal Nehru, one of the most popular leaders of the independence movement in India at that time (and who later became the prime minister of India). Emmanuel frequently visited Nehru's home as his guest in the early 1930's.

In 1934, Emmanuel accepted an offer by the Nehru family to stay at their newly purchased estate, "Khali," near Binsar, about 10 miles from Almora. He writes, "The Jawaharlal Nehru family had just bought an estate, Khali, near that mountain city, and offered me this as home and playground. I helped Ranjit and Vijaya Lakshmi Pandit (Nehru's sister and her husband) with the planting of fruit trees, corn and vegetables, and attending the hydraulic ram. During that time, the Pandits and Jawaharlalji were often in prison, resting or writing books. Ranjit translated Kalidas from Sanskrit into English, but prison life broke down his physical health and he left us early."

Emmanuel made the Khali estate of the Nehrus his new home. He worked voluntarily as caretaker and looked after the sprawling lawns with his horticultural skills. As he was a friend of the Nehru's and not an employee, he was free to continue his travels to the plains in the winter.

A glimpse of Sunyata's love of travel can be had from one of his journal entries:

> Soon I pass on to the caves of Ajanta and Ellora; to the Venice of India—Udaipur—and other marble cities of Rajputana (now Rajasthan), famed for beauty, bravery and chivalry. Then onwards to pay homage to Taj Mahal, to Krishna at Mathura and to Satyanand (Samuel) Stokes, 50 miles beyond Simla. In November, I am due at holy Benares (now Varanasi) with Malviya, on the holy Ganga Ma, with Bhagwan Das and with Chakrawarti Mataji (Yashoda Ma) and Krishna Prem, also near the Ganges. Later, I go to Gorakhpur and the Nirvana Stupa and Kushanagar where Gautama Buddha left his old body and to Lumbini in Nepal where he took birth. Thence to Kumbha Mela at Allahabad and to the Himalayan Khali estate to greet the snow and to fold my wings for a while, preparing a place for Jawaharlal Nehru and Kamla, who may be glad of a rest and respite from prisons and from the wilderness of European civilization.

It was at the Khali estate managed by him that he came to know more about Almora and its environs. Located about 250 miles northeast of Delhi, about 6,000 feet above sea level, Almora commands breathtaking views of the Himalayas with their snowclad peaks and lush, green, thick, calm and unravaged forests. It is close to the borders of Tibet and Nepal. Mahatma Gandhi, who stayed there for three weeks in 1936, wrote, "In these hills, Nature's hospitality eclipses all man can ever do. The enchanting beauties of the Himalayas, their bracing climate and the soothing green that envelops you, leaves nothing to be desired. I wonder whether the security of these hills and the climate are to be surpassed if equaled by any of the beauty spots of the world. After having been nearly three weeks in Almora hills, I am more than ever amazed why our people need go to Europe in search of health."

Emmanuel's close association with the Nehrus— Jawaharlal Nehru, his wife Kamla Nehru (who was alive then) and their only daughter Indira (who was in her teens); Nehru's sister Vijaya Lakshmi Pandit, her husband Ranjit Sitaram Pandit and their three daughters, Chanderlekha, Tara and Rita—resulted in a growing circle of contacts. Here Emmanuel came in touch with the Anglo Indian philanthropist E.T. Thompson, who owned a big estate at the Kalimath ridge in Almora. Eager to help him, Thompson offered Emmanuel a portion of his estate, which was picturesquely located. This generous offer was accepted by Emmanuel as a God sent opportunity. He could now fold his wings and grow roots.

Asked why he chose the Himalayas as his permanent abode, Emmanuel replied, "The Lord in the Gita says, 'Amongst the mountains, I am the Himalayas.' In Himalayan India, there is serene leisure to think and to contemplate and to go beyond thought, time and ego fuss. *Uttar* means North and Himalaya is the northern crown of India. Uttar is also called the throne of the gods. It is a special abode of Siva and Vishnu, *rishis*, sages, Sufis, silent *sadhus* and singing *paramahansa* swans. Mature mystics have wandered and dwelt here.

Many respectable extroverts from the middle to the far west come here and become simple and natural and they cultivate the grace of Silence.

"I was contented in Denmark though I could see that others regarded me as an oddity. In England, I felt freer. In India, I felt at home. But in Himalaya, I feel closest to heaven."

MEETING RAMANA MAHARSHI

In India, Sunyata was interested in meeting those mature souls who radiated spirituality. He was less interested in "semantic muddles, senti- or supra-mental wallowing in sticky concepts and glittering word symbols." Of all these great souls, he found the *darshan* of Ramana Maharshi to be one of his life's richest experiences. Emmanuel first heard of Ramana Maharshi from Lama Chow Chuji in Kashmir in 1935. He also read Paul Brunton's well known book *A Search in Secret India*, in which a detailed description of Ramana Maharshi and his ashram in Tiruvanamalai was given. Emmanuel's neighbor in Kalimaths' Ridge, Dr. W.Y. Evans Wentz, celebrated translator of the *Tibetan Book of the Dead*, gave Sunyata first hand information about the Maharshi.

During the years between 1936 and 1946, Emmanuel made four trips to Tiruvanamalai, staying for a few weeks each time within the bodily radiance of Ramana Maharshi. The first visit in 1936 was for two weeks. Here he met Paul Brunton (1898–1981), with whom Sunyata had hitherto been in contact only through correspondence. During his stay, Sunyata had *darshan* of Maharshi every day but never once did he ask any question. He would sit quietly in the back of the room. After he left the ashram, Maharshi told Paul Brunton that Emmanuel was a "rare born mystic." This remark of Ramana Maharshi about Emmanuel was quickly conveyed to him in a letter by Paul Brunton. Emmanuel's response to this remark was, "This seems to us enough recognition and grace for one lifetime." Emmanuel, who did not undergo much formal education, or what he preferred to call "headuction," said the mere presence of Ramana Maharshi in silence gave him much. Maharshi was, to him, "the *advaita* experience, whose chief language is radiant silence."

During his second visit to the Maharshi's ashram in 1938, Emmanuel was, as usual, quiet and left the ashram after a fortnight's stay. At a later *darshan* during his third visit in 1940, Emmanuel discerned a special radiance from the Maharshi directed toward him. "Ramana Maharshi did not give initiation in any ritualistic or orthodox form but he did transmit it by a look or in silence." Emmanuel continues, "Then, suddenly, out of the pure *akasha* and the living Silence, there sounded upon Emmanuel these five words, 'We are always aware, Sunyata!'"

So profound was the influence of the words "We are always aware, Sunyata" that Emmanuel had received telepathically from the Maharshi, that he took these as mantra, initiation and name. Since then, Emmanuel has used the name Sunya or Sunyata to refer to himself. In India, he now came to be known as "Sunyaji" or "Sunya baba" or "Sunyata." He was also addressed by other names such as "Sadhu Baba," "Sant Baba," "Sohan Singh," "Swamiji" and "Mahatmaji," but the names Sunyaji and Sunyata were most commonly used. Some did call him by his first name Alfred (as did Nehru and his family). His foster mother, Yashoda Ma, always called him Sorensen.

After leaving England and arriving in India, Sunyata never had to earn his living. Everything that was needed was simply given to him. Indians invariably extend warm hospitality, especially to ascetics, who are regarded in the highest esteem. It is the duty of house-holders to look after the needs of ascetics or seekers on the spiritual path.

It FALLS DOWN LIKE MANNA!

Sunyata did not marry. He had no possessions. He did not entertain any ambition. He did not join any exclusive religion. He said, "I have escaped 'education,' 'property,' 'marriage,' 'power,' 'ambition'—and 'special belonging' to any exclusive religion, association, organization, or society. I belong to the whole." Since Sunyata was now a full fledged ascetic, a *sadhu* in his lifestyle, it was possible for him to live completely carefree and independent. People accepted him as one of their own and graciously offered him money for his daily needs. Sunyata accepted only the bare minimum, just enough to meet his immediate needs. On money, he said, "If you don't chase it, then it chases you." Sunyata said, "I never had to worry for money in India.... It just falls down like manna. In India, the values are very different."

Sunyata embraced all that was best in Indian spirituality. Indians revered him as a saint, a baba or a *sadhu*. His reputation as a saint of high standing spread throughout the country. "My chief Viking assets were simplicity, adaptability, a certain intuitive light and a patient acceptance of the truth revealed in Vedantic lore. I had a passive uncritical attitude and the inwardness, the rich sahaj solitude," he said.

Sunyata's virtues of humility, simplicity and love charmed a large number of intellectuals, professors, politicians, ambassadors, rajas, holinesses and even military commanders. "They happened upon me and I could respond to my Self in all—even to millionaires like Birla and Jamnalal Bajaj; to *rishis* like Ramana Maharshi, Anandamaya Ma, Yashoda Ma, Neem Karoli Baba,

Swami Ramdas and many others, as also to rajas of princely states like Tehri, Aundh, Sivpuri, Kashipur and Ramgarh."

Recalling his numerous visits to the ashrams, Sunyata observes, "And with their *acharyas*, would-be holinesses and willful *shakti* business, I would be freely accepted as one of them. I would glide in and out of their company freely, without much effort, and sink into the light and the rhythm of this group or that. I fully comprehended their movements, their motives, their values, their maturity and their rightness in the joyous *jijimuge*—the *maya lila* shadow interplay."

In 1950, the Birla Foundation in India, established to provide grants to meet the minimum needs of *sadhus* (monks) engaged in spiritual pursuits, once offered Sunyata a lifetime grant of 100 rupees per month (that was equal to about $25 in those days). Sunyata accepted half that amount, saying that it would be enough. When prices rose with heavy inflation, Sunyata never asked for more.

Anandamayee Ma and Yashoda Ma

In 1937, Anandamayee Ma visited Sunyata's newly established dwelling in Kalimaths' Ridge in Almora on her pilgrimage to Mt. Kailash. She blessed his abode and then continued on her pilgrimage. Sunyata also had her *darshan* at Kishanpur, Kashi, Pit Kutir, Brindavan and Almora. About Anandamayee Ma, Sunyata wrote in his notes: "Anandamayee Ma is a simple village maiden and yet she embodies a culture, the fringe of which is never touched by the highly cultured people. She is practically illiterate, yet she is the repository of all wisdom. She never received formal initiation from any external Guru but was ego freely cultivated in natural spirituality."

On his experience of *samadhi* at the Kashipur

ashram, Sunyata wrote, "I remember how at Kashipur ashram, Ma Anandamayee expressly asked me to enter her silence room for meditation. I did. It was a *shunya darshan*—a relief like death."

Sunyata recorded his association with Sri Yashoda Ma, whom he called his foster mother. She had an ashram near Almora. Recalling a memorable experience he had in Brindavan in association with the two mothers, Sunyata wrote: "I remember a Himalayan silence—brief but eternal—in the *uttar* (north) Brindavan ashram. I happened to be with my foster mother Sri Yashoda Ma. It was there that Anandamayee and party stopped to greet the bodily invalid Sri Yashoda Ma, who was whole and free in the unitive life of *Advait* conscious awareness. It was marvelous to sense and aware the two Himalayan mothers together...and still more marvelous to be requested to stay on in the room, where the two mothers, "not two" were otherwise alone together. On this occasion, there was inner silence for half an hour. The *shunya* silence is eternally here and now. The silence at uttara Brindavan is one of my richest Himalayan experiences."

SUNYATA'S HUT IN ALMORA

Sunyata had the spare, wiry body of a man who lived just about as simply as it is possible to live. He lived in a little one room cottage which he built himself at his site on the Kalimaths' Ridge. Here he kept a small collection of books, an old gramophone and a few records, which included Ludwig Beethoven's four quartets. Often, when the sun had left all but the highest cliff of ice and the indigo came darkening up out of Nepal, Sunyata sat on the ridge and let the mystery and majesty of creation envelop him in silence.

The small room he built for his personal living was

surrounded by a secluded, spacious garden of flowering shrubs, mimosa and blossoming trees at the Kalimath ridge. It was roughly 12' by 12' with a low ceiling. Some photos of saints hung on the walls. There was a heap of books against one wall. The only furniture in the room was a worn-out wooden couch covered with a simple long cushion, an old armchair and three upturned wooden boxes—that's all.

Two or three other stone huts were later built by him on the lower slopes of his site. He accommodated his visitors in these huts. As there were then no arrangements for water supply by the local municipality to his cottage, Sunyata used to go down to a well to fetch water. The well was about half a mile's descent on a mountain trail. For washing, he made his own arrangements to collect rainwater and store it in his own self constructed tanks. His guests, if any, would get up in the morning, make a fire, prepare tea and sit in the sun for a while or do whatever they liked—meditating, reading, having tea, walking, or simply viewing the distant snowy peaks and diving deep into the scenic beauty.

From Sunyata's notes:

> Below is the Almora town, recently electrified. It is a sea of light in the surrounding dark hills. I rest awhile under the pine trees on the top of the cave. When I awoke, the 'morrow' had come from somewhere and was 'today' and with it came the thoughts of body needs and daily bread. Take no thought for tomorrow, say the lilies and the birds. But today I have to get water from the well, and flour, dal and vegetables from the village far below my cave.
>
> Natural activities and *dharmic* tasks are part of my constant contemplation, all accep-

tance and unity awareness. I get good contemplation when I walk in nature and when I
write at 3 or 4 a.m. in bed. I also get it when
I build and repair 5 or 6 small huts. Yes, food-
fuss and cave-cleaning can be a nuisance. I am
on good terms with dust! The sun and the
pure air disinfect. Emmanuel's body has not
seen a doctor here. I enjoy my walks during
which I induce good contemplation. Of food,
one needs very little when one lives harmoniously. One should eat slowly and masticate
well. A day of food fast can make a virtue of
necessity when provision is short or when one
is traveling. If one takes *satvic* food, one does
not expand or waste much. It is good to do
deep breathing in pure air. All this is nourishing for harmonious growth.

I keep my body fit and flexible in activities such as building huts, caves, cottages and
water tanks. This is natural 'yogic skill in
action,' without any rigorous *tapas* (ascetic
practices) or special yogic discipline.

Sunyata walked up and down a steep hill three or
four times a week between his home and the Almora
town, a distance of about four miles. Almora was 1,000
ft. down the hill. It took about two hours to walk all the
way— descent and ascent. Sunyata's body was strong
and agile even in his 80s. He did not feel any strain. The
walk was easy for him, as there was plentiful youthful
energy bubbling up in his young old body. He needed
only a little food. He writes:

I live on what happens to be available and
what comes to me. I feel that I am near heav-
en. There is vital nourishment in the pure

ether and the blue space around. I do not ask anything from anybody but I may accept whatever is offered for my needs in the right spirit. In Himalayan solitude, one does not think or talk about any ailments, dis-eases or ego woes. Within me, there are no sin complexes, frustrations or grievance complexes.

SUNYATA'S PRIVATE CAVE ON THE HILL

There were not only Sunyata's stone cottages on the ridge, but also a private place higher up. It used to be a cave under a tree. The back of the cave was on the rocks. The front was constructed by Sunyata. It contained two doors and a window. Inside was a fireplace with a chimney and a water kettle in it. A cot was the only piece of furniture. From the roof of the cave one could glimpse a panoramic view of the Himalayan peaks and sense the silence of the ridge and the steep valleys. One could also listen to the eternal music of the pine trees. This cave was used by him as an alternate dwelling. It was truly a place of undisturbed contemplation. There were not only colorful flowers at its door but also bright, scuttling lizards and birds. The singing mynah, the crow, came at breakfast time. The long tailed Himalayan magpie and the woodpecker tupping like a typewriter were also regular visitors. High up under the dark blue thunderclouds, one could sometimes spot snowy vultures.

Now and then, herdsmen came down the long track from Tibet or elsewhere. They brought their sheep, laden with borax and salt. At a great distance in that still air, one could hear the tinkling of a mule bell or the song of a grass-cutter. A rare note of the bell could also be heard at the little Kali shrine on top of the next hill. The evenings came. Sunyata was at peace. He scribbles: "Darkness enfolds us but the star suns radiate silently.

The planets seem to wink at us. I climb up to the cave around the big pine trees. The moon has appeared. Its light reveals the snowy summits hundreds of miles away."

CRANKS' RIDGE

Locals called it "Cranks' Ridge," although its real name was Kalimath Ridge, so named after the goddess Kali. Locals wondered why so many foreigners had gathered there, each living his own unique lifestyle. "What are a bunch of cranks doing here?" they wondered. The foreigners in and around Kalimaths' Ridge were mostly mature folks who were living the spiritual paths they had chosen.

Emmanuel had found a magnificient place to live in this region of powerful energy which attracted so many spiritual aspirants. Some of the more prominent residents from abroad were Evans W. Wentz, Lama Govinda (Ernest Hoffman), author of the *Way of the White Clouds* and *Foundation of Tibetan Buddhism*; Krishna Prem, Earl Brewster, an English painter; and John Blofeld, a Buddhist and Taoist scholar and author of *The Wheel of Life* and many other books. Sunyata epitomizes them in one of his pastorales: "The inmates in and around the ridge lead solitary lives. They are friendly but are inclined to avoid social mix up. Attuned to silence, they do not favor listening to the radio. They study Sanskrit, yoga, abstract painting and indulge in other spiritual pursuits."

Some of Sunyata's neighbors lived and died here. Apart from these Himalayan neighbors, many other foreigners came to Almora to stay with Sunyata in his abode, Turiya Niwas (the name he gave is dwelling), as his guests.

Hippies in Almora

In the 1960's, a great many hippies settled on Kalimath ridge. Some of them liked Sunyata and stayed with him in the two extra huts he had near his dwelling. One of them was Alan Marlowe, an American who maintained a correspondence with him from a Zen monastery in Carmel Valley. The well known hippie luminary, Timothy Leary, also came and stayed at the guest house called Tibetan View Estate run by a Tibetan family. Sunyata was away when Leary made his appearance in Almora.

Ralph Metzner also visited at that time. He provided Lama Govinda with his first and only acid trip as an experiment to see how it affected his consciousness. Lama Govinda, according to Sunyata, took the dose only to put it down. Sunyata said, "There is obviously no use taking it if you're not prepared to let go. People taking drugs fluctuate so much. The heightened consciousness is temporary. It is not abiding. I know many hippies who used to take drugs. Hashish has been used for thousands of years. It may be useful for many things but the fact remains that taking drugs is like playing with electric wires." For the most part, Sunyata was not in favor of this method of altering consciousness but he did say, "Drugs can give a glimpse of another reality."

Wuti

During his stay in Almora, Sunyata often had a pet dog, four of them that he kept at different times. The first was eaten by a leopard. Another one, named Wuti, would go to a butcher's shop and sit outside with his paws pressed together—a gesture of *namaste*—which was very hard for the butcher to refuse. Wuti was very well fed. Sunyata says, "Wuti became famous in Almora. Much more famous than I. I was a nobody. In fact, people started calling me 'The Dog *Sadhu*,' because there were so many *sadhus* in that part of the Himalayas and you needed to sort them out.

"After 10 years, Wuti was poisoned. It was one of those drug pushers who called themselves 'hippie heads.' There were a large number of them in the 1960s who came for the drugs and who committed crimes against the Himalayan silence, including rape and murder. The hippies had chosen to live in a house not far from mine and one day on a trip into the village, I noticed Wuti mooching about inside that fellow's door. Wuti must have found something very delectable there, for I had to call him away three times before he would come. By the time we reached Almora, I could tell he was poisoned. He vomited, cramped and shook. I carried him in my arms to the veterinarian's office, who was away and had to be sent for. He returned in quarter of an hour, but by then, Wuti had died. I carried him back to our hut where I buried him. It was his time to go, and so he went." Sunyata later changed Wuti's name to Wuji, adding "ji" as a sign of respect. After the dog's demise, Sunyata began using the name Wuji when referring to his own higher Self.

Sunyata's Word Symbols

Sunyata often used the words "ego-free," "time-free," "death-free," "age-free," etc., rather than "egoless," "timeless," "deathless," "and ageless," which are so common in ordinary language. The meaning he was trying to convey is that of being free *in* ego, free *in* time, free *in* death. He uses the word *in* and not *of* or *from*, which means the Self can be free *in* ego and not free *from* or *of* ego.

His other favorite expressions were "joyous ease," "delightful uncertainty," "affectionate detachment," and "innerstanding." "My term symbols such as innerstanding and mind freeness are not scholarly" he elucidates, adding, "but a simple carefree fool can play in words and can step immunely where angels and erudition fear to tread." For him, the word innerstand was a better substitute for the word understand as, for him, it went deeper, beyond the mental. He imagined that the word innerstand would one day be incorporated into the English dictionary.

VISITS TO DENMARK & EUROPE: 1964, 1970

In 1964, Sunyata visited his family and friends in Denmark after 34 years stay in India. A number of parties were hosted by his friends and admirers upon his arrival. At one of them he met Prince Peter of Greece and his wife. Sunyata, as usual, was dressed in a brown homespun llama robe and a turban wrapped around his head. He looked like an Indian wizard and quickly became the center of attention.

Sunyata also encountered a delightful older couple—Elizabeth Ratel, a Dane, and her husband, a Frenchman with Buddhist leanings. The Ratels invited him to visit France and to stay with them at their "Hill Farm" in the south of France. Sunyata accepted their invitation and visited them some weeks later. He stayed there for a fortnight before returning to India.

Six years later (1970), Sunyata once again left India for Denmark, this time to see his 92 year-old sister, who was lying critically ill in a hospital. During this visit, Sunyata attracted the attention of the media and some articles on him and his life in India appeared in the local papers in Copenhagen. After staying in Denmark for several weeks, Sunyata again made a visit to France on his way back to India, where he happily stayed with the Ratels for two more weeks.

SUNYATA VISITS THE USA

In 1973, a group of yankee "guys" and "girlies" from the Alan Watts Society met Sunyata at his Turiya Niwas in Almora and were impressed by what they found. They wanted him to come to the USA, to which he replied, "But I have nothing to teach and nothing to sell."

"That's why we want you," came the reply. In October of 1974, Sunyata agreed to fly to the USA on a four month sponsored visit as a guest of the Alan Watts Society, visiting California (Zen Center, Green Gulch, a sunny and sheltered hut in Druid Heights, and Palm Springs), Vancouver, Canada, Chicago and Buffalo, New York. He returned to India in early February, 1975. In 1978 the Alan Watts Society again arranged for him to come to the United States, this time for good, to live permanently in California as their guest. He was 88 years young.

Alan Watts' old houseboat, the S. S. Vallejo in Sausalito, became the center of Sunyata's weekly satsang. He would answer questions from a small group of people every Tuesday evening. Bill Keeler of the Alan Watts Society has preserved a number of taped recordings of the questions and answers from these meetings. A few extracts from his talk of June 2, 1982 (questions from the audience and replies by Sunyata), are given below:

> **Question:** *Why are you here?*
> **Sunyata:** Because the Alan Watts Society financed me here.

Q: *Why did you do that? What would you teach?*
S: I told them that I had nothing to teach and they said, "That's why we want you." Aha! How nice! So I am the Silence behind all this noise.

Q: *Did you want to come to America?*
S: I had no wish to go anywhere. The body was 84 and perfectly fulfilled, content that I would go to heaven rather than America. Utter contrast. It had to happen. I accepted it. I knew it could be done because they had financed Lama Govinda several times here. Bob Shapiro wrote saying, "Reality wise, Sunyaji doesn't need to do anything." That's why I'm here—to do nothing.

Q: *How did you get on in India?*
S: My utter simplicity was an asset there. And my adaptability. I could be at home anywhere.

Q: *How did you come to choose India to live?*
S: I didn't choose India. India chose me. Tagore invited me to "come to India to teach Silence." And now I come here to America to do nothing. Look at that. Poetic. Tagore felt that Silence. That Silence is a kind of reality to me. It was there in my childhood. It's not the Silence of sound but really the Silence of desire, willfulness, craving, fear.

When I came to Shantiniketan a year later, Tagore had forgotten about this simple fellow. When I'd been there for a week or two in the guesthouse, they put me in the long guesthouse, where people lived who were staying for a long time. And there I met Lama Govinda and his mother, C.F. Andrews, and many others. Then the heat came and I can't stand the heat even now. So I went to Darjeeling. Tagore had a house there and the first monsoon I spent there. Then I went to Burma for one month. Coming back from Burma, I went to Shantiniketan. There I met two Quakers who gave me letters of introduction to Indian people. I never made any plans. The Plan is there and I fit in, with joyous ease and delightful uncertainty!

Q: *How did you come to this Silence?*
S: I was born so. And that was what the great sage in South India [Ramana Maharshi] said of me—"a rare-born mystic." I didn't know what "mystic" was. I mean, what Ramana Maharshi meant by it. I built my hut in the Himalayas and lived there in solitude and quietness. I had no expression. No language to express it. Then the language grew up in letters to friends.

Every year in April, Sunyata would go to Chicago to give *darshan* to another group of seekers at Jungian psychiatrist Dr. Arvind Vasavada's home. Sunyata used to wear a big blue badge with the name "Mr. Nobody"

boldly inscribed on it. He loved the badge and would occasionally lift his shawl to display it with gusto.

Sunyata lived in Mill Valley until 1982, but later moved to William Pat Patterson's house in San Anselmo. In July, 1984, Sunyata again moved into a new house bought for him in Fairfax by Lottie Rose. Even at the advanced age of 93, he was agile and full of youthful vigor. Who knew that Sunyata would meet with an accident only a month later, on August 5, at a street crossing in Fairfax, California? The police report said that Sunyata was at the corner of Azalea Avenue and Sir Francis Drake Boulevard. A 1972 Toyota going at a speed of 30 miles an hour approached from the west, hitting Sunyata as he stepped into the pedestrian crossing. The driver, a young woman, slammed on the brakes, her car skidded and hit him into the oncoming lane of traffic. The police removed him to the nearby Ross Valley Hospital. The femur bone in his left leg was broken and fatty deposits entered his bloodstream. Sunyata's body went into a coma at midnight from which it never recovered, despite all efforts to save him. Eight days after the accident, Sunyata finally left his body at 9:27 a.m. on Monday, August 13, 1984. Autopsy of his body revealed all his tools were functioning fine, the same as a healthy man of 50 years. But for this unfortunate accident, Sunyata might easily have lived many more years.

For Sunyata, it was the triumphant end of his earthly journey. He finally went home where he always was.

Jawaharlal Nehru's daughter, Indira Gandhi, knew Sunyata while he lived in Almora. She had been prime minister of India since 1967 and, except for three years' break (1977–79), continued as prime minister until she was assassinated in New Delhi by a fanatic Sikh on October 31, 1984. It was a coincidence that Sunyata died the same year, only ten weeks before Indira Gandhi's assassination. On being informed by Dr. Ved

Prakash Khanna, an old friend of Sunyata's and chairman of the Sunyata Memorial Society in Almora, that Sunyata had died in a car accident in the USA, Prime Minister Indira Gandhi wrote the following letter, dated September 23, 1984, addressed to Dr. Khanna:

> It is good of you to let me know of Sunyata's accident and passing away.
>
> I met him first in the mid thirties, drawn by the notices asking for silence, which indicated the approach to his abode. He kept in touch during my stay in Almora and later was a regular winter visitor to my father's house in Delhi. Afterwards, I did not see much of him, though he did drop in a few times and often wrote.
>
> We had some interesting talks but perhaps I was not ready for his message. And, I must confess, I did not always understand what he wrote. Why did he call himself Wu? When he stopped coming or writing, I did not realize that he had gone to the USA. I regret that I could not benefit more from our acquaintance.
>
> His detachment was obvious and he felt at peace with himself and his surroundings. He proved that in matters of the spirit there can be no boundaries of any kind. It is apt that his ashes should rest in Almora. My thoughts will be with you on that day. It is sad that he is no longer in the body with us."

Sunyata's writings passed on

A few months before his departure for the USA in 1978, Sunyata visited Chandigarh, India, where I was then living with my family. He honored us by staying with us as our guest for ten days.

In the evenings, fifteen to twenty people would show up at our place to have his *darshan*. Sunyata was simple, unassuming, humble and easily accessible. He would give proper and convincing answers to the questions asked by seekers. His radiant, silent presence was enough to dispel any doubts they had.

Sunyata ate whatever was served to him. He did not show a preference for any special kind of food. Whatever food was normally cooked in a devotee's kitchen was acceptable. He liked Indian food and he ate it with his hands.

After Sunyata left Chandigarh, just prior to his trip to the USA, he sent me a small bundle of his selected writings from Almora. Going through these, I found them immensely inspiring and profoundly expressive, with an intuitive wisdom. Later, I met him twice in the USA— first, in early 1981 at his residence in Mill Valley and second, in May of 1982 at his residence in San Anselmo. We talked about his writings stored with me. Smilingly, he told me to do whatever I wanted to do with his work. Saying this, he handed me over a few more pages. This book is primarily edited and excerpted from these early works, with a few additions from later writing.

Gurubaksh Rai
March, 2000

Dancing
with Void
the

Editors' Note

Most of the essays in this book were written by Sunyata during the 48 years he lived in India (1930–1978), prior to his coming to the United States in 1978.

In Sunyata's original writings (and speech) he never used the words "I", "me", or "mine", when referring to himself. The editors have taken the liberty of changing the word "we" to "I" or "me" and the word "our" to "mine" when these words appear in the text.

Other changes have been to increase clarity and readability, leaving intact basic structure and context.

Definitions of Hindu terms used by Sunyata are given in the glossary.

1 🌿

Who am I?

I took human peasant birth in Jutland (Denmark). After a lovely solitary childhood in harmonious nature, I learned horticulture. As a simple gardener, I happily earned my livelihood for 20 years in various European countries. It was India's Poet Laureate Rabindranath Tagore who, during his stay at Dartington Hall, Devonshire (England), invited me to come to India. I arrived in India in 1930. After five years of constant travel in India, Burma and Ceylon, I have now been joyously settled in the Himalayan rich solitude, least lonely or lonesome when freely alone. I have built my simple abode, and call it a cave or a palace, according to mood.

In the *sahaja* [unity consciousness] sense, I seem to have happily died in Europe and was not in conscious search or quest of psychic healing or ease in the fabulous, esoteric and "spiritual East." Yet I was objectively interested in Indian culture and its cults, in the simplicity of Vedantic lore and in the simple, intuitive way of the so called Far East. I was chiefly interested in how life is lived in actuality rather than in theory, dogma, doctrine, ideal or perennial philosophy. Paradoxes and poetry

were easily digested and enjoyed. My mind did not spe-
cially usurp—and I had no ax to grind nor any urge to
assert. My chief Viking assets were simplicity, adaptability and a passive uncritical attitude. I was happily
blessed with the inwardness of rich *sahaja* solitude.

So, I could easily glide into the various *ashrams*,
institutions, and organizations—and was freely welcomed by their *acharyas* and would-be "holinesses" in
their willful *shakti* business. I could freely adjust into the
light and the rhythm of this group or that. By simple
identity, I could sense the values, the strength and the
Silence in these bubblings or stiffened life forces.

I had not been in conscious search of the masters
or the outer guides. But it was only Sri Ramana
Maharshi, living in the calmly glowing Arunachala Hill,
who seemed to me the most mature of the Himalayan
peaks. His silence seemed to be simple and real in quality, in effort-free radiance. He was always the same. He
was the same with the highest and the lowest, without an
idea of favoritism of any kind. If he spoke, it was out
from the whole rather than about It. He is Himalayan
and has been nearer to me ever since he left his visible
bodies.

I feel our word symbols must befit our experience.
Whether it is "mind" or "thought" or "time" or "ego," I
call it duality-consciousness. I am essentially free in
them and can be consciously so. Whether I am consciously aware or not, I am serenely poised in the "center." I am in the stillness which abides in the present. I
am ever free *in* rather than *from* or *of* the thing and the
quality.

I can be awakened and be consciously free *in* the
opposites. I can play in the complementary contrasts, in
the seemingly beautiful differences. I can play in "form-
free," "effort-free," "carefree," "time-free," "age-free"
and "word-free" rhythm. I am free *in* rather than *of* or

from; the meaning, if any, is in the feeling tone and in the vital, blank spaces or in the clear Silence between the black lines and the shadow words.

Merely "to know" and "to understand" seems to me to be far too mental expressions. I experience in "integral consciousness"—which includes subconsciousness and supra-consciousness—the whole of my being. I am weary of arbitrary abstractions like "love and hate," "East and West." My joyous *ananda* bubbles up because we are sharing a common Life. It is a *karuna* [compassion] bubble in *Sahaja Prajna* Light.

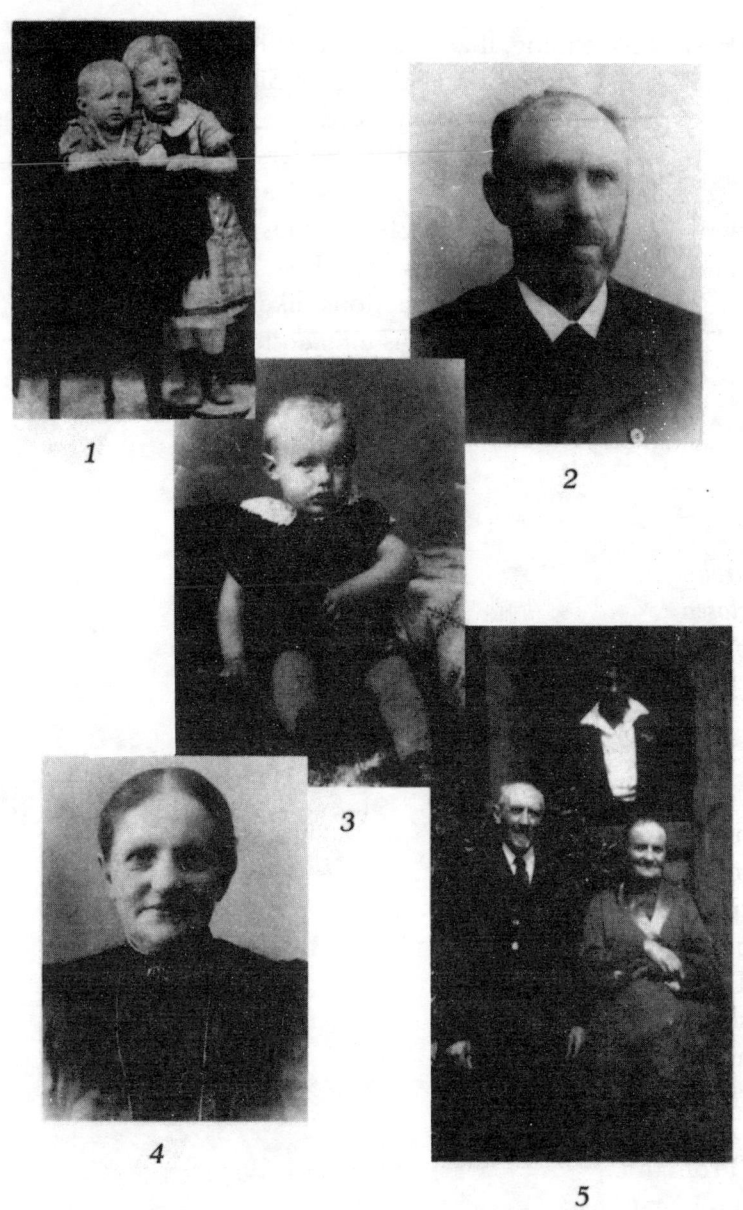

1. Sunyata & Sister 2. Sunyata's Father 3. Sunyata
4. Sunyata's Mother 5. Sunyata with his Mother & Father

2 ❧

Spiritual Practices

Did Sunyata acquire any mystic powers as a result of his natural sadhana *(spiritual practices)? Sunyata never openly disclosed to anyone that he had any such powers. In this essay his writing clearly reveals that he had the gift of healing.*

When different stages of *sadhanas* [spiritual practices] were being manifested through this body, what a variety of experiences I had then! I thought that there was a distinct *shakti* residing in me and guiding me by issuing commands from time to time. Since all this happened in the stage of *sadhana*, *Jnana* was being revealed in a piecemeal fashion. The integral wisdom (*Vijnana*), which this body was possessed of from the very beginning, was broken into parts and there was something like a superimposition of ignorance.

In my *sadhana* I was told by the invisible Monitor, "From today you are not to bow down to anybody." Later on, I again heard the voice within myself which told me, "Whom do you want to make obeisance to? You are everything." At once, I realized that the universe was, after all, my own manifestation. Partial knowledge then

7

gave place to the integral, inherent wisdom, and I found myself face to face with the Advaita One that appears as many. In the meantime, various *vibhuties* [powers] were being manifested through this body. These manifestations have occurred in various ways. Often, I found that as soon as I touched a particular patient, he came round in no time, but I did not know beforehand that he would come round in that way. Sometimes the manifestations occurred with knowledge mixed up with ignorance, e.g., on seeing a patient, I used to argue in this way: I know from my past experience that my touch has a healing effect. If, in this case, I touch the patient, he may come round. To verify this, I touched him and found he was cured immediately.

Manifestations of *vibhuties* have again taken place with full knowledge and consciousness on my part. I knew for certain that I could cure a dis-ease by a mere touch and I touched in full confidence of success. *Vibhuties* have now become a part and parcel of my *Swabhava*. This means that it is now regulated by *Swabhava* or the Supreme Self.

At this stage of *sadhana*, *vibhuti* first manifests itself as *ananda*, which comes from remembrance and recitation of God's name. When people get this, they think that they have got everything that *sadhana* can yield and their upward progress is thereby arrested. But he who keeps himself always on the move, without being tense, grasping or overwhelmed by such manifestations of joy, finds himself in possession of various "miraculous" powers. But those powers are not meant for display. They should be carefully kept under control.

Intuition reveals complete strangers from other races and realms. They may meet for the first time in their bodies and may intuitively aware their inner "essence." Busy bodies like prime ministers, commissioners, artists and millionaires who may be in that outer, or surface realm of forms, power and fussy importance, and the utterly simple fellow pilgrims who may be illiterate and uneducated, all can recognize the inner silence in word-free Self radiance. Words are often a nuisance or even a pest, when egojies try to explain. "Effort is your bondage!" said the Sage of *Arunachala* [Ramana Maharshi]. There is no fuss or exuberance in such mature recognition, but only calm, joyous ease in feeling tone and in word-free Silence.

Although I have made no vow of silence, I remain perfectly silent because I am usually alone, merged in the inner Silence and also in the silence behind the outer activities. I have no monastic rules to follow. My innerstances and circumstances give me little opportunity of breaking the laws. I give temptation a fair chance! The ladder from earth to heaven remains invisible to the egojies. Perhaps there is no ladder but an harmonious interfusing and unitary Self interplay.

Knowledge is not inherent wisdom. Love is not the same as *mahakaruna* [selfless compassion]. Learning and intellect are not mature awakening in "Self experiencing." The Asian greatness is in, more or less, conscious awareness of Maha Atmahood, of mature "awakening" and of calm "experiencing" into Selfhood. The archtype is the *muni* [a silent one], the sage, the sufi, the *rishi*, the *sadhu*, who have the *sahaja* intuitive "experiencing"—not the prophet, the hero, the powerful *siddhic* or tantric magician.

Alfred Emmanuel Sorenson
(Sunyata) as a young man

3 ❧

Pilgrimage
to India

The following piece written by Sunyata in 1932 contains his impressions and insights regarding some of the people and places he visited during his early travels.

I am a simple gardener, a peasant boy, who has traveled alone thousands of miles from flat Denmark to India, a lofty country of illumination. I have come with no conscious purpose and with no concrete idea of giving or of getting—but as a wanderer, a happy pilgrim, who knows that the goal is everywhere. We are being used and guided, but as Christ said long ago on his Cross: "Most of us do not know what we do or where and how we serve life."

I am interested in a culture that is wider than horticulture, and in art and literature as a living force in the present, or, perhaps it is simpler to say, that I am interested in Life itself as religious consciousness, or as pure awareness in all forms and functions and moods. In my long pilgrimage, it has been rich to see and sense that Life, to listen and to test my realization of its pulsations;

and I will try to tell you how I do it, although it may be rather personal and mystic.

My way cannot nor should not be yours. Each has his own rhythm and law of being to fulfill in interdependence. "To thine own self be true," says Shakespeare in Hamlet, Prince of Denmark. To me, that advice seems profound and valid in all levels of Self identification.

I have no remarkable talents and no money, except what I had earned in working with Mother Earth in a simple way; and in a simple way I have recently traveled through England, France, Italy, Greece, Palestine, Egypt, Ceylon, and now I am in India.

I have escaped education, possessions and cleverness. You may possibly find my language muddled, mystic and conceited when I, a simple worker, try to tell you, wise men and wise women on the Himalayan peaks of transfiguration, how I feel that one can see God. Our Bengali poet Rabindranath Tagore says:

> They knew the way and went to seek you along
>   the narrow lane,
> But I wandered abroad in the night, for
>   I was ignorant,
> I was not schooled enough to be afraid of you
>   in the dark,
> Therefore, I came upon your doorsteps unaware,
> The wise rebuked me and made me begone,
> For I had not come by their lane,
> I turned away in doubt, but you held me fast,
> And their scolding became louder every day.

In another poem he says:

> When the creation was new and all the stars
>   shone in their first splendor,

The Gods held their assembly in the sky and sang:
"Oh, the picture of perfection!
    The joy unalloyed!"
But someone cried all of a sudden, "It seems
        that somewhere there is a breach in the chain
        of Light and one of the stars has been lost."
The golden strings of their harps snapped, their
        songs stopped and they cried in dismay;
"Yes, that lost star was the best; she was the glory
        of all the heavens."
From that day, the search is unceasing for her,
        and the cry goes from one to the other; that in
        her the world has lost its one joy.
Only in the deepest silence of the night, the stars
        smile and whisper among themselves:
Vain is this seeking, unbroken perfection
        is over all...
Sometimes this hidden perfection which cannot
        be described,
But for the existence of which we are certain
        beyond mental knowledge and factual proofs.
In direct perception we see the beauty of
        perfection in all forms and are in touch.
It is not the beauty of form of color or sound:
It is altogether subtle, more transfused,
        more whole.
It is in things a simple light, and loveliness
        (which if we can focus it steadily) of a
        universal harmony.

The beauty of unbroken perfection is revealed to us
as Reality here and now and at once we can see God.
Siddhartha Gautama knew when he said, "Do not complain and cry and pray, but open your eyes and see. For
the light is about you and it is so wonderful, so beautiful, so beyond anything that man has ever dreamt of or

prayed for—it is forever and ever."

The "hidden" light shining in every creature and every form is not hidden if we open our eyes and live wide awake with Life. It smiles through every fellow pilgrim, every tree, every stone or every form we pass. It seems free and aglow with the light of loveliness. Yet it does not seem strange. All is accepted naturally and nothing is seen as ugly, mean or dull.

I can live in natural correspondence and steady consummation. Each face and each form that I greet through my senses responds. It is as if Life smiles across in recognition of Itself. Life is seen by me as the "One"— exceedingly rich and freely nourishing.

The old Hebrew said, "He who sees Jehovah dies." It is true in the light of ego-consciousness. The consciousness of "he" and "she" and of the "ego" must die and transform itself into Life awareness. The much older Vedas have a truer Self identification when they declare again and again that the "Lord is to be seen" and that only the pilgrim who has realized and who sees Him everywhere is religious. Only when we can see Life steadily and centrally does real conscious life begin for us. Our seeing is lovely and is such wealth that we can never feel lonely or lost. But rarely are we really alive, alive to feel our oneness with the "lowest" or with the "highest" and to see that pure love knows no degrees. We are not pure enough. To the Pure, everything is pure. "Blessed are the pure in heart, for they shall see God."

I have escaped education and the often stiffening burden of learning, lore and cleverness. I am rich in having few needs, a simple faith in Life and a feeling at home with most fellow pilgrims on our lovely earth. When this pilgrimage to the East commenced, I had no friends en route and no letters of introduction. I knew not the addresses of nests and sleeping places which eventually I made mine. Only our Bengali poet

Rabindranath Tagore had befriended me. In Europe I enjoyed the delightful uncertainties of the road and the sure Life that is One and that is everywhere. Life knew its way and things happened beautifully.

I had no special talents but I had time, love, a certain freedom and a sure faith in my *Dharma*. I was richly alone but never lonely. I passed slowly through the lands of Europe, Egypt and the near East, over the Red and the Arabian seas to the lovely pearl of the Orient, ancient Lanka. Thence in eastern robes—always in third class—I tracked the coast of Mother India, touching her lovely temple towns and her myriads of lovely fellow-pilgrims on the way to Calcutta and Shantiniketan.

In April, the heat in the plains of Bengal became too strong for even a Viking and I took shelter in the Himalayas (Darjeeling), a guest in grandeur, purity and peace. Here as everywhere else, my pilgrimage had been royal and rich in beauty.

In India, I have felt equally at home with princes, with men of intellect and character, and with simple fellow workers and with the common people. How little difference there is if we can see through the forms and the natural weakness to the royalty of our fellow travelers and to their gift of Life. We have not really met our fellow beings until we have seen their "little Lamp," their Self. Life shines through and reveals itself through all masks. Each face and each form is like a poem of life, a hymn of life to Life. We can feel the inner response and the central recognition in all forms—if we are harmoniously free of the parts, and the ego.

Every city, every town, every village has a life-rhythm of its own—aye—every tree, every aspect or mood of nature has a gift and a life of its own in the "Whole." It is up to us whether we are open to recognize it.

We are in Life and what we are and what we have is

so much more than what we think. How lovely it is to greet Life, the same Life, in varying and strange forms and to feel our kinship with it! At times, it seems moving, merging, intermingling in the phenomenal world. Life and death are one. And then suddenly lo! All is seen as a meaningful light-suffused Whole, of which we are a due and inevitable part. Then parts move and merge. Perfection is there—the parts glide into a pattern. Our blinkers fall and we see!

The whole of my day can be lived in the noisy myriad life. I may move among degrading poverty and disease. I may work among the prostitution of bodies, of emotions and of minds. I may see the pathetic strutting and assertive egos, the physical, emotional, psychic and mental bullying. I may see death and suffering in the streets and in the hospitals with all their pangs and pities. Yet there is a ray of light, a flash of rightness, a meaningful rhythm in all these movements and noises in the cities. It is like the surging silence of nature in the sea. All is forgiven and it seems strange not to forgive. In that awareness I have known my truest reality. In it I have found my richest freedom in life. How lovely it is to wander quietly and freely in new places and among strange faces until they are no longer strange and new, until Life is recognized and the smile of Life exchanged.

So a simple Viking pilgrim may be greeted and accepted by royalty or poets, by scholars or artists and he may find them interesting. There is much royalty even in slums and wondrous beauty in simple ignorant fellow-beings.

What a direct recognition I had from lovable common folks and fellow workers in Greece, Arabia, Ceylon and our India! They seem to come out, shining through their forms. There was sometimes a thin crust of civilization, of possession and of specialized blinkered mentality. There was also often an expression of an inner dignity and joy—a natural, spontaneous recognition and free acceptance of my love. Words or lack of words did not matter.

In truth, nothing is ugly or dull if we can open our eyes and see. Things open out and nothing is inarticulate to us if we can be still, open and free (from ego-consciousness), if we can live with Life and listen.

Once upon a time, the animals did speak. They still do, but neither in Hindi nor in English and we shall hardly learn their language until we have learned our own language of being. It seems that it is we who have fallen from grace and awareness. It is we who have lost the faculty, the power and the truth of eloquent silence and organic being. It is not because we do not know deeply enough that we jabber and get excited. We really do know what we practice. What we are is self-evident. In our form and being's rhythm, It shines through and life speaks to life in a language truer than words and fashions. But we must be silent and still to hear the Word and to contemplate with God, face to face.

If we know our *dharma* enough, we need not fuss or flutter, enthuse or fear. We can Be and let Be. If we listen freely, we can hear the sheer silence of a deeper and richly satisfying life, the joyous harmony of a creative symphony in all actualities. We can listen with our whole being and then words neither help nor disturb. The unbroken perfection of Reality must, by its very nature, be incapable of expression in any language, except that of Being if we can but live it. Those who know, know and those who do not yet know, cannot be told. We can touch and taste a joy and a freedom which neither death nor fellow pilgrims can possibly destroy or scatter.

India is near the cradle of an Aryan race and still she guards our deepest treasures—our richest heirloom. So little of her real wealth has yet been touched in spite of the wave after wave of conquerors who were attracted by gold and an outward glory. The real and central values can only be ours by recognition and appreciation. They can be shared and increased by being shared. We can come back to the fountain, the pristine source, to drink of immortality-awareness.

India has eternity in her rhythm. Her stiffened forms may protect pearls and her rottenness and decay may make good manure. Life moves on and it knows its way. Life and Death are one and "we and our Father are One." Our awareness transfigures our values and sets us free to "belong" to all, and to recognize God beyond ideas, ideals, assertions and egos.

It seems that our gift to Life is just this liberation— this recognition of *It*, the unbroken perfection, the pure Love, which knows no degrees.

4 ❧

Snow Maiden

Sunyata retells the Hindu story of Shiva, Parvati and the killing of Manmatha, the Hindu Cupid

When the Himalayas were new, they were the abode of gods. Then, as now, Siva, the King of kings and the destroyer of ignorance, was here—stilled in *sahaja samadhi*—radiating calm benediction. The children of men recognized and worshiped him then, just as the fellow-pilgrims of today are aware of the truth of Siva's Reality, and the unsullied purity of Sri Himalaya.

Once upon a time, Lord Siva was, as usual, in a state of pure contemplation. His crystal clarity reflected all the actualities in the phenomenal world. He saw through mere facts and mere forms to the reality within all things, beyond the veils, prisons and delusive bondage. He liberated the pure Life flow by his dynamic silence.

Among the queens of the Himalayas was the lovely daughter of the Snow, who loved and served the King of kings, but who also loved herself and subtly yearned for the admiration and attention of her Lord. Every day, she

19

brought him delicious fruit and nectar and she beamed on him warmly like a small sun. But the King of kings heeded not. He saw her no more than the golden eagles and the fleeting cloudlets in the blue and green valley below, for Pure Love knows no degree.

One day, in her desire to be noticed and wanted and loved as giver, the queen dressed her regal beauty in all the wondrous, softly changing hues, which she had gathered from the valleys and the mountains around, and from the colored and sun suffused Himalayan dawns and sunsets. In order to attract her Lord and to "do him good," she decked her exquisite form with pearls and marvelous rare gems and with beads even more colorful than those worn by hill women here today. Her rubies and diamonds, emeralds and sapphires radiated like a clear dawn over Kanchenjunga and thus, in entrancing loveliness, exquisitely tender and innocent looking, she disguised her subtle, unconscious guile, and her terrible feminine will to give and to get, in a smile which was reflected far into India and Tibet and all over Nepal.

Confident of her power and sure of victory, the royal daughter of the Snow approached the King of kings, carrying sun kissed apples and other luscious fruit from the valleys. And she called in a voice, sweeter than the heard melodies, "My Lord Siva, Behold, I Serve."

As Siva was aroused from his deep contemplation, the roof of the earth quaked and cracked, while avalanches of snow rushed from his hair into the blue valley and swelled the silvery streams.

At first, the King of kings stared unseeingly at the apples of rare knowledge and at the lovely, but gem bedecked and vain daughter of Sri Himalaya. He saw only her Essence, her Reality, the *mani* jewel within. Slowly emerging into the vision of forms and duality-consciousness, he discerned the outer charm of the queen. He saw that she was not open and simple, not

Real. Behind her stood the winged king of love [Cupid], lifting a huge bow of bees and forthrightly pointing an arrow of rubies directly at Siva's royal heart.

The Queen also felt the little god, and in the triumph and ecstasy of her approaching victory, she drew nearer to serve her King. Suddenly, as Siva looked into the eyes of the love god, there was a tremendous crash, and lo! the bow and arrow and all the queen's finery flew into millions of fragments and were scattered all over the Himalayas.

Siva awoke from the *maya* to pure awareness, and he no longer saw the outward splendor of the royal daughter of the Snow, except as pure essence. Again he merged into *sahaj samadhi* and real Life play, while the so-alluring Queen turned ashen grey in desolation and despair. All seemed lost. All her guile, her giving and her gaud were of no avail. She sobbed so profusely that the seven rivers overflowed their brims, and the lotus lake Manasarovar became slightly choppy and salty. But the daughter of the Snow realized her falsity, her cloying egoism, and how her truth (in the greed and stress of her emotion) had become plastic, blinkered and blurred.

For a while, she hugged her hurt and her feminine truth and nourished her lie by ego pity. But all was not lost. Siva had focused upon the virgin soul within the bedecked form of royalty; it awoke into conscious awareness, like the sleeping beauty in all of us may awake at the glance of the Eternal. The contrite queen was really brave and she decided, "I will make a good death and be born again worthy of serving the King of kings in true simplicity and pure beauty. Unnoticed, I may serve him in a love which shall know no trying, no want, and no fear. I shall always be near my Lord, clear enough to see Him everywhere. I shall radiate the pure Love, which knows no degree and needs no reciprocity or reward. I shall be myself in simple dignity and naturalness."

So it happened beautifully. The Queen died into Life and became the Snow Maiden, Uma Haimavati, whose Silence is radiant *sunyata*. Like Sri Omanandaji, she sings softly in Himalayan rhythm:

Lo: Thy vast Self we name but do not know,
And in the naming break the mystic spell.
O Siva: If the Silence is thy Hymn,
Teach us to sing it well.

The blue necked Siva, destroyer of ignorance, is ever in Himalayan contemplation, dancing his cosmic rhythm of transmutation and change of forms. "The form of the *shakti* is all *ananda*," mutely radiating the Love which knows neither fear nor degree. The children of man pick up the fragments of the arrow and of all the scattered finery of the Himalayan queen, who now shines the freer in purity and joyous grace as the Snow Maiden, Uma Haimavati.

Sri Himalaya still has grandeur, vastness and richness of delicate gem colors which make Siva's realm a noble crown for our worldly consciousness. His snowy ranges frame our vast panorama in translucent purity, and Uma Haimavati smiles in gorgeous sunsets and in heavenly dawns.

5 ❧

Meeting with Rabindranath Tagore

Sunyata's first meeting with Rabindranath Tagore occurred in 1929 when he was working as a gardener at Dartington Hall in England. Tagore was a guest there, and when they met, there was instant recognition. It was Tagore's invitation to "come to India to teach silence" that served as the impetus for Sunyata's's travels. India would eventually become his permanent home.

The name of Rabindranath Tagore still echoes in my memory with a fragrance of serene grace. When the Nobel Prize for literature had been awarded to the Bengali poet, his name and fame became known and widespread in Europe and so also appreciated by a solitary peasant lad in Denmark. It was especially his poetry that I loved. In it, I recognized an awareness of kindred values, of intuitive insight and of integral experience and I responded in loving gratitude to the simple beauty of language and of feeling tone.

My solitary childhood on a Danish farm had been harmonious in natural contacts and in contemplative, integral experience. My Danish mother had called me Emmanuel and had, no doubt, told me the meaning of this mystic term symbol. A Jewish maiden, Miriam, the mother of God, was told by the archangel Gabriel, "Ye shall call his name Emmanuel—the immanent and indwelling Christ." This Christ had assured me: "Lo, I am always with you. Be of good cheer. Seek and find ye first the inner realm of integral grace. Experience the Christ within your Self. Whatsoever you have done unto one of the least among you—that also ye have done unto Me, Emmanuel."

Even as a child I loved the truth of this mystic wisdom, which is pure *Advaita Vedanta* [non-duality]. All mature mystics, sages and *rishis* intuit this wisdom. In ego humility, we can aware and experience the Self in every changing form and interplay of *swalila* [divine play]. I found this inherent sense of *swadharmic* wisdom and living awareness of its immanence and integrality gracefully revealed in Rabindranath Tagore's poems, especially in "Gitanjali," "Fruit Gathering" and "The Gardener." In intuitive empathy, I could "go with" at joyous ease.

My first personal meeting with the poet happened beautifully in 1929 at Dartington Hall in Devonshire, where he had come to rest and to heal in "nature" and in "creative painting" after strenuous travel abroad and talks at Oxford. It was a momentous meeting with a living embodiment of the Vedantic wisdom, which I already loved dearly.

I had many poetic talks with Tagore. We also had many word-free and ego-free contemplations alone together. I responded to the poet's wish to share Beethoven's last intimate quartets played on my own gramophone. He often read to me some of his favorite poems in which I sensed his almost plaintive yearning for "Home," the Himalayan Bharat, or was it a nostalgic longing for the integral God Experience—the grace of *sahaja samadhi*? Tagore had eternity in his eyes and in his being's rhythm. He felt easily depleted by our externalized superficial activities, our duality values and our ego fuss.

Rabindranath Tagore invited me to come to his "Abode of Peace,"—Shantiniketan—there to teach "Silence" at joyous ease and in integral sympathy. A year later, I was free and able to visit India. I experienced that Gurudev [Tagore] was right. Bharat [the ancient name of India] is my Home. I am among kindred brethren in India. My few months holiday in India eventually grew into 30 years! [This piece was written by Sunyata in 1960]

I lived with Tagore for a while at Shantiniketan and in the Himalayas, feeling richly fulfilled and contented, but it was our first body meeting in England in 1929 which drew me home to Himalayan Bharat. I am profoundly grateful for Gurudev's recognition, inspiration and evocative *karuna* love. This empathy in *karuna* experiencing gives a new dimension to my conscious Self awareness in integral living.

One poem of Gurudev's illustrates my home freeness:

Thou hast made me known to friends
    whom I know not
Thou hast given me seats in homes not mine own
Thou hast brought the distant near and dear,
    a brother of a stranger
I am uneasy at heart when I leave my
    accustomed places
I forget that there abides the old in the new,
    and there also Thou abides

Through births and deaths in this world and
    in others, wherever thou leadest me

It is thou, the Same, the companion of
    my endless life
Who ever linkest my heart with bonds of joy
    to the unfamiliar
When one experiences thee, then alien there
    is none, no door is shut
Oh, grant me my prayer, that I may never lose
The bliss of the One in the play of the many.

6 ✿

In the Light of Tagore's Radiance

Sunyata's observations at a students' conference at Lahore, 1935, that was presided over by Rabindranath Tagore, and other meetings with the poet.

I am in a whirl of feasts and vital Life play. *Notre soleil brille toujours.* [Our Self-sun always shines] At night, there are moons and comets, fixed and untamed stars in cosmic dance and in universal play. I am reminded of Blake's "Whirlwind of Lovers" with Rabindranath Tagore as the Sun, the center and the focus of all our festival activities.

"Rabi" means "the Sun"; how rich an Eastern sunset can be! The Poet looks a regal, ripe and cultured soul as he moves or rests among us. His poetic sensitiveness and delicate perceptions are shrouded and protected, like a snail in its shell. There is eternity in his eyes and dignity in his inner, integral rhythm. His rich, silent life awareness often shines in his face, and in his form and in his words. Hundreds of fellow pilgrims gather each day at his home to pay him homage in silence. On festive occasions, he wears a golden robe with touches of sun-shine. Pure winter calm and serene clarity are in his mien, as well as in his locks of snowy hair and long sil-very beard.

On the first evening, with a youthful vigor of voice, Rabindranath Tagore delivered the convocation address to the students. He read it naturally for one full hour, in a clear and harmoniously modulated voice. It was well received by the audience in spite of the torrential down-pour and patter on the tin roof. The applause was loud, especially when the poet paid homage to Mahatma Gandhi, and again when he referred to his own gesture of returning his once accepted knighthood honor as a protest against the official butchery and degrading inhu-manity in Jallianwalla Bagh at Amritsar—where hun-dreds of peacefully protesting Indians were shot dead by British Colonial troops. In his address, I did not find any playing up to the giddy gallery nor any playing down to the vulgar pit.

At the final meeting of the students' conference, we had a poetic symposium with recitations by Rabindranath Tagore, Sarojini Naidu and other lesser known poets. The first part of the symposium was pan-demonium. The doors and the windows were broken, as there was no more room for the impatient and disap-pointed crowd in Lahore's largest hall. The young men tumbled in, eager to listen to the poet. With or without tickets, they were in layers, one on top of another. I sur-vived, as though in a steambath, and with a few bruises. "Music hath charm" and, to judge by such scenes, our Rabindranath might rank with a great football hero, a famous cricketeer or even a boxer or a political Fuehrer.

The poet is looking well in spite of strain of travel and bodily age. He is young at seventy-seven and has long since attained the recollectedness of the ageless Life aware Self. It enables him to recuperate quickly and to smile serenely the Smile of Life. Childlike, he is open to new things, to new forms and to new experiments of life, which helps him to keep well, alert and fresh.

The Punjab seems to agree with the Poet. Again and again, he is prolonging his stay here. He is always going "tomorrow," but that tomorrow fortunately is elastic. The poet's four days' stay has now already stretched into fourteen. He says that never before has it been his wish to stay for so long in a private home.

Every morning we have readings from his "Gitanjali" by the poet himself. Afterwards, he talks about the meanings of his read poems. Everybody present enjoys his prosaic and informal talk. Music is played by talented Indian artists. Three to four hundred people usually find their way to this outlandish place every morning. Rabindranath loves this contact with the youth and also with the other simple, unpaying and unexpected guests. The poet reads and talks in Bengali and in English while a Pundit translates it into Punjabi. The poet's personality, life rhythm and awareness are transparent in his form and features, in his voice and movements. Some of us also find his Silence the most rich.

In Allahabad, he stated that he was "a born exile." It is only when we become aware that we too are exiles that we, like the prodigal son, turn our pilgrimage consciously homewards. Rabindranath is fully conscious of the impermanence of our temporary homes and personal loves. The poet sensitively fluctuates on the surface in calm awareness, beyond the seeming division of age and ego, of matter and spirit. He is often "exiled" in moods and in the layers of meaning.

I can feel the poet Tagore intimately in all his changing moods and circumstances. I can feel one with his "innerstances." I can discern his fleeting feelings. His reactions to others are reflected in his sensitive face in regal radiance. His fellow travelers are often infantile

and adolescent in their ego craving. Most of us are subjective, ego assertive and blinkered in our desires and
values. Yet he says:

> My desires are many and my pride is pitiful
> They try to keep me in bounds who love me
> But it is otherwise with Thy love
>   which sets me free
> So sings out the poet's clear and silvery voice

I have followed the poet to the conferences, to the
festive banquets and to many simple and trying functions in public and private realms. I wonder at the old
body's strength to endure and his age-free spirit's ability
to keep calm and "life giving." In his rhythm and beneath
his outer movements and shadows, I am aware of the
poet's inner quietude, Self recollectedness and his rich
Silence, which I first experienced in the stately
Devonshire home by the river Dart. It was the summer
of 1929 and he was completely free from all his engage-
ments, duty complexes and the harassing ego cravings.
He had there the time that, in Europe, is money.

Free for a while from his Oxford duties and the pes-
tering egos, he could simply be the Self. He could find
the true, vital correspondence in nature and in melodies
heard and unheard. He painted. He and I also shared in
the life of Beethoven's intimate, last four quartets and
"Grosse Fugue." Most richly did we share in the living,
dynamic silence. In his life play and his rich silence, I
could feel his Indian background of an ancient and
unbroken culture. At Dartington Hall, he had the charming wistfulness, the joy of longing, the pathetic beauty of
the "born exile." The born exile, like Life itself, was
never static or at rest for long but ever creative, finding
itself joyously in new forms everywhere.

Later on, my initial three months stay as Tagore's

guest at Shantiniketan and my seeing him daily in his own setting did not efface my memory of our close association at the Devonshire country home during our first meeting in 1929. The sharing and recognition of integral Life awareness in Silence was the richest bond between us.

My third intimate meeting with Tagore was also chiefly a "wordless" sharing, a rich interchange in vital Silence. It was an untrying recognition in worth-ship rather than in words and worship. It feels good to be in the poet's radiance and to meet the cultural elite of Lahore that come to have the light of his darshan. All communities and strata of society seem united in paying homage to the poet. Their petty differences are sunk in the light of the poet's intuition and synthetic vision. Students, especially lovers of literature, artists in life, as well as the money-rich folks—all come to see Tagore. It is a rich honor for a simple unlearned Viking to be asked by India's poet to come to India to teach Silence. And is it not rich to be able to afford to decline?

The poetess Sarojini Naidu (1879–1949), popularly known as the nightingale of India who wrote lyric verses, was among those who visited him several times. Uday Shanker, a classical dancer of great repute, came with his troupe to perform the exquisite Indian dances for the aged but ever young poet. The Bhalla home does represent the money of a self-made man, but it is not the vulgarity of the newly rich. I find in it nothing gaudy or vulgar, incongruous or jarring. The newly erected private temple in the Bhalla home is beautiful in fitness of line and of proportion, with marble wrought screens and carved woodwork. The atmosphere within is pleasing.

At dawn and at dusk we have chanting and music and burning of sandalwood. Ghee and *samagri* [incense powder] are offered to the sacred flames of fire in the *havan* [a Vedic ritual ceremony], which symbolizes the eternal living spirit, the Holy Ghost. But why have symbols when we are the Real itself and can simply "Be"? I prefer the living temple outside—with the clear blue sky as the dome with infinite *akasha* [ether] spaciousness, nature's harmony and pure air.

When Tagore is seated or talking, we forget the fragility of his aged tools. He is often like a huge yet miniature snow capped hermit mountain in his Being's rhythm, serenely sunk into awareness of inner realm, the invisible Real—that is beyond sound, desire, thought, ego and mental consciousness. At times, the "born exile" may strike one as aggrieved and truculent. But his semi serious tone easily turns into one of fun and joyousness. It is as if the illuminated soul, through the poet's frail body, shines richer and clearer. It is now mature and ripe. His face is lit up from within and there is the gleam of eternity in his eyes. I feel the *Lila* [divine play] in his accents and in his nuances of moods. The spirit play animates the form of his body and the sound of his voice, yet I find that the real touch, the real force, is in his Silence.

I had my last darshan of Poet Tagore's body in Himalayan Almora. We celebrated his birthday, one of his last in his frail body. He himself was serene and calmly ready for departure. The born exile was near Freedom. His poetry was fragrant with delicate beauty and grace. He had awakened into Self awareness. Let us rejoice in gratitude—and in glad humility.

7 🌿

Meeting with Mahatma Gandhi

In October of 1935, Sunyata met with Mahatma Gandhi at his ashram in Maganwadi, Wardha. He came in contact with some important personalities staying there, including Frontier Gandhi (Khan Abdul Gaffar Khan), his brother Dr. Khan Sahib, Seth Jamnalal Bajaj and Mira Behn.

I nestle with Mahatmaji, Gandhi or Bapuji [beloved daddy]—basking in the radiance of India's uncrowned emperor. He lives in a mud hut and is undisguised except for a scanty loincloth. Bapuji is a practical mystic and a karma yogi. His keen mind, intuitive insight and central harmonies make his relationship and his touch just right. He puts everybody at ease and at his best. His wonderful toothless smile and innate courtesy melt the surliners (i.e., the hardcore politicians and intellectuals).

At present, all is peaceful here. I feel I am in India at its simplest best—in its living rhythm which cannot really be fully expressed in words and images. The *ashram* is bustling with creative activities and vital doings.

33

Day's Routine

Mahatma Gandhi rises at 3 a.m. and at 4, we gather on the roof for prayer. At 6:30, we partake of porridge, milk and fruit. Then we go around to the villages and teach for some hours by practical work. At present, we especially concentrate on sanitation, hygiene, diet and village industries. Armed with bucket and stick, shovel and broom, we are daily cleaning the roads and village greens of human excreta and filth. Mahatmaji, Mira Behn, I and all others doing this work are at first looked upon despisefully by the other "untouchables." They prefer to live in the idyllic stench of their own filth rather than to remove it and keep the bosom of the earth clean and tidy.

At 10:30 a.m., we dine on chapatis, cooked vegetables and curd. From 2 p.m. to 5 p.m., we again do work such as spinning, corn-gleaning, typing etc. Supper is served in the evening at 5:30 (rice, dal, milk and salad). Mahatma Gandhi has his frugal meals with us on the verandah. He also partakes in our village activities. He is ever active and one wonders at the old body's energy and endurance. Evening prayer on the roof is at 7:30 p.m. And bed is shortly after.

Mira Behn

Strong featured, with shaven head and in Eastern dress, Mira Behn, daughter of a British admiral, is doing well here. She has the peace, the poise and the calm of having found her real home in Gandhiji's *ashram*. It is joyous to hear the cheerful spontaneous shouts of the naked children running and stumbling in their eagerness to greet her—"Mira Behn, Mira Behn!" She is having a cottage built in the village nearby. Bapuji follows her in the squalor to share in the rhythm and the needs of the poorest.

In a middle-aged body, Mira Behn is shining with beauty. She is happy and richly fulfilled. She will never be Miss Slade (her original name) again. She has some of the features, the self-possession, the dignity and the charm of the British breed at its best. Her childhood and early womanhood were spent in desirable mansions, in the comforts and luxuries of civilization. Now, as a mature person, she has attained the art of simple living and the soul comfort of love culture in a tiny one roomed mud hut.

MAHATMA GANDHI'S ROOM

Bapuji's room is light, airy and pleasant. It has no striking features. There is no wooden furniture except a tiny writing table, only a few inches high. There are no pictures on the wall, no ornaments and no objects of "art." Bapuji's face and life-play alone are a series of living pictures. The doors are wide open for any stray wind or any visitor. Visitors here come and go, some staying at the Satyagraha *ashram* for hours, some for days and others for weeks. Some inmates live in huts or cottages and make their own food arrangements; others sleep in dormitories or under the trees or the starry canopy—and all wash their own utensils after each meal.

Every other evening, all of us walk some three miles to another *ashram* or to a girls' school for prayer. On the way, Bapuji chatters and laughs happily with us. My arrival was unannounced and unexpected but Bapuji said, "We need not advertise when we are going home." We talk on all subjects that float in the air—on diet and Denmark; on Mussie (Mussolini) and soya beans; on

Gita and geology—all the while, God is not far off. Like other cultured Hindus, Bapuji does not favor proselytizing. His feelings toward other religions are not only of tolerance but also of respect. Each one is essentially right and true for those born within its respective realm. Each is a dialect which emphasizes various aspects of the universal language of the soul. It does not mean that the individuals who are thus urged from within should not go to the fold and be nourished to function where they find life richer and more abundant. It does, however, mean that the practitioners of one belief should not be aggressive at the expense of those who come on a different road to the many mansions in the inner kingdom of harmony.

Gandhiji says, "What I want to achieve, what I have been striving to achieve these 30 years, is Self realization—to see God face to face, to attain *moksa*. I live and move and have my being in pursuit of this goal. All that I do by way of speaking and writing and all my ventures in the political field are directed to this end. I find a solace in the *Bhagavad Gita* that I miss even in the Sermon on the Mount. When disappointments stare me in the face and all alone I see no ray of hope, I go back to the *Bhagavad Gita*. I find a verse here and a verse there and I immediately begin to smile at the overwhelming tragedies (and my life has been full of external tragedies). If they have not left any visible scars on me, I owe it to the teachings of the *Bhagavad Gita*."

Bapuji does not smoke. He does not drink. He does not take any stimulants. Knowing them as poisons, he does not put these into the building of his house and his tools. Bapuji fasts frequently for purification and enjoys silence every Monday. He advocates *Brahmcharya* [celibacy in thought, word and deed] and ego restraint for spiritual sight and for the darshan of the Self. Birth control by contraceptives is racial suicide, says Bapuji.

Gandhiji was never too busy to withdraw temporarily from business affairs. He will do so during intermittent periods of contemplation. Mondays are the days he would observe word silence. If he had not made this practice, he might not have managed to do his business (dharmic task) because his spells of contemplation were the source of his inexhaustible spiritual strength. His example shows that it is possible to do arduous practical work without allowing one's spiritual life to be smothered and choked by the cares of the world of banality and ego fuss. This is perhaps the greatest lesson that India has to teach the present world. The art of contemplation is really another name for the art of living.

I leave Maganwadi at dawn after a last darshan of Mahatma Gandhi.

*F*RONTIER GANDHI

I am again in the central Indian town of Wardha and have fallen into the bosom of two Mahatmas—the Northwest Frontier one (Khan Abdul Gaffar Khan)[1] and the all India one (Mohandas Karamchand Gandhi). This little gaily whirling globe of ours, so silently singing, fosters quite a sprinkling of Mahatmas. They may be nearer than we know. It takes a potential Mahatma to recognize a real one. I see and sense the radiation of such simple and mature souls as Swami Bholanath, Anandamayee Ma, Ramana Maharshi—all "uneducated" persons in whom the universal Light and Self awareness shine through. By our side are now two all-India figures—great souls who are deeply religious despite being political leaders, the one rejoicing in "Krishna" and the

---

1 Khan Abdul Gaffar Khan (1890-1988), popularly known as Frontier Gandhi for his belief in nonviolence and for building the Khundai Khidmatgar (Servants of God) movement in the Northwest Frontier Province, now in Pakistan.

other in "Mohammed" and both have escaped "education," as we know it in the West.

Frontier Gandhi and I walk together a distance of five miles from Wardha to Segaon. We plan to visit Mahatma Gandhi, who has withdrawn to a typical, isolated village. We stride over the bare, hot fields. At first, we hardly talk during our walk over the fields. We trot along with speedy pace, testing each other's silence. I wonder how Frontier Gandhi could keep his silence so well. There was no strain, no trying but only a free communication between us in harmonious speed and in silence. Prison bars and Pathan hills teach the soul wordless lessons; "Those who are learned do not know and those who know are not learned" or "He who speaks knows not and he who knows speaks not." We trot mutely, attuned to our complementary rhythm of silence. After covering about two miles of rich silence, we descend into sharing of words. We talk about corn, crops and the undernourished, helpless millions that represent the real Hindustan—the fabulous India.

We also talk about Almora, the Himalayas, Jawaharlal Nehru and other loving friends. Then the Pathan Chief waxes eloquently about the simple and grand virtues of his people of the Frontier. His love for a number of his own children, so abundantly reciprocated, shines through and makes his handsome frame finely radiant. His love also includes the larger family and fellow beings in other parts of India—aye, it includes all humanity, all Allah's projections of pure Self. Now we see Bapuji at a distance returning from his morning walk. He receives us joyfully, radiating his wonderful toothless smile upon us. I watch the two royal souls meet and embrace. Bodily they are very dissimilar but inwardly how alike and sharing in work and suffering in the service of the people! While the two Gandhis talk jokingly in Hindi, I pick up a copy of the *Koran* in English translation. It is heavily marked and commented upon by Bapuji in his own handwriting. Together with Bapuji, we now inspect the new mud huts and the bamboo shelters. Whenever Bapuji moves and settles for a while, I greet Mira Behn from a distance. She is leading a goat. Later, I see her teaching a class of village spinners.

We retire with Bapuji to his one roomed cottage that is beautiful in its simplicity and its vibrations. I see some artistic clay designs over the niches depicting village life. Bapuji has a shave and listens to our news. Mahadev Desai [Gandhi's secretary] has come by *tonga* [carriage] and, while he usurps the talking, we whisper softly while spinning. Time passes. Men say, "Time passes" and Time says, "Men pass." What does Eternity say? Its speech is Silence. Bapuji turns to me and apologizes for having neglected me. He pierces through my form with his keen eyes, so restless and so different from beams and flashes of intellectual fireworks. Mahatmaji smiles mutely at the talking Viking and his eyes say, 'Now we are quits"—equally rich in Silence.

SETH JAMANALAL BAJAJ

Possessed of a heart of gold, Seth Jamanalal Bajaj, the millionaire businessman, is Mahatma Gandhi's right-hand man. From his early boyhood, he has been favored by the goddess Lakshmi with plenty of wealth. He owns lands, schools and a number of industries. He is totally dedicated in the service of Mahatma Gandhi. Despite enormous riches, he has remained utterly simple in his lifestyle. He wears simple dress like an ordinary person. His wife, old mother and children also live in simple dress and rhythm. He and his family would be inconspicuous figures in an Indian slum or bazaar crowd.

I first met Mrs. Bajaj and one of her daughters

accompanying her at a lone Himalayan castle belonging
to the Nehru family. The millionaire lady and her daughter did not live in the very well-built and splendidly located main building. They preferred to live in a little part of
the chicken house. It was otherwise a simple, neat and
clean room. It had not housed any chickens for years.
Mrs. Bajaj and her daughter did their cooking in this
quiet corner room—very simple vegetarian food—the
ladies teaching me how to make lovely toffee from ghee
and gur.

A Visit to Wardha Again in 1941

I nestle again at Wardha at the invitation of Seth
Jamnalal Bajaj. I observe that the political leaders here
have chosen freely to go to prison in their struggle for
freedom. Mahatma Gandhi is leading and directing the
campaign of quit India against the British rulers. The
loin clothed emperor of India is a practical mystic. He
works and relaxes, lives and moves in the light of the
intuitive visions that are revealed to him during his tests
and trials, failures and triumphs.

At Wardha, I am sharing a room with Rajendra
Babu, ex Congress President and first President of
the Republic of India. During the day, most of my
time is spent at Sevagram. The evening prayers with
Bapuji are simple and serene. Sevagram is creative in
manifold activities. Mahadev Desai is here. Acharya
Kripalani is staying at our guesthouse. Genial and
pleasant-voiced when not shouting from a platform, he
seems to be too involved in politics and imprisoned in
intellect. Peareylal, Gandhiji's secretary, is in jail. In his
place, it is the real Indian princess, Rajkumari Amrit
Kaur, who is serving the Mahatma.

Bapuji's one-room hut is pleasantly artistic in its

utter simplicity. A few reliefs on a mud wall depict palm trees and typical Indian village scenes. There is one mural painting done by the visiting students from Tagore's university—Shantiniketan. Above Bapuji's seat that also is his bed on the mud floor is a lotus with the symbol *Aum*. By his side hangs a single motto urging us to "Be quick, be brief, be gone."

Yesterday, I had hours of brilliant talks in eloquent Silence with Bapuji as it was his day of Silence. Refreshed by yesterday's fast of food and silence, he was in a joking mood. Yet he would quickly and playfully switch on and off to grave and vital decisions, answering queries and listening to reports from Rajendra Babu, Kripalani and two or three secretaries. In between, he would look up his letters. I felt like a fool jester at a Royal Court! Bapuji's jokes, like his Silence, are richly creative.

I also visit Sabarmati Ashram where Gandhiji and his wife Kasturba Ma lived for 20 years. The Dandi March began from here, which awakened multitudes of Indians to dignified awareness of Freedom.

Sunyata was on a visit to Benares, staying at Yashoda Ma's old house "Radha Vilas." Tandra Devi, now Swami Omanand Puri, was also in the house. The news of Mahatma Gandhi's assassination was conveyed to him in the evening. Sunyata penned down his reaction to the murder of Gandhiji in the following extracts in his diary. (editors):

January 30, 1948

As I pen this diary in the moonlight at 9 p.m., an ashramite lad on the balcony sticks his head through the open window and tells a shocking news: "Mahatma Gandhi died today; he has been shot." Who killed him? Nobody knows. I hope that the killer is not a Mohammedan! Mahatmaji is a saint to be worshiped for centuries to come. An apostle of non-violence and now a victim of violent assassination, he has become a martyr! Perhaps his death is a fitting crown for his long, spectacular yet simple life.

One knows he would die as he lived, as a dignified human, dimly aware of the mystic truth. It was just last week I saw him there at the prayer meeting in Delhi and feasted upon his keen sense of humor and fun.

India will not let him die. He will be immortal. He may perhaps attain avatarship. The leaders of the nation that he united promised him last week to be good boys and girls. May they keep their promise like true Aryans.

Bapuji was everybody's father. He was a unique and disquieting figure in a world of sordid power politics. It was his sincerity, ego humility and integrity that disconcerted bewildred egos. The real India responded and saw its Life revealed mystically in Mohandas Karamchand Gandhi.

8 ❦

Jawaharlal Nehru

*In 1953 Sunyata became a naturalized Indian citizen.
Hailing his decision to embrace Indian citizenship, Prime
Minister Nehru remarked at a function at the Danish
embassy in New Delhi, "Brother Alfred has paid us the
highest compliment by becoming one of us."*

I was often a guest in Jawaharlal Nehru's ancestral
home—Ananda Bhawan in Allahabad. This was during the period 1933–47. I was befriended by
Nehru's talented sister Vijaya Lakshmi Pandit
(1900–1990) and her husband Ranjit S. Pandit. I was
also quite familiar with their three daughters—
Chanderlekha, Tara and Rita. During the Freedom
Movement in India, elder members of the Nehru family
were periodically sent to prison by the British government on political grounds. Jawaharlalji, who was leader
of the political movement in India, remained in various
prisons for many years. I met Jawaharlalji at intervals
while he was in Almora jail. For a while, I stayed as guest
of Dr. R.K. Kakkar, Superintendent of Bhowali
Sanatorium, where Nehru's wife Kamla (who was alive
then) was undergoing treatment for tuberculosis, then

considered a dreadful disease. Jawaharlalji was let off
from prison now and then to see his ailing wife. When
Kamla's condition further deteriorated, Nehru was let
out of jail by the British authorities in 1935.

Freedom was won by the Indians in 1947.
Jawaharlal Nehru was the unanimous choice for the
Prime Ministership of India. I used to visit Jawaharlal
Nehru frequently at his residence in New Delhi during
my winter forays from Almora. I was always welcomed in
his house. Jawaharlal's daughter, Indira Gandhi, gave me
a standing invitation to visit her in Delhi during my winter raids and I remember her generous hospitality over
many teas, breakfasts and lunches there for 15 years.

I never intruded upon Nehru's privacy nor did I
ever ask for any favor. We experienced each other's
silence—that's all. I often wrote him letters in my
obscure mystic style.

Nehru was cultivated in many cultures, Eastern and
Western. He was at home in all and was verily a world
citizen. Frank, gracious and utterly unsnobbish, he could
lash out at dying traditions and sickly sentimentality. He
could sometimes decry the idle brand of "*sadhus*" [wan-
dering, homeless monks] in India as "thieves and para-
sites," as they seemed to abuse and sponge on India's
economy. He could also be harsh on panditic blinkers
and learned ignorance.

What was the common link between us? Any special sharing? Any kindred awareness? Yes, it was a kind
of mystic light of integral wholeness, a love of India and
Indian people and of writers like Kalidas, Shakespeare,
the ancient Greeks, the Red Indian cultures, Goethe,
Shelley, Keats, Herman Hesse, Eliot, Carl G. Jung and
Albert Einstein.

I was once graciously invited by Prime Minister
Nehru (India's darling) to bless Rita Pandit's wedding in
New Delhi. I had known the now charming and sophis-

ticated lady Rita since she toddled about at Anand Bhawan as a tiny kid some 20 years ago. I had to "brave" the wedding as I descended to suffer the fearful civilization and to heroically endure its noise and heat and terrible ego fuss. Sri Jawaharlalji was at his cultivated and unsnobbish best. The wedding was solemnized at Vijaya Lakshmi's home in the cool hours of midnight. The house and the grounds were lavishly and beautifully illuminated but there was no extravagant display or food fuss. The Vedic wedding ceremony was rather prolonged (as usual in India).

On the following evening, a grand reception was held at Jawaharlalji's house. The "Himalayan plebeian" again mingled with the Delhi elite! The President and the Vice President were gracious by their presence. I knew them as simple Congresswallahs, as prisoners and heroes in Bharat's cause. They appeared now somewhat stiffened in solemn rigidity and fixed smiles.The Prime Minister, as a genial host, mingled freely with the guests, civilized or otherwise.

Indira Gandhi had returned from her Russian and Scandinavian galivanting and looked gracious and serenely at ease. I made quite a "corner" here with the foreign ministers and the ambassadors. The Afghan Excellency was known to me previously from peace conferences and Gandhian seminars. He and the Prime Minister introduced me to other Holinesses and some funny selves. Imagine this Viking body in golden guise, in Buddhist orange robe and dignified gait and mien, floating in these snobbish Sri dollar worshipping realms, where evening dress at meals is not optional.

I could hardly imagine that Jawaharlal Nehru could be graciously and charmingly playful with me on this occasion. He began to tell a number of lively, somewhat exaggerated tales about me, my *sadhana* and my spiritual life. For a few moments in the distinguished gathering, he put me in the spotlight. I wondered why, moving around in this gathering, Nehru could be so playful about me! Some of the VIP guests present were carried away by Nehru's eloquence. I remember how the Nepalese Prime Minister there and then dropped an invitation to me to visit Kathmandu. The Japanese ambassador started conversing with me about Zen and urged me to visit his realm of Sunrise. I felt especially attracted to the Chilean envoy, Don Miguel Serrano. He looked very much alive and talked about his love of the Himalayan mountains. He has written well on his beloved Andes and on the Invisible Real. (He later visited Almora and I had a few meetings with him. He featured me in a chapter, "Brother of Silence," in his book titled *Serpent of Paradise*.)

Jawaharlal came a second time to our group to chat for some 40 minutes. Next to us in the group was a terrible-looking pure, powder white girlie, some 60 years young, gaunt and gaudy. Another yankee girlie looked half naked and gross, bulging with fat and oozing money power. Was it vulgarity of the superior, pure (or is it deadly white?) race? The girlie was flurried but she, of course, was not red except in lip service—how odd and ugly such feminine creatures of the Far West look in an Indian setting and in the home of our cultured Prime Minister!

The Syrian ambassador appeared to be a congenial Sufi type. He took me for tea and lunch at the snobbish Imperial and Ambassador Hotels. Later, I glided everywhere in ministerial cars. I was at joyous ease. I was only slightly bemused when Svetoslav Devika Rani hosted a lunch for me at the Imperial Hotel.

I saw Nehru frequently at meetings, seminars, embassies and other social gatherings. Once I was walking barefooted on the streets of New Delhi when I saw Prime Minister Nehru's car passing by. Nehru stopped the car and dragged me inside. I was lovingly "kid-napped" to his house in Teen Murti.

Nehru was once addressing an election meeting in Almora at a gathering of many thousands. I was also sitting in the crowd, a little far off from the platform, but Nehru spotted me from the stage. Suddenly, my name was boomed through the loudspeakers to the consternation of many, one of whom remarked, "What! That cranky Sorensen—a friend of Nehru's?"

My last meeting with Nehru happened in November, 1963, in New Delhi. Nehru was about to enter his car when he spotted my royal turban amongst the watching crowd. He came back quite a distance, grabbed my hand and blurted out, "Oh brother Alfred! Have you become a politician?" My reply was emphatic, "Oh no... Instead a peace maker!" Nehru smiled and that smile of life remains in the Self radiant *Sunya* Silence as real as it is. [Nehru died six months later on May 27, 1964.]

Ramana Maharshi

9 ❧

Ramana Maharshi

Ramana Maharshi was to Sunyata the living embodiment of all that is great in India. He remarked, "Never before have I awared such a radiance in any human form."

The celebrated psychoanalyst, Carl G. Jung, is said to have expressed his views on Ramana Maharshi thus: "Sri Ramana Maharshi is a true son of the Indian Earth. He is genuine, authentic and in addition to that, something quite phenomenal. In India, he is the whitest spot in a white space. What we find in the life and teachings of Sri Ramana is the purest of Bharat [India] with its breath liberating humanity. It is a chant of milleniums, the melody is built upon a single motif which, in a thousand colorful reflexes, regenerates itself within the Indian spirit and the latest incarnation of which is Ramana Maharshi. The life and teachings of Sri Ramana are not only important for India, but also for Westerners. Not only do they form a record of great human interest, but also a warning message to the humanity which threatens to lose itself in the chaos of its unconsciousness and lack of (ego) self-control."

When Miguel Serrano asked Dr. Jung about his

book entitled *The Undiscovered Self,* what he meant by the Self, he was told, "The Self is a circle, whose center is everywhere and whose circumference is nowhere. And do you know what the Self is for the Western man? It is Christ (Christ-consciousness), for Christ is the archetype of the hero representing man's highest aspiration. All this is very mysterious and at times frightening."

Yes, it is frightening to clever, mental egojies, but not to mature Indians who aware that God, Guru and Self are synonymous term symbols and that the "Source" and "I" are One, or rather a non-dual ego-free 0. Sri Ramana Maharshi recognized in Emmanuel "a rare, born mystic" and said unto him, "We are always aware, Sunyata." Ye must be a poet or an intuitive mystic to *innerstand* awarely Wuji's musing and mystic consciousness. I do not write and expect to be merely understood or overstood. I innerstand at joyous ease whether I am awared or noticed at all or not. There is divine indifference in Wuness.

St. Augustine made the mystic wise statement, "That which is now called Christ, or Christianity, existed from the very beginning. There was never a time when it was not." Yes, the Word, the Logos, Sophia, the alone-begotten Sun, Christos, is from Eternity. "In the beginning was the Word, and the Word was with God, and the Word was God" is St. John's Gospel truth and is a universal Truth. The Godhead is before and beyond the beginning, Self radiant beyond being and non-being—Self-created, Self-sustained and Self-projected into *Swa Lila* Self interplay.

Ramana Maharshi said, "What is all this talk of Masters and disciples, Gurus and chelas?" To one who has realized the true Self, there are neither Masters nor disciples. Such a one regards all people with an equal intuitive eye. The intuitive light reveals Reality. Self recognizes Self through all persona masks and disguises.

The Guru Master is awared within ourselves. The *Rishi Jnani* [Poet Sage] awares the Self in all beings—in all things. "*Tat twam asi*." "I *am* equal with the lowest and therein is my strength. They think I am the body. What a pity," says Ramanaji.

The body mind and the ego soul are good tools, but the tools are not our Self. We are all the divine spark—the spiritual no-thing-ness—and may regard our bodies, minds and psyches as instruments. If we do not identify our Self or God with them, we can be free in them, mind-free, body-free, guru-free, God-free, death-free and care-free—free *in* life—because we "awarely" are Life.

"Each man his prison makes," but we can awaken into ego freedom, Self awareness, affectionate Grace awareness and thus also into affectionate detachment from things, events, egojies and prison chains. We are the death-free Spirit, awarely, in intuitive Light and Grace awareness.

Says Sri Ramanaji, "It is the surest way to handicap oneself, this burden of the mind with inordinate desires and with fears of failure and loss. Every man is divine and strong in his real nature. What is weak and faulty is his habits, his desires and his thoughts, not himself. Aware the essence, get hold of the main thing, that the 'world' and the 'Self' are One and that is *purnam* [perfect]. Only your attitude is faulty and needs readjustment. As a whole, the world doesn't need saving. Man makes mistakes and creates sorrow. When the consciousness of a *Jnani* enters awareness, it is set right spontaneously. He is an unjudging Witness in the divine dharmic *Swalila*." All is right that seems most wrong to mental, confused egojies. Aware the All-Rightness.

"Bhagwan, as ye call me, is your Self. You have not a correct picture of your Self. You have too long identified yourself with the body and with the brain. Pursue the inquiry: 'Who am I?' When you truly aware your Self and be the Experiencing, your ego-self vanishes like a shadow in the Light of the 'Self Sun.' Whosoever shall seek to save his ego life shall lose it.

"Ego oblivion is Self awareness. The Self is that out of which the sense of the 'personal' arises and where it shall disappear. Go inward until the last thought of 'I' vanishes. You will awaken into the consciousness which is immortal, and you will be truly loving and wise when you have naturally awakened to your true Self, which is the real nature of Man.

"If people comprehended the real meaning of what they repeat, they would not do all this *puja*, *mantra*, *tantra* and ego power play. How often is the mantra repeated here? Were people to find out the meaning and put it into practice, it would be good, but who will do it? Some rituals are being performed for worshiping God-Self in the invisible Real. It is, after all, a good thing. There is nothing lost in my touching the *puja* articles and so I do it."

Find out "who" was present at your birth and "who" will witness your death—the Source from which you came and whither you shall return Home. Evil is no more real than you are. All happens to and is contained within the little bubble of consciousness called I. The real world lies beyond the ego soul, beyond time and actualities. Aware that which is always present—and your problem of spontaneity and perfect response will be solved.

Although the *Jnani* [the Enlightened one] is consciously one with the Absolute, his trait of character continues to exist outwardly as a vehicle of his manifestation, so that *Jnanis* can have quite different characteristics. Ramana Maharshi said he had no disciples and no Guruship. A mature, Self-realized *Jnani* awares no essential difference between himself and others. To him there are no "others." Consciously or unconsciously, we

are all *Jnanis*, Buddhas, Christ-conscious Emmanuels—
one with the Self. The Source and I are a non-dual 0, and
thou art thy Self–the object of thy search. But one who
is unawakened, unenlightened, unliberated, awares all as
dual or multiple. He awares all is different from himself.
To him, Guru-disciple relationship is a reality, and he
needs the presence and the Grace of the Guru to awak-
en him to Reality. If he is ready, ripe and mature,
Ramanaji could initiate by touch, by look and by silent
radiance as he did to me. "I have never said that there is
no need for a Guru," said Ramana Maharshi. "The Guru
need not necessarily be in human form. Dattatreya had
24 gurus—the elements, etc." That meant any form in
the world was his guru. He surrendered egoji to the unitive Self in All.

Guru, God, and Self are synonymous word symbols. The Real Guru, like the realm of Grace, is within,
is the Self. An external guru can awaken us into Self
awareness. Ramana Maharshi could say: "The
Upanishads say that none but a guru can take us out of
the jungle of mental and sense perceptions. I might have
had an external Guru at one time or another. Did I not
sing hymns to *Arunachala*?"

Ramana Maharshi's initiation by look was a real
thing. He would turn to a devotee—his eyes fixed upon
him or her with blazing intentness. The luminosity of his
eyes pierced into one, breaking down the thought
process. Sometimes it was as though an electric current
were passing through one, sometimes a vast peace, a
flood of Light that could "tease us out of thought as doth
Eternity." One visitor reported: "Suddenly Bhagwan
turned his luminous, transparent eyes on me. Before
that I could not stand his eyes–for long. Now I looked
straight back into those terrible, wonderful eyes, how
long I could not tell. They held me in a sort of vibration
distinctly audible to me."

Ramana Maharshi once said, "Bhagawan, as you call me, is your Self. To comprehend this matter, it is first necessary for a man to analyze himself. Because it has for long been his habit to think as others think. He has never faced his Self in the true manner. He has not a correct picture of himself. He has too long identified himself with the body and the mind. Therefore, I suggest you pursue the enquiry 'Who am I?' "

What can be said about this true Self? Ego is the disease. It is possible to go inward until the thought "I" gradually vanishes. You will awake, aware, attain into that consciousness, which is immortal. You were never born and so cannot die. Man will be truly wise and Grace aware when he has awakened to his true Self, the real nature of man. The sense of I pertains to the persona mask, the body mind, the ego. When a man awakens to aware his true Self for the first time, something also arises from the depth of his being (depth-consciousness). That something is beyond the mind. It is infinite, divine, eternal. Some people call it "the Kingdom of Heaven," "the realm of Grace," or "Grace awareness." Others call it *Param Atman*, Nirvana, *Sahaja Samadhi* and Eternity. When this happens, man has lost his illusory ego in Self awareness. Ego oblivion is Self awareness.

Unless and until man embarks on this quest of his true Self, doubts and disease will follow throughout his life-span. What is the use of being knowledgeable about everything else when you do not know who you are and what you are? Men avoid the inquiry into the true Self, but what is there more worthy to be undertaken? Realize the unconditioned, absolute Being that you really are. *Tat twam asi*.

Ramanji stated, "I did not know that there was an essence or impersonal Reality underlying everything (innerstanding all) and that *Ishwara* [God in the personal aspect] and I were both identical with it. Later on, I found that the books (the *Shastras*) were analyzing and naming what I had felt intuitively without analysis or name. In the language of the books, I could now describe the state I was in after the awakening as *Suddha Manas* [pure stillness], *Vijnana* or the intuitive, illuminated, thought-free, contemplative *Samadhi* (*Sahaja Samadhi*), which is not so much 'thought' as 'shutting out of thought.'" The message left by Ventakataram [Ramana Maharshi] when he left his home was, "I have set out in quest of my Father Source in accordance with his command. It is a virtuous enterprise that this body has embarked upon; therefore, let none grieve over this act and let no money be spent in search of this."

A *Jnani* does not identify himself with the body or with the mind: The Self is in us—as we are in the Self. "If there is pain, let it be. It is also the Self and the Self is *purnam* perfect." Occasionally, Ramanaji protested at the amount of attention bestowed on his body. Several times, when there seemed to be an improvement in his condition, he declared that he wanted no more treatment. The tumor, diagnosed now as sarcoma, sapped his little remaining vitality, and yet, as his body weakened, his face grew gentler, more graceful, more radiantly beautiful. The beauty was almost painful to behold.

He said, "They take this body to be Bhagavan and attribute suffering to him. What a pity! They are despondent that Bhagavan is going to leave them. Where can He go and how? He is always here. Have I ever asked you for any treatment? It is you who want this or that for me. If I were asked, I would always say, as I said from the very beginning, that no treatment is necessary. Let things take their due course.

"A *Jnani* may be relieved of his mortal body, but he is not curious to shed his body. He is indifferent alike to existence and non-existence of the body, being almost unaware of it. Who is there to will the recovery?" The other, the individual that would oppose the course of destiny, no more existed in Ramanaji. There is no going and no changing for that which *is*—Bhagwan—the intuitive Ocean, the cosmic Self. Feel, sense, intuit and aware the inner Presence, *Tat twam asi*. Em-man-u-El innerstands. Awareness is All.

You omit the element of *Chit*, pure cognition of awareness, that is free from all personal and mental distortions. Unless you admit and accept the reality of *Chit*, of pure cognition, ego-free, mind-free, will-free and choice-free, you will not aware, recognize and consciously *be* the unitive Self. You assert your "self" to be what you are not and deny your Self to be what you are.

In Grace-awareness, questions and problems resolve themselves; there is no planning, no striving, no worry, no fear, no inordinate desire, no dis-ease but joyous ease and delightful uncertainty. Spontaneity becomes a way of Life. Mere happiness turns into abiding Grace, *Ananda* awareness. If you awarely innerstand, you will aware the Self—everywhere and nowhere. All things and all egojies change and pass, but your Self is not a thing. It does not change and pass.

In my childhood, there seemed to be unconscious awareness, unmental, intuitive intelligence, inherent Wisdom and calm Grace awareness. Neither mind nor ego obtruded. No sin complex, no sense of guilt, no greed or lust, no bondage and no search for freedom, salvation or enlightenment. There was contentment, harmony, and integral wholeness and so I had no quest of God or Guru, Truth or I-dentity.

Everything moves according to its own pattern. You can distinguish in your life-play a pattern or you can aware merely a chain of accidents. Explanations are meant to please the mind. They need not be true. Reality is indefinable, indescribable, name-free and form-free, a world of consciousness and awareness. *Prajna* and

Mahakaruna [divine wisdom and great compassion] alone are Dharmic Law.

"I do not ask for love, I radiate it. Such is my nature. A child just grows. He does not make plans for growth, nor has he a pattern, nor does he grow by fragments, a hand here, a leg there; he grows integrally and unconsciously—because he has no imagination, no fixed images, no ideals. You can grow likewise, but you must not indulge in forecasts and plans born of memory and anticipation." "Unless ye rebecome childlike (not childish) ye can, in no way, re-enter the divine realm of Grace." So it was said and experienced by the Christ conscious Jew, Joshua ben Joseph, and likewise also by many sages, *Jnanis* [enlightened ones] and mature mystics in all religions in all the present and past realms—all in due *prarabdha karma*.

"I was literally charmed here to *Arunachala*," said Ramana Maharshi. "The same force which drew you to this place, drew me to it. I left in search of my Father Source and in obedience to an inner command. It was only embarking on a virtuous enterprise." It was his due *prarabdha karma*, and he bid that his mother cease to moan about it. He seemed to have fallen into a conscious trance, wherein his egoji became merged into the very source of Selfhood, the very essence of being. Afterwards, he lost most of his interest in studies, sports and friends. His chief interest was centered in the sublime consciousness of the Real Self, which he had awared so unexpectedly and unsought. The "depth experiencing" happened upon him. Mundane desires and fear of death vanished. He experienced the inward serenity and spiritual strength of integral wholeness and unity awareness (Grace-Awareness), which never left him.

When he was asked to desire his body's healing from malignant cancer, he explained it was impossible. "There must be something called mind or ego to create a desire, but there is no such thing (in me). The clever, learned doctors advised the amputation of the diseased arm. An artificial limb would have been another ornament for me. If there is pain, let it be. It is also the Self, and the Self is *purnam* perfect. I told the doctors from the beginning I feel no pain. So there is no need for an operation."

The essential message of Ramana Maharshi is to enquire "Who am I?" and to awaken to that real "I" which is not the ego but the eternal blissful Self. There is nothing to achieve, attain, conquer or control, nothing to be obtained or to be possessed. Only this mature and abiding awakening into conscious Selfhood is needed. The method advocated is to be still, to be ego still, to inquire, "Who am I?" What is I? What is the mind-ridden, lustful and troublesome ego? Sincerely ask the Silence, the inner Stillness and you will reach the Source, the Self. You need not kill or control ego. It will drop away of its own accord or you will be consciously free in it and in all other tools. Nothing will be left but the eternal, blissful Self.

Be *Still*, but do not *try* to be still. Simply *be still* to reflect purely "Being Awareness Grace." Ramana Maharshi always stressed the one essential truth that was necessary for the integral awakening, that there is only one Self and nothing but the Self.

10 🌿

Peer A. Wertin
(Ramana Giri)

Peer A. Wertin, who was given the name of Ramana Giri by Maharshi Ramana in the mid-1940's, was often Wuji's guest in his Himalayan sanctuary in Almora. After eight years of intense yogic sadhana, he flew beyond as a real and full fledged Paramahansa. Did Peer try too intensively and too immaturely? After eight years in Himalayan Bharat, Peer's body had to go, the physical one depleted by tuberculosis and left behind for Sri Agni (God of Fire) to consume. But Peer himself had transcended body awareness, and he "came through" and "beyond". One in a hundred thousand, or perhaps one in a million, comes to Realization like this.

—Sunyata

It was on a sunny winter day in holy Benares in the early 1940s that I met Peer A. Wertin. He came gliding along by the shore where the washer men were busy splashing the dirty linen of respectable egojies. I was sharing my leftover food with donkey friends, as human friends would always give me too much to eat. Peer seemed touched by my donkey friendship. Birds of

59

a feather and kindred asses flock together! Peer was in a body of some 25 summers—tall, dark-haired, and slim.[1] He was studious-looking, civilized, respectable and balanced. His upper lip was slightly damaged by some explosion during military duty. I detected a slight stoop, but no sign of T.B. then or later when he visited me in the Himalayas.

We went together to see some sadhus, gurus and learned Pandits in the holy Benares. One Guru fastened on Peer the name "Sri Hanuman." I was not much impressed by the competence of that Guru nor with the name he gave to Peer. Since Peer had been in holy Bharat only a brief while then, I felt he would eventually find his due path. "Step by step as thou goest, the Way will open unto thee."

Peer came to my Himalayan retreat in the Spring when the heat came upon the plains. He stayed in my upper Sunya cave on the hill's crest. It had vast scenic views and a vaster expanse of silence. He imbibed the gracious solitude in the pure, Krishna blue *akasha* realm, while Paramhansa wings grew and unfurled. He had the psychological urge towards stark openness and nudeness. It was the need of being natural, without the rags of ego deceit, artificial respectability or artistic hiding. In this purity, the mental fig leaves become positively indecent or a kind of vulgar prudery.

Peer felt right in that Himalayan setting with nature, with books and a rich inner life. In the outer play, there was the singing self-radiant Silence, the winds in

---

[1] Peer A Wertin was born into an aristocratic Swedish family in 1921. He became a wandering Pilgrim in India in 1945 and subsequently renounced his property worth about eight million dollars. He was related to the king of Sweden. He practiced the "who am I" technique of Ramana Maharshi with intense zeal. He had a direct experience of the Self on Sivaratri day in 1949, after he had undertaken intensive yoga practice for 40 days in Bhagavan's presence in the ashram in Tiruvanamalai. Ramana Maharshi gave him the name Ramanagiri. After eight years in the Himalayas Peer died, his body depleted by tuberculosis.

the pines below, and the crescending of *Aums*. I left Peer
lovely alone except for an occasional service and chat.
Sometimes we played naturally, nakedly together raking
pine needles or cutting grass or wood—all part of our
Himalayan contemplation.

Peer Wertin was awarded a two-year scholarship in
India to study religious and philosophical lore, but he
renounced it all when he took to yoga and intensive Self
inquiry. I had introduced him to Maharshi Ramana in
Tiruvanamalai. In and through Maharshi, he eventually
came to full "awakening," conscious "Self awareness" or
"Advaita experiencing." "Hanuman," the name given to
him in Varanasi, dropped off and "Ramana Giri," con-
ferred on him by Ramana Maharshi, emerged.
Comparisons are odious, yet Maharshi Ramana is
Himalayan to many current molehills and tinpot, claptrap gurus. Peer was blessed in Maharshi's grace and
sahaja recognition.

When I met him first, I asserted nothing. Himalaya
and Sunyata have no need to assert. I could sense in him
a certain Swedish occultism and an intense longing to
realize the Truth. Ramanagiri later came through an
ancient road, a homeward way, frequented by the wholly awakened ones. Here all mental concepts and ideals
vanish. Only awareness remains, bereft of all theories
and ideal abstractions. It is the serene state of exalted
calm in absolute Silence. It has been called nirvana or
turiya or *sunya*. Ramanagiri was in this state of "advaita
experiencing." I did *pranam* [salutation] to Ramanagiri
in glad homage, in *karuna* love and in Himalayan *ananda* gratitude. Upon leaving my place, he went on a pilgrimage. His "*Jiva Yatra*" [soul's journey] was lived mostly in South India, by seashores, in jungles and at the grail
glowing, holy mountain Arunachala.

A few years later when he was still in his 30s,
Ramanagiri left his body. He is deified and worshiped in

a shrine or small temple on the seashore near Madras. Ramanagiri was in my Sunya cave in Almora and he is still here. Blessed be the name Sri Ramana Giri.

The following letter received by me was one of Peer's last:

Dearest Sunya,

In this letter I must tell you that I have sailed away. I have sailed to a far-off place, a place which cannot be described by words. To describe it is to pollute it. The steamer on which I sailed is a very powerful one, but it rolls hard in the sea if the weather is stormy. The place is called by many names, but still no name can cover its Reality. Some used to call the place *Nirvakalpa*, others *Satchitananda* or *Nirgun Brahman*—some call it God or Self, others call it Pure Consciousness, or the ego-less state. To describe it is to put up a big wall before it. The name of the Steamer is Mind. With the help of *Prana*, one reaches the place that for the *jiva* seems so far away, and really speaking, is nearer than one's own breath. If the sense weather is stormy, the steamer will roll badly in the *samsaric* ocean. By now, you must understand the art of my sailing and why I have been so silent.

Let me tell you what happened and why I have been so silent. The same day as I was going back to North India, I visited the Theosophical library at Adyar, and while walking in the garden, Shri Bhagwan Ramana Maharshi appeared before me. He asked me to follow him. I went along the seacoast to a little place where I sat down for meditation, when there Sri Bhagavan's voice told me that my only duty (*Dharma*) from now onwards was the Self. Further, he gave me some *upadesh* [spiritual instruction] which I followed for some days. One night—between 12 and 2—*Kundalini* was aroused to *Sahasrara* and the *jiva* merged into the Self. On account of the sound O*m* from the waves of the sea, I was brought back to body awareness; otherwise, I would have left my body because in that state there is no one to come back—and no one to make any effort. After having regained body consciousness, I discovered that I had lost all my memory.

All events before the time of Sri Bhagavan's appearance in the garden had gone out of my mind. Friends who had been very close to me looked like strangers. People whom I thought that I had never met before came and told me that we had met in Madras only a few days before. Everyone and everything looked so new and strange and unreal. Now I am getting back my memory, but mostly recollections connected with spiritual experiences and deep love. That is why I am writing to you, because those who are near my heart turn up again in this mind, which is so very different from the previous one.

The village people here have built a little hut for me, but there is no post office in this little fishing village, the name of which I do not even know, so I cannot give you any address yet. I don't think any postman will take the trouble to come down to the sandy beach, but I shall let you know later.

With all my love—
Ramanagiri in Him

11 ✤

John Blofeld

John Blofeld, born in London and considered an expert on Buddhism, was at one time a neighbor of Sunyata's on the Himalayan ridge. He lived in Almora for a few years, along with his Chinese wife and two children. He wrote many books including The Wheel of Life, People of the Sun, *and* The City of Lingering Splendour *(Peking).*

J ohn Blofeld's experience in ego abeyance may be temporal, but it was real. The mystic experiencing which he underwent was actually induced by the intake of mescaline. His mind-ridden ego was influenced and subdued by this drug. The use of mescaline and other synthetic drugs, now so much in vogue, seems to be a second– or a third–best mode towards "heaven," "nirvana" "or "the mystical experiencing of God." It may well be only an artificial short-cut for certain fellow wayfarers in whom intellect, erudition and other conditioning seem to be obstacles in their *sadhana*.

There is use and abuse of everything—and of every invention. Whether it is mescaline or any other kind of drug—like nicotine or alcohol, trash novels or even excessive sex—it is a bid to escape from unsatisfactory ego life. John Blofeld accepted mescaline religiously and in stark seriousness. One must be simple as one is simple before God. His integral experiencing was but a temporary elimination of ego and duality. How could it be otherwise when artificially evoked by drugs?

John Blofeld speaks well about his dream or death experience which made itself upon him. He has the word technique (just as Beethoven had the tone technique) in his maturity to express the almost inexpressible. I like his passages as a whole. I admire his attitude, his light of awareness, his feeling tone and the choice of word symbols. What Paul says about Peter tells us more about Paul than about Peter. What John says about his inner, mystic experiencing reveals him—as consciousness. Isn't consciousness more of our Self than our physical, mental and feeling bodies?

John's "surrender" is a kind of simple ego surrender. It discards all that hinders the "ecstasy." Here the ego is subservient to the Self. It sets one's ego-free from all the mental tension and emotional stress. Ego knows itself as non-existing, yet it is at ease. *Ananda* pervades. One innerstands consciously and serenely. No shouting, no raptures, no ego fuss!

Higher and lower states of consciousness are also ego terms, ego concepts and ego values. It is the swell and clever ego consciousness which arrogates itself a higher status. Fundamentally, "there are no others" but there is only the "I *am*." Once a Bengali youth shouted to me, "In the whole world there is nothing but God." This statement pertains to an impersonal ego-free universality, which is beautiful, but it is discouraged in orthodox Churchianity, Judaism, Islam and other dualistic creeds. In Buddhism, the term symbol God is hardly mentioned. It is too vague, too ambiguous and too elastic a concept. All depends on what we mean by the term symbols such as "God," "Soul," "Self," "Spirituality," and the like. Are the concepts, ideals and precepts sentimental restrictions, or are they concrete valid experiences in the play of the universe (*swalila*)?

Read John Blofeld's death experience as he tells it. It is not a joke, or a frivolous fancy to die—or to take mescaline in order to experience a heightened, widening and more vivid consciousness. It may be taken sacramentally and simply, as one is simple before God or Self. "Egoji" must be willing to die and mature enough to surrender. Even then, there can be Hell to pass through unto Heaven. Read Aldous Huxley's *The Door of Perception, Heaven and Hell* and *Island*. His trouble was "intellect" and "erudition" and mere "mental beliefs," which are a hindrance to integral awakening. Preconceptions, preconvictions and mere beliefs must go, giving way to intuitive light, "*karuna* love" and empathy. The meaning of Yoga is union, awareness and ego-free *satchitananda*; or is it power, knowledge and ego swellness?

John Blofeld's integral "experiencing" was but a temporary elimination of ego and duality. How could it be otherwise—when artificially evoked by drugs? Ramana Maharshi's experience, on the other hand, was the *Sunya* Silence and he lived it. He also radiated it gracefully. He spoke out from the Silence. He answered our questions—always directly, tersely and simply—rather than in flowing eloquence.

[John Blofeld's "Experiencing," in his own words as found in Sunyata's records, is as follows]

"Prior to the experiment described here, I had entertained some doubts as to the claims of Aldous Huxley and others, which imply that mescaline can induce yogic experiences of a high order. The experiment which took place on 25 May, 1964, at my Bangkok house under the supervision of Jonathan Slokes, who had previous experience (direct and as an observer) of the effect of mescaline.

"At 9:50 a.m., I took a half dose (0.25 gr). For some time, there was no remarkable effect, but a slightly heightened sense of color and form as exemplified by the vividness of the patterns seen upon my eyelids when I closed my eyes, after gazing through the open slats of a Venetian blind. At 10:40, an unpleasant state of mental tension supervened. I found myself in a struggle to preserve a hold on my "I," which seemed to be in a process of disintegration. The schizophrenic effect was accompanied by a sensation of cold (although the temperature in the room must have been about 100° F), and by an increasing lethargy, which discouraged the smallest action. After a while, these unpleasant symptoms abated and I was able to enjoy attending to what was happening to me.

"At 11:10 a.m., I took the second half-dose (0.25 gr). Shifting colors of form danced upon my closed eyelids. Some of these were patterns of great intricacy, such as those which embellish certain parts of sacred buildings—mosques, temples etc.—or sacred objects of various kinds. These elaborate patterns were abstract, floral etc. Figures of deities, humans or animals formed no part of them. I recognized each one for what it was— Islamic, Tibetan, Siamese—but now, for the first time, I saw them not as arbitrary decorations, but as profoundly meaningful. I felt that, in spite of belonging to widely varied traditions, they are all really valid, and all derived from a single source.

"Presently, I tried to visualize the Tibetan Mandala of the Peaceful Deities, but succeeded only in conjuring up some rather metallic looking demons, although they were far from frightening and not even very lifelike or realistic (being something of a cross between metal statues and living beings), they did convey to me (as though mockingly) that to expect a profound religious experiencing as a result of taking mescaline was presumptuous.

"Soon after that, the sensation of a rapidly fragmenting personality returned to me with frightening force. I grew alarmed for my sanity and should have hastened to get an antidote for the mescaline had one been available. Though J.S. persuaded me to eat some lunch, I was in no condition to enjoy it. By then, things seen and heard presented themselves as independent visual and actual experiences with no seer or hearer to link them into one of those single compositions which, at any given moment, form the content of normal consciousness. The food went down my throat as usual, but it seemed to be disappearing into a receptacle connected with me only to the extent that it was too near to be visible. The mental stress grew agonizing. My fear of permanent madness increased and I suffered especially from the feeling of having no inner self or center of consciousness into which to retreat from the tension and to take a rest. An additional discomfort was the sensation of bright lights, shining now and then from behind me, as though someone were standing there flickering a flashlight off and on. The movement of my man servant, who came in several times with dishes of food, sweets and coffee, occasioned great uneasiness. Whenever he was out of sight, I felt he may be standing behind me for some vaguely sinister purpose. And since he knew nothing of the experiment, I was afraid he would suppose that I was mad. Anyone else's uninvited presence would have made me equally distrustful and uneasy, though I was not bothered at all by the company of J.S., because he was in the know and I felt the need of a nurse or guard.

"No words can describe the appalling mental torment that continued for well over an hour. All my organs and sensory experiences seemed to be separate units. There was nothing left of me at all, except a sort of disembodied sufferer, conscious of being mad and wracked by unprecedented tension. There seemed to be no hope of being able to escape this torture, certainly for many hours, perhaps forever. Hell itself could hardly be more terrifying.

"At about 1 p.m. I dragged myself to my bedroom, shut myself away from everyone like a sick animal and fell on my bed. In my extremity, I suddenly made a total surrender and called upon my "I am!" Come madness or death or anything whatever, I would accept it without reservation, if only I could be free from tension. For the first time in my life I ceased to cling—to cling to self, loved ones, sanity, madness, life or death. My renunciation of my self and its components was so complete as to constitute an act of unalloyed trust in my "I am" (Christ within).

"Within a flash, my 73 was utterly transformed. From hellish torment, I was plunged into ecstasy—an ecstasy infinitely exceeding anything describable—or anything I had imagined from what the world's accomplished mystics have struggled to describe. Suddenly there dawned full awareness of three great truths which I had long accepted intellectually but never until that moment experienced as being fully self evident. Now they had burst upon me, not as intellectual convictions, but as experiences no less vivid and tangible than are heat and light to a man closely surrounded by a forest fire.

"There was an awareness of undifferentiated unity, embracing the perfect identity of subject and object, of singleness and plurality, of the One and the Many. Thus I found myself (if indeed the word symbols 'I' and 'myself' have a meaning in such a context) at once the audience, the actors and the play. Logically, the one can give birth to the many, and the many can merge into the One or be fundamentally, but not apparently, identical with it. They cannot be in all respects one and many simultaneously. But now logic was transcended. I beheld (and myself was) a whirling mass of brilliant colors and forms, which, being several colors and several forms, were different from one another and not altogether the same at the moment of being different. I doubt if this statement can be made to seem meaningful at the ordinary level of consciousness. No wonder the mystics of all faiths teach that understanding comes only when logic and intellect are transcended. In any case, this truth, even if at an ordinary level of consciousness it cannot be understood, can, in a higher state of consciousness, be directly experienced as self evident. Logic also boggles at trying to explain how I could at once perceive and yet be those colors and forms, how the seer, the seeing and the seen, the feeler, the feeling and the felt could all be one; but to me all this was so clearly self evident as to suggest the words 'childishly simple.'

"Simultaneously, there was awareness of unutterable bliss, coupled with the conviction that this was the only real and eternal state of being, all others (including our entire experience in the day-to-day world) being no more than passing dreams. This bliss, I am convinced, awaits all beings, when the last vestige of their selfhood has been destroyed—or, as in this case, temporarily discarded. It was so intense as to make it seem likely that the body and mind would be burnt up in a flash. Though the state of bliss continued for what I later knew to be three or four hours, I emerged from it unscathed.

"I shall now attempt to describe the entire experience in terms of sensory perception, though not without fear that this will cloud rather than illuminate what has been said, for the content of my experiences, being supra-sensory and supra-intellectual, can hardly be made understandable in terms originally coined to describe the mental and physical content of ordinary perception.

"Reality, it seems to me in retrospect, can be viewed as a plasma of no intrinsic color or form that is, nevertheless, the substance of all colors and forms. Highly charged with vivid consciousness, energy and bliss, it is engaged in eternal play. Or it can be viewed, not as plasma, but as an endless succession of myriads of simultaneous impulses, each of which rises as a wave mounts and dissolves in bliss within an instant. The whirling colors and shapes which result produce certain effects that recall flashes of rare beauty seen sometimes in pictures, dreams, or in the world of normal everyday consciousness. It can be deduced that the latter are, in fact, faint recollections of this eternal beauty. I remember recognizing a well loved smile, a well-remembered gesture of uncommon beauty, etc., though I perceived no lips to smile, no arms to move. It was as though I beheld and recognized the everlasting abstract quality to which such transient smiles and gestures had owed their charms.

"Again, Reality can be viewed as a good dancer with marvelous vigor, his every movement playfully producing waves of bliss. From time to time, he makes stabbing movements with a curved knife. At every stroke, the bliss becomes intense. (I remember that the plunging knife made me cry aloud, "That's it! That's right! Yes, yes, yes!") Or else Reality can be viewed as a whirling mass of light, brilliant color, movement and gaiety, coupled with unutterable bliss; those who experience it cannot refrain from cries of "Yes, yes, yes! Ha ha ha! (Wu!) That's how it is! Of course, of course!" I felt as though, after many years of anxious search for the answer to some momentous problem, I was suddenly confronted with a solution so wholly satisfying and so entirely simple that I had to burst out laughing. I was conscious of immense joy and of credulous amazement at my own stupidity having taken so long to discover the simple truth.

"Within the 'Play of the Universe,' there is endless giving and receiving, though giver, gift and receiver are, of course, the same. It is as though two deities (who are yet one) are locked in ecstatic embrace, giving and receiving with the abandon of adoration (the Tibetan Yab Yum representations of deities hint at this). The artists who paint them must be forgiven for their inability to indicate that the giver and the receiver are not only one but form-free, although indeed some artists manage to suggest the oneness by blending the figures so well that the Yum is not seen unless the figure is given prolonged and careful scrutiny. During the experience, I was identical with the giver, the receiver, and the incredible bliss given and received. There is nothing sexual about this union; it is form-free, the bliss is all-pervading and giver and receiver, giving and receiving, are not two but one. It is only in attempting to convey the experience that the imagery of sexual joy suggests itself as perhaps coming a little closer than other imagery to the idea of an ecstatic union in which two are one.

"Some of the conclusions I drew from the whole experience are as follows:

a) Fear and anxiety as to our ultimate destiny are needless, self inflicted torments. By energetically breaking down the karmic propensities which give rise to the illusion of an ego and of individual separatedness, we shall hasten the time when Reality is revealed and all hindrances to ecstatic bliss removed unless, *Bodhisattva* wise, we compassionately prolong our wandering in *samsara* so as to lead other beings to that goal.

(b) The world around us, so often gray, is the product of our own distorted vision, of our ego-consciousness and ego clinging. By casting away our selves, together with all our longings, desires, qualities and properties that pertain to them, we can utterly destroy the illusory egos, which alone bar us from the ecstatic bliss of universal consciousness. The key is total renunciation, but this, also, cannot often be achieved by a single effort or will because each of us is hemmed in by a hard shell of karmic propensities, the fruit of many, many lifespans. The three fires—desire, passion and ignorance—are hard to quench. And yet they would be quenched in an instant could we but make and sustain an act of total renunciation (ego death). Such an act cannot result from effort or longing, because these would involve our egos and thus effectively strengthen them. Thus, in the ultimate stage, even effort and longing for nirvana must be abandoned together with everything else. This truth is hard to understand.

(c) The Buddha experience indicates that when enlightenment (i.e., full awareness of that blissful Reality, whose attributes include inconceivable wisdom, compassion, light, beauty, energy and gaiety) is obtained in this lifespan, it is possible to continue carrying out human responsibilities, behaving as required, responding to circumstances as they arise—and yet be free in them all. So it is with a talented actor, who in the part of Romeo, weeps real tears when his grief for Juliet threatens to overwhelm him. Yet he can withdraw inwardly from his role long enough to recollect the unreality of Juliet and her death and yet continue to give the same performance.

(d) A single glimpse of what I saw should be enough to call forth unbounded affection for all living beings for, however ugly, smelly or tiresome they may seem, all that is real about them is that glorious blissful shining consciousness, which formed the center of my experience. Hatred, disdain, dislike, aversion for any being sharing that consciousness (i.e., any being at all) must amount to blasphemy in one who has seen Being itself.

"It may be objected that my description of the experience is too closely reminiscent of *Vajrayana* [Tibetan Buddhist] imagery and that what I perceived was not Reality at all, but a mere subjective illusion based on the content of my previous studies and practices. The answer to this objection, as Aldous Huxley brought out so well in *Perennial Philosophy*, is that, in all ages and all countries, everyone who has undergone profound, mystical experience, even though in essence its content is apparently the same in every case, has been compelled to fall back on the imagery of his co-religionists or of those for whom he writes. The experience itself is unlike anything known to us in ordinary states of consciousness. There are no words to describe it. Moreover, while my own experience fully confirmed what my Vajrayana teacher had taught me, it was much too foreign to my previous understanding of those teachings to have been a subjective illusion based on them.

"As to how it happens that a dose of mescaline can make such an experience possible to someone who has not attained it by profound and prolonged practice of Yogic meditation, I just do not know. The way I explain it to my own satisfaction is that the effect of mescaline is to free the consciousness temporarily from the obstacles to true realization of universal unity, normally imposed by that karmic structure which each of us takes to be his individual self."

12 🌿

Grecian Lila

Lila had no income, no money, and no curse of property. She accepted no fee for her healing work except food and shelter and fare to her next destination. She was frequently called to hospitals, institutions, ashrams, nature-cure health centers, occupational therapy centers, holiday camps for insane and disabled children and to some of the leprosy colonies. She was often teaching her artful art and skill of touch in healing. Jawaharlal Nehru [Prime Minister of India] noticed her selfless work and called her "the woman with the wonderful touch."

—Sunyata

S ri Lila, a Grecian, was born in Istanbul (then Constantinople). When she grew up, she learned and developed a special skill in the method of oil massage for the healing of feet ailments, skin diseases and psychic ailments. She successfully practiced massage therapy in London during the second World War. She had also briefly been in Boston, Paris, Vienna and Salonika. Finally, she developed a flourishing practice in Athens.

It was in Athens that she suffered a deep shock

upon the death of her mother. When her mother died, Lila too died, in a way. It was actually her ego that died. An imperious inner voice came unto her, "Sell all that thou hast and follow me." Whither goest thou? "To India!" was the thunderous and surprising reply. She had no special feeling for going to India, as she knew nobody there. But there was no why about it and no dallying, no telling of plans or any program and no knowing of what to do or what to be. She had no aim, no object, no purpose. It was only "Go!" Lila simply obeyed the inner call. She trotted into the unknown and the unknowable. She had ceased to be ambitious or ego will-ful. Her practice in Athens was sold or dissolved. She was left with her body, which had become a no-body.

Traveling alone by the cheapest locomotion possible, Lila set out via Cyprus, Israel, Jordan, Iraq, Iran and Pakistan—to Himalayan India. All passages opened up. Strangers became friends and all happened beautifully. It had to happen that way because her attitude and *karuna* approach were right. Lila was a friend to all in India and she was equal with the lowest. She had no ax to grind. She had no grade to make. She had no swelled or bumptious ego. *Ananda* could bubble up within her being, ego-freely.

Lila had rather hard but salutary experiences in *ashrams*. She preferred the practice of unitive relationship with lepers, *sadhus* and simple fellow pilgrims in our richly poor Bharat. Blessed are the poor in spirit, the purely ego-free, and blessed are the meek.

In private and public institutions, Lila taught her art and healed the patients. She lived the wisdom of insecurity, taking no thought for the "morrow" or for the next meal or shelter. There is eternal surety in the calm awareness that we are being used and led, safely guided and worked through. "Step by step as thou goest, the way will open unto thee." We are the Tao and may well

drop the blinkered conceit of agency. Lila was consciously God-led and Self-dependent in *Swalila*. Guru
Wuji opines that she is safely dead. Such a death is enter-
ing into realm of Self awareness. It is leaping into integral living, the secret of eternal life, here and now.

Lilaji moved in Bharat for four or five years in
delightful uncertainty. She was joyfully adapting with the
situations and was healing, soothing and loving all egojies she encountered in India. She worked selflessly and
made no demands. She did not pay much attention to
the ego opinions of others. "Blessed is he who expecteth
nothing." "Pitiable are they who work for fruit." "To
dharmic work thou hast the right, but not to the result
thereof." "Lo! I *am* is always with you! Be of good cheer!"
sayeth Emmanuel. So trot along or bounce fear-freely.
Drop your blinkered conceit of agency and be not
attached to results, property or any special form or concept in anandful *swalila*.

Swadharma is our chief concern. Like the Grecian
Lila, be consciously aware in the non-dual experiencing—then live it in all the ego fuss, duality antics and
seeming bondage. Free in it all as is the Grecian Lila.
Wu!

Lila contends that all our bodily (emotional, mental
or physical) dis-eases and ego woes are due to wrong
thinking, false disciplines, and false values. The cause is
always in the psyche. The illusory egojies want love,
wantto be wanted, to be used and noticed. Some, in
order to get attention, pity and power, make their bodies
ill, thus getting flattery, importance, attention and
power—of a kind. Yet Lila loved egojies. She healed and
harmonized them by giving her time, skill and charm,
spontaneously at joyous ease, clogging along in the most
menial and tiresome tasks.

Lila had but two cotton dresses (white skirt and
blouse) and no headwear except her hair and some-

times a kerchief, à la peasant woman of Europe and China. Often she washed her robe while waiting for some hours or whole nights, at railway stations— always traveling third class—and carrying her own bag and bedding. Her body was never ill, but from the civilized respectability and Western conditioning there was still left what Tibetan Guru Wuji calls bathing rituals and excessive mania: a fear of bugs and fleas and flies, and a war with the dust that is in India. "There is nothing either good or bad but thinking makes it so," quotes the mind-free and thought-free fellow. I am on good terms with pure, Himalayan dust and dirt. I have also never needed a doctor. "I" is naturally spiritual— and "to the pure all is pure."

Beholding Lila so often washing and disinfecting her hands, clothes and even the whole body, we could see Wuji think feel and wonder, "What a terrible sin complex or staining guilt inhibition Lila must have!" She had the power of healing, of evoking love and of stimulating Self-dependence, God dependence and psychic health. Constantly, she effected marveleous healing miracles, without hardly trying. It is the attitude, the contact touch or empathy that matters. Lila was skilled in doctoring, especially in foot and skin dis-eases and massage, but it was her efficient and efficacious touch that healed rather than the fluid and the ointment used. And she who wanted, needed and solicited no money attracted showers of money as a lightning conductor attracts the lightning.

Lila swam into our ken in Almora in May, 1956, after she had already experienced Bharat for a couple of years. Some Himalayan Holiness had pushed an Australian named Allen upon her. She usually had some lame dog or a lamb—or an ego—in tow or under her wing.

She and Allen came trotting along from the motor

bus station, leaving their things and not knowing where or to whom they were going or whither to lay their heads in slumber or in *samadhi*. Mrs. I, a native and to them a complete stranger, met them on the road and offered heart room and house room for both, amongst her other orphans. Also, on her second Almora visit, all of us stayed with Mrs. I. We were taught massage, practicing on one another's bodies. On three other occasions, with Dr. Sen and French Mata Karuna Mayee, they took shelter in the Sunya caves at Kali Math. At our first meeting, we remember Lila saying, "I am dead!" not boastingly or assertively, but simply stating her coming to Bharat, her attitude to values and her purpose-free, will-free and unplanned doings here. Being weary of constant travel and constantly craving egojies, she hoped to find a Himalayan, natural heaven in holy Uttara Kashi with only a small dispensary and a few patients (but patients would flock around her wherever she went).

At Uttara Kashi, I feel, she got her worst psychic shock while in India. The holy holinesses and the native money egos there would, on no account, tolerate leprosy treatment going on in their holy realm. And by a woman—a Western one, who was even pretending to be holy, though living simply enough. She must be a witch, a spy or something even worse! Let's eliminate her! Wu!

Although Lila was sponsored by Bharat Sevak Samaj and by the ministers of the state government, the half finished dispensary she had was eventually abandoned. Doctors were jealous of her many miracle cures. They were unkind towards her because of her popularity. Nobody could discern her ego freeness. She and Karuna Mayee were lucky and glad to get away alive. From thence, she began to sense inner calls from the Greek Orthodox convent in Bethany, where she is now sheltered. But it is all due, dharmic and karmic *Swalila*. Wu!

Sunyata and Wuji

13 ❧

Rudolph Ray

Rudolph Ray, a gifted painter of great repute, and his wife, Joyce Ray, lived in Almora for two years (1958–59) as Sunyata's neighbors on Cranks' Ridge.

O ur gifted and gracious Himalayan neighbor, Rudolph Ray, is a lovable creative artist. He paints the lily purely and reveals the soul scapes and the sound shapes. He has also creatively revealed our funny psyches. All the inmates on the Cranks' Ridge have been "done" by him. He has abstracted us psychologically. "Oh mother of God, what funny guys and girlies ye do look without your usual masks, body disguises and respectable fig leaves! Such lovely crackpots and pure fools ye be—to be sure!"

Rudolph goes out of the ego-ridden mind or mind-ridden ego quite freely. He simply lets the psychic symbols re-create themselves through his tools, talents and technique. He lets them come through in color tones. All things are our Self in this or that form and in mutual interpenetration. Rudolph Ray is naturally, or by yogic practice, sensitized. He is susceptible to the vibrational outpouring through his art. He lets the various psychic vibrations reveal themselves in cosmic and in abstract symbols.

I had no natural, intuitive key to the symbolism of Rudolph's art but Lila of Greece and the French Mata [mother] Karunamayee had. It was in their presence and in their talks with Rudolph, as also in my own solitary sensing of our various soul portraits, that I began to innerstand and intuit in mystic clarity. Rudolph's soul scapes and his greatness as a mature artist.

Lila and Karunamayee recognized and interpreted the characteristic symbols of the gentle soul of Lama Govinda, and also the abstract psychological images of other friends. They "awared" the essentials even in the two soul scapes of our sweet selves. There they are— hanging just inside my front door—the two excellent portraits of Karunamayee Ma and the two images of my otherwise usually invisible, real psyche!

In Rudolph's revealing of my soul in mystic color blots, I seem to discern a pleasing glow of ego humility, *ananda* grace and gratitude—a self-pleased, self-radiant plenum void! This especially is in the abstract and integral painting. In the other, there are certain features of what Wuji calls human, mortal ego faces, and it is rather funny and untamed, with a "devil may care" and distinctly unrespectable mien. There are often two or more paintings of the same person—one with some facial human features and the other purely abstract of psychic integrality. I saw all these paintings—psychological and abstract portraits of myself and of our neighbors in the Cranks' Ridge—come into being by Rudolph. Are the portraits the ego exhibition of the inmates living in the Himalayan Cranks' Ridge? Wu!

Rudolph may be called a mystic artist. Karunamayee innerstands his art. She can share with him in analytical wordiness because she has come with Rudolph on a similar Yogic path. But Lilaji (Grecian

Lila) had the more integral and spontaneous experiencing, as she had been gifted with silent contemplation and inner awareness since her infancy. Such *sahaja* contemplation is simply a thought-free, concept-free, effort-free, purpose-free integral contemplation. It is a mode akin to *sahaja samadhi* or ego-free *advaita* practice.

The whole is in the part play. The microcosm, like Christ, is within. I have been a tree within a wood and many a new thing I innerstood that was rank folly to me before. It is not self hypnotism, auto-suggestion or integral wholeness awareness. It is indeed a pure, receptive play in positive passivity, negative capability and ego-free, non-critical attitude.

I have recently been living with my books, *The Wheel of Life*, *Commentaries on Living*, *The Flying Saucers* and three minor but important ones, with very similar titles: Carl Jung's *The Undiscovered Self*, Alan Watts' *The Supreme Identity* and L.C. Beckett's *The Undiscovered World*. I do not practice any effort-ful meditation *asana* [yoga posture], pose or rituals or any lustful grasping at meaning. I just contemplate effort-freely and in pure receptivity. Be open and desire-free till ye awaken integrally. Innerstand at joyous ease. Be the "I"-free, non-dual experiencing.

Our foremost doctor of the ailing psyches speaks of the Unconscious Zeitgeist, the shadows of sin complexes, guilt complexes—and psychic dis-eases. We cannot dissolve and dare not face—in fear of the undiscovered—the integral Self that seems to be a dire danger to our persona masks and mental egohood. The schism, fissures and discords in our psyches are symbolized in the divisions of countries.

[The following passage is quoted by Sunyata, although the source is not mentioned. The passage is most likely from the writings of Carl G. Jung. –Editors]

The unconscious Zeitgeist compensates the attitude of the conscious mind and anticipates changes to come. An excellent example of this is modern art. Though seeming to deal with artistic problems, it is really performing a work of psychological education on the public—destroying their previous views and concepts of what is beautiful in forms and meaningful in content. The pleasingness of the artistic product is replaced by chilling abstractions of the most subjective nature. This tells us in plain and universal language that the prophetic spirit of art has turned away, for the time being, from the old object relationship towards the dark chaos of subjectivism. As far as we are aware, art has not yet discovered what it is that holds all men together and could give expression to their psychic wholeness. Great art, till now, has always derived its fruitfulness from the myth, from the unconscious process of symbolization, which, as the primordial manifestation of the human spirit, or integral psyche, will continue to be the root of all creation in the future.

The development of modern art with its seemingly nihilisthic trend towards dis-integration must be understood as a symbol and symptom of a mood of world destruction and of world renewal (Shiva's transmuting dance). This mood makes itself felt everywhere—politically, socially and philosophically.

Rudolph Ray seemed to be a medium, a channel being used for and by projections from the vast unconsciousness. He had no conceit of agency and said to a critic, "We think we push—but we are all the while being pushed or pulled. Intuitively we are being used, led and guided."

Rudolph spoke at one of his exhibitions saying, "During my work in India, it became clear to me how important it is to reach sources of inspiration that do not belong only to our time and civilization, but are arche- typal and universal. My art is based on the belief that Art is Being. That Being is preceded by cognition, which, transcending all limitations of time, space and mental structure, arrives at the formless, which is the image of the infinite molding the finite."

Rudolph Ray seemed to go naturally out of his mind or ego, out of will and desire and trying, and allowed the symbolic language of psychic art to come through.

Rudolph Ray said of his work: "This is a return to the transformed beginning, a regeneration, a new cre- ation which never was before, yet related from whence it started. The human seed never perishes. Immortality is the destiny of Man. We possess it in our body organs, the structure and function of which is known. Besides we have in us the most subtle particles which are free from material dependency and not accessible to intellect. The intellect is too rough an instrument to catch them. They can be discovered only by intuition as inherent vibra- tions. Released, they have immense creative power. In the mystical stage, all forms dissolve into nothingness, which may be termed as non-ego. The process of arriv- ing at 'soul scapes' by intuition is an enigma. We probe much deeper into our mind, where the intellect cannot enter. The result is the experience of a metaphysical real- ity. I dissolve the shapes in limitless space. Subsequently, the duality of knowing is transformed into oneness, into Being. The apparent images that arrive are images which make the reality transparent. Reality is then simultane- ously revealed and concealed."

When Rudolph was asked about painting the pictures of Dr. Suzuki in six stages, he said that he had been intensely influenced by the *Maitreya Upanishad* which described these stages as (i) wakefulness, (ii) dreaming, (iii) deep sleep, (iv) individual cosmic-consciousness, (v) intellectual cosmic-consciousness and (vi) spiritual cosmic awareness.

Referring to the achievements of the West in the outer world and outer space, Rudolph pointed out that the inner realm or integral Self was completely neglected and ignored by it. It is only in India that the spiritual values of the inner Self are realized through Yoga. "I have realized this great truth while living in India and my paintings have changed from the early expressionism of 1954 to the intense, transcendental phase of my intuitive experiences in India," said Ray. His earlier works are exhibited in museums in New York and Tel Aviv.

While opening Ray's exhibition of paintings in New Delhi on November 6, 1959, the then vice-president of India, Dr. Sarvapali Radhakrishnan, said, "I am very happy to be here today and to open the exhibition of Dr. Rudolph Ray's art. His approach to the problem is very distinctive and characteristic—and new. All works are fragments of autobiography. They reveal the artist's own experience."

Dr. Ray, like many others, was greatly inspired by the Himalayas, the transmitters of India's classic wisdom.

14 🌿

Passings

Sunyata here gives a description of a few deaths of some of his Himalayan neighbors—Earl Brewster, Adele Stulterheim and Jean Lyon Dhawan—that he witnessed in Almora.

Earl Brewster

Earl Brewster's body was cremated at the holy Vishwanath sangam. He left his body very peacefully and it all happened beautifully like his ideal, artistic, Himalayan life play among us here during the last 22 years. He was solitary, quiet living and invalidish for a long while with bodily impediments and occasional pains and suffering, all a due part of his ideal Himalayan *sadhana*. On the whole, his life was harmonious, artistically enjoyable and *ananda*ful. Although his body at 79 was frail and discomforted at times, there was not much acute or prolonged pain. Until a few months ago, he was able to enjoy and to paint the gracious and ever changing face body and soul of Sri Himalaya. But a minor and a very urgent operation became imperative and was duly performed. It gave him instant relief, but the clever doctors diagnosed so many internal complications and warring woes that they gave the body but one month of lastingness. Earl knew, and since then he kept mostly to his bed at "Snow View," quietly and cheerfully preparing for his homeward journey, saying it would be a relief.

He was visibly weakening and rapidly withdrawing from our realm of values—and of ego play. His consciousness did no longer stand to the alert attention of our important trifles and loving solicitudes. He felt it irksome to listen to our mental concepts, ego reasons and opinions. His memory and imagination wandered, and he seemed to be communing, listening or contemplating in modes of awareness, of Being and of realities, away from our actualities and mundane ego fuss. He preferred to be left lovely alone along the border realms, contacting inner values and more real relationships. Blessed is he who is left happily alone to be "All One" in the flight of the alone to the Alone. Wu!

As pain increased and nights were cumbersome, a dose of morphine was administered and Earl slept for 22 hours. On Thursday evening, he suddenly came back, his consciousness perfectly clear and pain-free, for some 15 or 18 minutes. He was again himself at his charming and gracious best. It happened beautifully, as if by chance, that the neighbors and intimate, local friends called just then to inquire about him. Lama Govinda (Ernest Hoffman) had been his intimate friend for 40 years. Earl greeted all—each one separately in gladness and gratitude. Daughter Harwood's birthday letter was read aloud to Earl, and he was glad and grateful to all and for all, saying cheerfully, "I am going now. I feel as if I were between two worlds. All is arranged well. All is as it should be. I am thankful to you all. '*Grazie per tutto.*'"

Apparently, he had been in touch and had full assurance that "All Is Well." The doctor and Boshi Babu had come only a few minutes before the end. Earl tried obediently to swallow some fluid, but could not manage.

With a slightly convulsive movement, he gave it up, and, at the same instant, also his body. A few hours later, his friends were on the way down to Vishwanath ghat, two steep miles below our holy Himalayan city set on a hill, and by dawn "*consummatum est.*" The well used body had been transformed, transmitted and translated into ashes and *akasha.* While in the inner vastness still sounded the reassuring "*Ram Nam Satya Hai*" (Christ! Christ! Truth Is) [Mantra commonly chanted at Hindu funerals]. There is no death of the Real that we ever are.

I remember quite a few friends and lovers, Ma Sri Yashoda Mai, Narayana, Webbia, Bertram, Michael, Ranjit, Adele, Arpita Devi, and now Bob and Earl and Jean, all leaving their bodies. Some did so in my solitary presence—and wished to do so. Not once did I wish or will to hold back death nor did I grieve or regret in ego pity. Somehow they seemed nearer and freer, relieved from blinkered prejudices, preconceptions and delusive chains. The song goes on in eloquent silence! "I love you beyond mind and meaning and measure. Oh, what a love it is! How free, how new, like nothing else on earth." Empathy transcends the trammels of earth and of egos. Experience and empathize with the Himalayas, with Maharshi Ramana, with any fellow pilgrim, tree friend or with your Self in any blessed form. In empathy with fellow pilgrims, there is no apartheid. I cling not to bodies and minds. So we can have gay Himalayan funerals. Wu!

Adele Stulterheim

I remember the festive passing of the body of our *Amma* [mother], Adele Stulterheim. It was celebrated in October radiance, in autumn's fulfillment and serenity. It so happened beautifully that the town had been preparing, just then, for the visit of some official guy, and the roofs of the houses in our narrow two mile-

long upper bazaar had been gaily bedecked with
women and babies in their gorgeous best rigs, out, like
a colorful flower spread, as our procession came along
from the Cantonment. We passed through one mile of
the uneven bazaar, where the streets were paved with
pebbles and flagstones. Visibly on the bier was Adele's
strong, motherly head uncovered, shaking and bobbing
up and down, as if still alive, in a last, joyful greeting—
contentedly, thankfully nodding to the town, the simple folks and the Himalayan nature that she loved so
dearly. Then the two steep miles down to the holy
Sangam, the wedding place of two Ganga streams,
where her body is washed in charity and in grace. (All
rivers in Himalaya are Gangas and holy).

She was part of the intersuffusing Himalayan
empathy. Om! Om! Ram! Nam! Sat Hai! sounded in the
vast vistas and in the still vaster, integral silence within
all, as Sri Agni's flickering tongues dancingly transmuted
a disused tool into ashes and ether space. Purifying
akasha, earth and air, smoke and fire, water and ether
space consciousness, all the elements participated in the
Aryan rites of the exuberant Himalayan *lila*. Sri Nataraj
ever dances cosmically and transmutingly in sure poise
and at joyous, integral ease.

Wuji enjoys the eternal *Now*, in grace and gratitude.
He awares in *Swalila*—the free self interdependence, all
acceptance, grand affirmation and natural *sahaja* grace.
It is no earthly use asking Himalayan Wuji to be solemn,
mental, respectable or pandit faced. He bounces freely
in existential leaps and bounds and in Himalayan ups
and downs.

This is all a play, rich and right and graceful. When
ego has died integrally and maturely a few times, one can
die again and again, fear-free, fuss-free, body-free and
carefree. Having practiced and experienced that there is
a Ground, a Source, a pure, integral *alaya* [source of

being, God], our deaths may become a due habit, a healing bath in the Source, as is deep dreamless sleep. There is mind freeness, ego freeness, and ego oblivion in such integral experiencing. "Die before ye die!" advised Mohammed. Such a death is the secret of eternal life.

JEAN LYON DHAWAN

Jean Lyon, author of a book on India titled *Halfway Across the World*, was nice, kind and warm-hearted. She came to our Himalayas some 10 years ago to finish this book. She fell deeply in love, not only with the Himalayas but also with Kakoo Dhawan, who was doing research here on the "within" that is also "beyond" the transcendental Himalayas. Only last Saturday, Jean left her 50 year-old body, and within 10 hours, it was duly consumed by Sri Agni's glow at Vishwanath. "We seem to have a habit of dying here," says Wuji.

Jean was a Yankee, born in Peking but now happily and naturally "gone native" in simple empathy with Kakoo Dhawan. Her last five years as Kakoo's helpmate were surely the happiest fulfillment of a richly eventful ego life. Her respectable, scientific and rather mental compatriots were naturally perturbed, dismayed and somewhat shocked—a swell, cute and prawd (proud) girlie going native! Wu ha da!

But did they perceive her integrity, her integrality and her ego-free natural face? Did they aware the living grace? Egojies blunder in blinkered subjective truths and in semantic term symbols. Only the Self can effortlessly aware, recognize and appreciate the Self within—and everywhere.

We see no more in anything, or anybody, than we bring with us and have sensibility and maturity in realized experience—to see through to, in intuitive insight and comprehension. That which regognizes its Self is within. He who sees greatness passing by himself is great. The mature mystic in life sees through his eyes rather than with them.

Jean's inner silence and unassertive acceptance like her simple empathy with Kakoo and Sri Himalaya were, to her fellow compatriots, a complete loss of face, of persona mask and of individuality.

15 🌿

Albert Schweitzer

I n recent years, few men have caught and held the public imagination so well in bringing back to civilization the lost sense of culture, of *shraddha* [faith], the living faith or reverence for all life, as has a German-born jungle doctor, Albert Schweitzer (1875–1965), in equatorial Africa. A legend in his lifetime, he lived the ethic of compassion, empathy and love in action in the service of African primitives until his body was 91. He was the one man in whom Western humanity's conscience had become articulate.

Albert had been sensitive to all forms of pain and suffering since his childhood. When he, like Joan of Arc, heard the evening bell, it seemed to tell him, "Thou shalt not kill." When he went to bed, he added a prayer of his own, "O good Lord, protect and bless all things that breathe. Preserve all living things from evil and suffer them to sleep in peace." He seemed to have retained a light of awareness, a memory of pre-ego, an integral consciousness, and a strong feeling of unity in and beyond union and opposites.

It was something like mystic intuition as "In the whole world, there is nothing but God" and "All that

95

lives is holy (one integral whole) and all is alive." He was obsessed by the feeling that he had no right to personal happiness so long as others suffered. Even as a child, Albert's inner voices induced in his consciousness the *Boddhisattva* mood of awareness, an awareness of his *swadharma* [God's Will] in his Being's law and guidance.

As a Doctor of Philosophy, he wrote a brilliant thesis on Kant; as a musicologist, he wrote a book on Bach (and he used to be one of the best Bach performers); as a doctor of (ailing) divinity, he wrote a theological interpretation of the Last Supper. His other theological works such as *Search for the Historical Jesus* and *Psychiatric Study of Jesus* kicked up such a dust of violent controversy from orthodox elements, that Schweitzer had to assure the colonial authority in French Congo that on eschatological issues he would keep mum, a promise kept until he left his body.

He had already become a doctor of mentology, psychology, divinity and musicology when he received the inner call to go to the African Jungle brethern, to whom love and medicine and surgery would be more useful and serviceable. Schweitzer also studied for years to qualify as a doctor of bodies. There is no such thing as real chance or real choice, but it happened during a brief visit to Paris that his attention was drawn to an article which lamented the lack of trained personnel in Africa and begged someone "on whom the Master's eye already rested" to respond. Schweitzer decided to be that man.

Did he choose Africa or did Africa choose him? He had the inner call to expiate for the sins of Europe, the power, greed and abuse of the "civilized man." He said openly and with rare courage, "We are burdened with a great debt. We are not free to confer benefits on these people as we please. It is our duty (dharmic debt). Anything we give them is not benevolence, but atonement." Remember Rabindranath Tagore's poem on

Africa? "Is it also a suppressed or unconscious guilt complex which makes adolescent Yankee gifts often seem to be benevolent bullying and charitable patronage?" asks Himalayan Wuji. Civilization is not culture. Knowledge is not wisdom.

In 1913, Albert Schweitzer set up his hospital at Lambarene in the heart of French Congo. Except for brief visits to Europe, he lived and practiced there until he left his 91-year-old body in 1965. Africa accepted him without difficulty and, no doubt, taught him a great deal. Slowly, the surgery and medical work he understood developed from a primitive beginning to a great hospital with extraordinary improvisations.

During one of his brief visits to Europe (1931), he was asked to give the Goethe Centenary Address at Frankfurt and he took the opportunity to warn against the pernicious philosophy (Nazist, Fascist and Communist), in which the individual must give up his own material and spiritual personality and must live as one of the spiritually restless and materialistic multitude. The Nazi regime frowned upon him. His *Hibbert Lectures* at Oxford were even more startling. Speaking on the role of religion and modern civilization, he stated, "Is religion a force in our life today? I answer in your and my name 'no!' Proof? The War. Nothing could be simpler and more devastating."

Out of My Life and Thought was also published by him in 1934. It is possible to differ from many of his ideas, findings and interpretations, but not from the sane suggestion that "today there must arise a philosophy—profounder and more living than our own—and one possessed of a greater spiritual and ethical power. In the terrible age through which we are passing, all of us, both of East and of West, must watch for the coming of a more perfect and healthier form of thought, which will conquer man's heart and compel all people to acknowledge its sway. Our aim must be to bring this philosophy into existence."

In 1948, Schweitzer was awarded the Nobel Prize, and the money he received was used by him to open a leperosarium close to the hospital at Lambourene. His address in Oslo in 1950 summed up his faith and life work thus: "The human spirit is not dead. It lives in Solitude. The human spirit knows that *karuna* [compassion], in which all ethics must be rooted, only attains its full flowering when it embraces all living creatures, including human beings."

Once when his wife, a true helpmate, asked him, "How long are you going to go on working like this?" "As long as I draw breath," was his brief answer. Dr. Schweitzer kept his word. On the occasion of his ninetieth birthday, a Life magazine correspondent had wanted to know if he, as an Alsace man, felt himself to be more French or German (Jean-Paul Sartre is his cousin and oh, the difference!). "*Homo sum!*" (I am man) he said quietly. Few humans can truly say about themselves—"I am integrally whole—the Universal man." The jungle doctor lived his *swadharma* consciously, simply and unassertively, and the world seems poorer without him and without such fellow pilgrims as Jawaharlal Nehru, Carl Jung and Albert Einstein.

Such statements as: "To know and understand everything is to forgive everything" and 'Homo sum. Nihil humanum a me alienum pluto!' [I am man. Nothing human is alien to me.] are still assertive ego boasts. Knowledge and understanding are not wisdom or mature "innerstanding" in empathy. What is there to forgive? Who forgives but the illusory egoji? Who accepts insults and responds to malice, but egoji? In integral awareness, we experience that we "are more than human, mortal egojies." Wu! This ego transcendence or non-dual awareness or Grace has been courted and experienced in

Himalayan India by individuals during millieniums. Grace is within and all around us—everywhere and ever present. It is not ours to give or to receive, but integral awareness and experience of It gives meaning, not only to the individual *swadharma*, but to the entire Life process (the *ananda*ful *Maya Lila*), to the actual phenomenal world as a stage on which mental, emotional and lustful egojies strut and suffer, lust and love.

The invisible Real plays in and through it all—and is our Self. It simply *is*—whether we aware it or not. Ramana Maharshi says: "Grace is the Self. It is nothing to be acquired from others, nothing you can have, possess, conquer or control. All that is necessary is to aware and experience its existence in you."

As consciousness of Being *Swabhava*, you are never out of *its* operation. Grace is ever here. In *it*, we live and move and have our Being. *It* is not manifest in our conscious awareness because of ignore-ance—the prevailing false identification with *egoji*. With *shraddha* [faith] in ego-free, intuitive light, it will become manifest in pure consciousness. *Karuna* is desire-free Love. Grace, Light, Life, Spirit and God are all synonymous term symbols with Self, Truth, the Real, the Eternal. "Experiencing" is all.

16 🌿

Milarepa– Tibet's Great Yogi

Milarepa (1052-1136) was a foremost mystic sage of Tibet. He was a poet, saint, rishi, Sufi, mahatma and an artist— all rolled into one. A Mahayana Buddhist on the lofty Tibetan plateau, Milarepa was deeply revered by the people. His intuitive thoughts burst into blossom with his writing of poetry, precepts and songs. —*Sunyata*

Those on the spiritual path should read the exciting adventure of this mystic. His own account of his mystic pilgrimage in consciousness is beautifully mentioned in the book Milarepa, which is translated into English by Lama Kazi Dawa Samdup. The feeling tone, the rhythm and the light of awareness take on a universal hue. The individual becomes the individuum (the whole). The account is esoterically true. It matters little whether or not the life is actually true in details and mere facts.

His pilgrimage through sin and ego crucifixion to transfiguration and simple awakening into conscious awareness is fascinating. It culminates in natural living *samadhi* (simple, pure, active contemplation), which has the authentic signatures and seal. The stages, the happenings and the obstacles (which are helpers) are faced by all esoterically. But since our approach and our reflective light are not similar to Milarepa's, we get stuck in ego-consciousness. We wallow in the bog of ego wills; we flutter in whims and conceit of agency, while Milarepa's attitude reveals his maturity of consciousness.

Few have Milarepa's flair for the Eternal. His sins were adolescent play with vital forces in occult, tantric and *siddhic* tricks. They were juvenile *shakti* busyness, ego lust for power, and the abuse was chiefly through his infantile ego pity for Ma's and sister's tribulation. But what a steady and constant faith in the Real Guru within and a mellow charm and saintly, kind humor Milarepa reveals in his retrospective musing and telling! Marpa, the Guruji he reveres, is essentially within all of us. It is nirvana, freedom and grace. It is here and now. We simply need to awake to be consciously aware of the Experience.

Milarepa was pestered and poisoned like Jesus and Socrates by the jealousy and non-understanding of the scheming pundits of the time, to whom intuition was "sour grapes" and "taboo." It was not the consciousness that was killed, only the forms called Jesus and Milarepa.

Our Christ is revealed by suffering and by our attitude to crucifixion of egos. Christ is death-free. Behold Milarepa's attitude to his body's transformation, to shame and to pedants. "My life in this form has reached its completion; therefore, must I meet the consequences of having been born."

When the fearful disciples begged him to take healing treatment, he said, "It is commonly the rule that illness befalling a sage is to be looked upon as an exhortation to persevere in devotion (dedication), and he ought not have any special prayers offered for his recovery. He should utilize illness as aid to progress (awakening) on the Path, ever ready to meet suffering and even death. Now I need neither forces (*shakti* fuss) nor mediators. I need not the making of prayers nor expiatory offerings, nor exorcism nor propitiatory rites. The maladies born out of the five poisons I have changed into the bliss of the five wisdoms. The time has come when the visible illusory physical body merges into the realm of pure light, and for this no rites of consecration are necessary."

Milarapa was (consciously) the mystic *sunyata* light. He who has one end or Reality in view sees what all things and events serve and also our suffering and ego crucifixions. The things needed are maturity, stillness, and patience. This implies being sincere (to reflect or contemplate purely) and ego humble. Only egos suffer and they are illusory. They are nothing. We are no-thingness: the full, solid, radiant emptiness, *sunyata*.

Milarepa gradually wakes up. His joy bursts forth in rhythmic fragrance. His broken earthen pot (and the last possession) becomes the guruji, preaching unto us the wondrous Sermon of Impermanence. Quietly he sings: "Within the temple of the Bodhi hill, is my body. Within my breast, the altar is.... The horse of mind (vital forces) doth prance about. Knowledge is not wisdom. Much telling is of little profit. A contented heart is the noblest king."

When sister Peta is ashamed to see his naked, natural form, Milarepa sings to her the song of true shame and dignity:

> The contemplatives on the mystic path see no need to hold to codes of shame conventional. Therefore, do not, O Peta, seek to add unto thy present miseries, but let thine understanding flow within its natural channels. (Be conscious of innerstanding. Know intuitively by

identity). Therefore, Peta, do not speak in that fashion. Thou regardest my naked condition with shame, because I have cast aside clothing and covering and cannot cut off the part which thou lookest upon as shameful. I am glad to have obtained the truth (awakened to Reality) through being a man and there is no shame in it. Knowing what is really shameful, I have devoted (dedicated) myself to right *dharma* and have kept my vows rightly. I am the worthiest of human beings, for I am engaged in turning to the best account the previous boon of blessed human life.

If thou speakest of shame at seeing my body, then thou shouldst feel shame because thy breasts, which did not exist at the time of thy birth, have developed so prominently. Seeing that it is better to do away with an object of shame than to keep it on, please do away with thine own—as quickly as thou canst. That which is really shameful are evil deeds and wily deception, artificiality and vanity.

Listen to Milarepa's song to the Geshe (the learned, blinkered, bookish and proud pundit):

I have never valued or studied mere sophistry of word knowledge set down in books in the conventional forms of questions and answers to be committed to memory (and fixed at one's opponent). These lead but to pride and mental confusion and not to such practice as bringeth actual realization of the truth (real-ized experience and conscious awareness of the Eternal). Of such word knowledge, I am ignorant, and if ever I have known it, I have forgotten it long ago.

Accustomed to contemplation of the whispered chosen truth, I have forgotten all that is said in written and printed books.

Accustomed as I have been in the study of common science (intuitive self quest) within, knowledge of erring ignorance I have lost.

Accustomed long to contemplate all visible phenomena as the *dharma* says, I have forgot all mind-made meditations.

Accustomed long to contemplate *Mahakaruna*, I have forgot all differences between myself and others.

Accustomed as I have been to contemplate this life and the future life as one, I have forgot the dread of birth and death.

Accustomed long to the study all by myself of mine own experience, I have forgot the need of seeking the opinion of friends and brethren.

Accustomed long to application of each new experience to mine own growth (awakening), I have lost all creeds and dogmas.

Accustomed long to keep my mind in the uncreated state of freedom, I have lost conventional and artificial usage.

Accustomed long to humbleness of body and mind, I have forgot the pride and haughty manners of the mighty (the trying display of *shakti* business).

Accustomed long to regard my fleshy body as my hermitage, I have forgot the luxury of retreats and of cities.

> Accustomed long to know the
> meaning of the word-free *sunyata*, I have
> forgot the way to trace the roots of verbs
> and the source of words and phases.
> May thou, O learned one, trace
> out these things in standard books.

This last ironic squib refers to the spiteful, sleek and already learned pundit, who provokes the Song. Irony can be part of gay, winged humor while sarcasm and sadism cannot be so and cynicism is a sure sign of defeat.

Intuition and *mahakaruna* shine through Milarepa's words. The light is authentic. The song is of realized experience. The humor is cultured and kind. The rhythm is that of the joyous and the free. What excellent losses and forgettings in the "cloud of unknowing" and in the "game of unbecoming." What blessed unaccustomedness, what serene joyousness as our Milarepa walks on— and reveals the way—simply and consciously self aware! Om! Om! Om!

Milarepa is radiant, fresh and mystically alive. It seems he is listening to the Invisible Real. He moves out of the prison of mind with graceful ease. He takes a leap out of time to fall into the Eternal. No wonder his inner visions burst into poetry, precepts and songs. It is so natural for him to use his tools harmoniously. He innerstands. He is aware of the cosmic Being.

> Discover the non-existence of the personal
> ego and the fallacy of the popular idea that it
> existeth. To realize the non-existence of the
> personal ego, the mind must be kept in quies-
> cence, in repose. That is a state of stillness of
> mind. The eternal is reflected in such a state.
> The mind is bereft of all ideas and thoughts.

Cognition ceases to blur. Mind passes from consciousness of objects, of time and of ego. Days, months, years may pass without the person perceiving it. Mind is now risen to a state of *samadhi*. There is tranquil rest in timeless trance.

Yoga is balance—poise, ease and skill in action. It is the ineffable, indescribable mode, transcending the duality of words and of I notions, wherein the personal consciousness (ego) becomes merged, but not lost, in the cosmic All consciousness. It is like a raindrop merged in an infinite ocean, or like the light of a lamp in the light of the Sun. "Be ye lamps unto your Self."

It is possible to remain in abiding *samadhi* and to be freely active in the phenomenal play. Seek ye first the realm of Self awareness within and ye will aware it (Eternity) also everywhere. As awareness dawns in our consciousness, our other tools—mind, body, thoughts—harmonize in pliable use and we are free in their spontaneous functioning. We are aware that they are neither us nor our Masterji's. Simply we are time-free, thought-free, carefree, ego-free and gay in the joyous play of projection and of withdrawal. We simply, consciously Are. Milarepa expressed it thus:

All phenomena, existent and apparent, are ever transient, changing and unstable but more especially the worldly life hath no reality, no permanent gain (in it), no lasting satisfaction or fulfillment. The realization of this makes me seek, in the contemplative, intuitive consciousness, *that* which is—without corruption, without being shattered, without withering. Many seeming thats are not *that* (suchness). Much talking about it is of little prof-

> it...(It is dissipating, blurring, duality distrac-
> tion! Experience it!—Sunyata). No time have
> I to waste in futile talk or in painting word
> symbols. Grant that this Yogi may hold fast to
> solitudes successfully.

But still *samsara* [the world of birth and death] and nirvana [the state of Freedom] are one. The world, the Devil and the Word made flesh are all imbued, sustained and comprehended by "spirituality." Spirituality is our flair for awakening into eternal awareness of the Whole.

Spiritual life is a matter of mystic conscious inner-standing. It is a matter of body-free, *dharma*-free, *lila*-free awareness. Learning is not insight. Knowledge is not wisdom. Sages never quarrel nor argue but they rejoice in the inner Self revealing Silence.

For 20 years, I saw Sri Yashoda Ma suffer in bodi-ly pain and discomfort. Her disciple, our Himalayan Masterji, Chrisander, for that reason, completely reject-ed her guruship, saying that a "real Guru cannot be ill." This is true in a way. The Real cannot be ill nor does it suffer. That is why I say that spiritual suffering is a con-tradiction in terms. But what about the bodies of Gurus? The bodies of Self realized *Atmas* may be full of woes and dharmic retributions. Gurujis who have expiated or neu-tralized their own sins successfully and so may be free in their *karmas* may well accept and may even reach out for the sufferings of their disciple's bodies. The love of Jesus for the fellow human beings made him suffer and die for them (three years—and three agonizing hours). The *mahakaruna* compassion of Buddha made him live for the world 40 years after his Self illumination. That is the price one has to pay in ego life. Pure love and compas-sion invite vicarious suffering and At-one-ment.

A jealous Pandit contrived to send poisoned food to Milarepa so as to finish him off. Milarepa knew it. At

first, he declined to accept the feast but said that he
might accept and eat the curd later on. Accordingly, he
did eat and did suffer greatly in his body from the recognized, accepted and swallowed poison. He says,
"Generally speaking, a yogi's illness (referring to his pain
as a result of swallowing the poison) and that of the ordinary person is not of the same character. To the former,
it may seem to be accidental. But in this particular
instance, mine illness to me is an ornament. The round
of births and deaths and the deliverance are seen (ever
purely reflected) within the realm of the Clear Light.
When the hands attain their natural posture (when the
tools are harmonized), the great *mudra* upon them
placeth its seal. Thus is there (in me) great indifference
and courage—knowing no impediment. Disease, evil
spirit, sin, obscuration but tend to beautify me greatly.
They lie within me shaped as nerves, as humors, and as
seed gifts I use to ornament the signs of my perfection.
May this sin of evil thought be expiated. This illness
which becometh me so well I could transfer, but no need
is there to do so."

Like Socrates, Milarepa drains his cup of poison
without saying, "Thy will be done!" He knew it is ever
"done" and so he had no conceit of agency. He said:
"May all thy share of miseries too be taken over by me
and likewise be neutralized. Compassion have I for him
who doth injury to his Guru or preceptor or his parents,
and may the evil karma born thereof be partaken by me
and thoroughly digested." It cannot be absolved but can
be neutralized by repentence (which means awareness)
and by an equal amount of good karma. One can suffer
and redeem the evil for another—in the calm light of
mahakaruna. Milarepa sings:

Hold your peace and no litigation will
arise. Maintain the equipoise in *samata* and

distractions will fly off. Dwell alone and ye shall find a friend. Take the lowest place and ye shall reach the highest goal. If ye tread the secret path, ye shall find the shortest way. If ye realize voidness, compassion will suffuse your heart. If ye lose all differentiation between your selves and others, ye shall attain to Buddhahood.

To me and to Buddha and to the brotherhood of my disciples, the three jewels are (1) the light within, (2) the wisdom of the way of awakening unto it, and (3) the body of the awakened self luminous ones (*rishis*, sages or merely the wise ones). Pray ye (dedicate your ego) earnestly without distinguishing one from the other. The mortal relics of a man who hath realized thatness hath no need of rituals conventional. Let him remain in peace.

17 🌿

Kabir

Kabir was born in Benares (Varanasi) in 1440 of Mohammedan foster parents who gave him his Mohammedan name. In his early life, he became a disciple of the celebrated Hindu sage Ramananda. He earned his living as a simple weaver. In 1518, with hands so feeble that he could no longer make the music he loved, he left his body at Maghar near Gorakhpur—acclaimed as a saint by Hindus and Mohammedans alike.

—Sunyata

The words of two simple men of the past can still be heard in every village in India. These are Tulsi Das, the abandoned child of an untouchable beggar, and Kabir, the despised Mohammedan weaver of Benares, who, when safely dead, was acclaimed as Sufi or Rishi by two world religionists.

Kabir lived at the moment in time when the poetry and deeply philosophized experience of the Persian mystics, Attar, Sadi, Jalaluddin Rumi and Hafiz, were exercising a powerful influence on the religious thought of India. In his own spontaneous songs, music and poems, Kabir reconciles the intense and personal Mohammedan

mysticism with the traditional theology of *Brahmanism*.
It is one of the outstanding characteristics of his genius
that he was able, in his poems, to fuse them into one. It
is as a mystic poet that Kabir lives on.

His fate has been that of many revealers of Reality.
He was an opponent of religious exclusivism and sought,
above all, to initiate fellow pilgrims into the Eternal
Present. His millions of followers have honored his
memory by re-erecting, in a new place, the barriers
which he labored to cast down. May the Lord preserve
us from our disciples, followers and understanders!

But Kabir's songs survive. They are the spontaneous expression of his authentic Self experience—in
homely metaphor and religious symbolism, drawn arbi-
trarily or indifferently from Hindu and Mohammedan
phraseology. It is impossible to say of their author that
he was *Brahman* or Sufi, Vedantist or Vaishnavite. He is,
as he says himself, at once the child of Allah and of Ram,
a simple totality or fulfillment who revealed himself to
the sincere lover in all creeds, according to their maturity and measure.

The personal and impersonal aspects blend and are
inter suffused by "God." Narayana represents the impersonal aspect of our divine nature, or experienced Self
Identity; Kabir himself represents that mystical experience of Love or *Mahakaruna*. It is this identity which
makes its appearance at a certain level of spiritual culture and ego maturity, and which the creeds and philosophies are powerless to kill.

When Kabir was beseeched by a devotee to reveal
the way to liberation or *Mukti*, he answered, "There is no
way except yourself. Simply awaken into Self identity
experience. The fishes are content in their element. Why
are you not content in yours?" Implying, it seems, that
awakening into conscious awareness in our element (of
Eternity here and now), is all we need to experience the

unbroken perfection in and over all. We innerstand all the Eternal while. Simply awaken and experience that there are no problems, no bondage.

Very few of Kabir's simple songs are well translated into English or even into Hindi. Rabindranath Tagore's translation of "100 Poems" deals chiefly with the aspect of transcendence rather than with the experience of the living *Sahaja Samadhi* in actual immediacy. Kabir had awakened and so he could play freely and simply in the shadow play of word-symbols and other phenomena.

Kabir says:

> Within the Projector is all and the Projector permeates all. Without the secret, we are all sunk in error: Only wholeness, maturity and purity can experience the Holy. Only *sunyata* comprehends.

> Wherever one looks there is He too, the same. Why perform so many ceremonies? God is no plaything. Why shout? God is not deaf. Forsake all other words, quaff the Word, the 'letterless,' the word-free, the ineffable.

> The name-free was first space, *Sunya*, and from space *Purusha* [original, eternal person] projected *Sabda* [the word] and *Kala* [Time]. They are really one.

> Through fear of *Kala*, devotion of various
> kinds arose, but by experience of the mystery
> of *Nama* [God's Name] fear vanishes...The
> outward eye and the mind's eye perish."
> Narayan innerstands and Sunyata compre-
> hends and radiates freely.

Kabir was a weaver, a simple and unlettered man, who earned his living at the loom. Like Paul, the tent maker, Boehme the cobbler, Bunyan the tinker and Yesuah the carpenter, he knew how to combine vision and industry, skill in action, in Yogic balance and in psychic wholeness or holiness. The work of his hand helped rather than hindered God awareness.

Kabir's contemplation was actual and practical. He was no ascetic indulging in bodily austerities, but a married man, father of a family, and it was out of the heart of the common life that he sang his rapturous lyrics of Prem, and *Mahakaruna* [divine love and pity-free, possessive-free compassion]. His was wisdom by identity and freedom by experience. Again and again, he extols the simple life and the value and Reality in existence. He lived Eternity awareness in immediacy, from moment to moment.

> O Pilgrim! Where dost thou seek me? Lo! I am
> beside thee. I am neither in temples nor in
> mosques. I am neither in Kaba nor in Kailash.
> Neither am I in rites and ceremonies, nor in
> Yoga and renunciation. If thou art a sincere
> pilgrim, thou shalt surely find me revealed.
> Thou shall meet me in a moment of time.
> Kabir says; O *Sadhu*! God is the breath of all
> breath.

So long as man clamors for the 'I' and the 'mine,' his works are as naught; He is the breath, the word and the meaning. He is the limit and the limitless. In and beyond the limit is He. The limit-free, the sex-free, the name-free.

There are no words to tell that which 'he' is: I must withdraw my veil and my will and meet Him starkly with all my bodies.

There the wise are speechless, for this truth may never be found in Vedas or in Bibles. Only he who is the Way has surely transcended all sorrow. Wonderful is that realm of Ease which no merit can win. Kabir says: Experiencing It, the ignorant man becomes wise and the wise man becomes speechless and silently at Ease. He drinks from the source of the inbreathing and the outbreathing of love.

You have slept for numberless ages. Put all dreams and imaginings, ideals and mere opinions away and stand fast in that which you *are*.

O *Sadhu*, the simple way is the best: All contradictions, problems and questions are solved. Still your mind to silence before that splendor. It should not be given a name, lest it call forth the error of dualism.

O Brother, when I was forgetful, my real Guru within revealed the way. Then I left off all rites and ceremonies. I bathed no more in the holy waters. Then I learned that it was I alone who was mad and the whole world besides me was sane, and I had disturbed these wise people.

Your speech is simple, Beloved, but not theirs, who speak of you and explain. I innerstand the voice of your stars and the silence of your trees, and my life has fulfilled itself at a hidden fountain.

He who can open the bud into a blossom does it so simply, patiently and maturely. Why renounce or flee a world pervaded by love, joy and beauty, in order to find the One Reality, who has spread His form of love throughout all the worlds?

"The Yogi of professional sanctity," Kabir says, "has a great beard and matted locks and looks like a goat."

The images are all lifeless, they cannot speak.
I know for I have cried aloud to them. The
Purana and the Quran are mere word symbols: the veil dissolved, we are consciously
aware in our Self.

It does not take much experience in ascetic literature to recognize the boldness of Kabir's attitude in such
a time and place. He lived and sang from authentic experience. But Benares and Mecca and the ecclesiastical
powers feared and disliked him. From the narrow point
of view of orthodox sanctity and ego power complexes,
whether Hindu or Mohammedan, Kabir was plainly a
heretic. His frank dislike of all institutional religion, of
all external observances, which was as thorough and
intense as was that of the Quakers, completed his reputation as a dangerous fellow, so far as ecclesiastical opinion was concerned.

His stay at Magar was a form of exile or banish-
ment from Holy Kashi (Varanasi). The "simple union" in
Eternal Reality which he perpetually extolled as the duty
and the joy of every soul was independent both of rituals
and of bodily austerities. The God whom he proclaimed
was not especially in Kaba nor in Kailash. Those who
sought "Him" (the sex-free, form-free and name-free)
needed not to go far, for "He" patiently awaited discov-
ery within and then everywhere, more accessible to the
washerwoman and the carpenter than to the ego-right-
eous holy man and the learned scholastica.

Innerstanding is also transcendence. "Freedom
experience" and "joyous ease" radiate in the "simple
way of awakening." Therefore, due to his Self-experience, the whole apparatus of piety, Hindu and Muslim
alike, the temple and the mosque, the images and the
holy water, the scriptures and the priests, were
"denounced" by this intuitive and Self-experienced

poet as mere substitutes for Reality—dead things inter-
vening between our awareness and our Self. We are apt
to cling to ideas and traditions and to stick to our tools
and media, rather than to court the real and abiding
Self-experience or wisdom in Identity.

Everything is part of the projection withdrawal play
in "God" and therefore, even in its humblest detail, capa-
ble of revealing the player in the intuitive vision or purely contemplative experience. It is a special vocation of
the mystical consciousness to mediate between two
orders, going within and going out in unity awareness.
The secret of life is our mystic death or awakening. In
Self-awareness, we innerstand and are not caught in
forms, divisions, media or functions. We are aware and
free in them. Bondage is delusive and pertains to minds
and eyes in shadowplay.

Those who experience share (although they may
never tell) the joyous and ineffable secret—of the
Eternal, in time and in spontaneous play. Kabir says,
"*Brahman* and the forms and the play are ever distinct
yet ever united," and *jijimuge* [ever intermingling] guards
or reveals the same mystery. This mysterious unity in
separateness is common to all sane and real mysticism.
In Zen Buddhism, it is "*jijimuge*" and "*sunyata*." The
Plenum Void comprehends.

For the mere intellectualist, as for the mere pietist,
Kabir has little approbation. The whole creation is the
manifestation and play, projection and withdrawal of the
Eternal, the living, changing expression in radiant joy
and in *Mahakaruna*. In and beyond the mist of pleasure
and disease, failure and fulfillment of egos, is the divine,
joyous Ease in rhythmic rightness. "Om Aum is the
Everlasting Yea."

Our normal human consciousness, very partial and
limited at its best, is so completely committed to dependence on the senses, mind and prejudices, that the fruits

of intuition itself are instinctively referred to them. Even great contemplatives and genuine self-experiencers, in their effort to convey to us the nature of their experience in the super sensuous, intuitional realm, become mental, intellectual or rational in their word symbols. They are driven to employ some form of sense imagery—coarse, inaccurate, blinding and often falsifying, as they know such imagery to be even at its best.

Everywhere Kabir discerns the tactful rhythm and the "unstruck music" of the universe. His favorite symbols are Krishna, the divine flute player, and Nataraj [Shiva in the form of the Cosmic Dancer], the visual embodiment of rhythmic movement and transmutation, that mysterious, joyous dance of the universe before the Lord, before the face of *Brahma* or *sunyata*, which is an act of worship, a radiance and an expression of the infinite calm rapture of the transcendent in the immanent. Do we experience our symbols? Do we live in the name-free, form-free, time-free and effort-free Self in joyous Ease?

In his wide and rapturous experience in God, Kabir never seems to lose touch with ordinary experience, nor does he forget the "common" life. His feet are firmly planted upon earth. His lofty and passionate apprehensions are simply controlled by intelligence and by the inherent discipline. This alert, common sense is usually found in intuitive persons of real mystical genius.

Kabir discards abstractions and philosophizing and external religion (or religiosity), and he insists on simplicity and directness. "God is the root from whence all manifestations—material and spiritual alike—emanate. Happiness (*Ananda*) is yours (consciously) when you come to discover the root." Hence, to those who keep their intuitive eye on the "one thing needful," denominations, creeds, ceremonies, the conclusions of philosophy and the discipline of asceticism are matters of comparative indifference. They represent merely different angles from which the soul may approach its "dissolution" or "awakening" and are only useful insofar as they contribute to this consummation.

So thoroughgoing is Kabir's eclecticism that, in his effort to tell the truth about the ineffable apprehension, he seizes and twines together symbols and ideas drawn from the violently conflicting philosophies and faiths that illuminated his life—whether it be Vedantist and Vaisnnavite, pantheist and transcendentalist, *Brahman* and Sufi—just as he might have woven together contrasting threads upon his loom.

> Experience radiates through opposites and reveals the Unity. All are needed. All the colors of the spectrum are needed if we would demonstrate the simple richness of white light.

> The discovery of God is the simplest and the most natural of all things if we could but grasp and experience it. He may best be found in the here and now, in the normal, human bodily existence and 'mud' of material life.

> The sincere seeker is he who mingles in his heart the double current of love and detachment, like the mingling of the streams of Ganga and Jamuna. In his heart, the sacred waters flow day and night, and thus the sound of birth and death is brought to an end. Look within and behold how the moonbeams of that Hidden One shine.

It is needless to ask a sage the caste to which he belongs. The priest, the warrior, the tradesman and all the thirty six castes alike are pilgrims in Eternity. It is but folly to ask what the caste of a caste-free sage may be. Hindus and Muslims alike have awakened into the realm where no real marks of distinction remain.

Do not go to the garden of flowers! O friend, go not there! In your body is the garden of flowers. Take your seat on the thousand petals of the lotus and there contemplate the infinite Beauty. The unstruck drum of Eternity is sounded within me, but my deaf ears cannot hear it.

The Guru comes and bows down before the disciple. Wonder of wonders! The disciple chooses the manifold fruits of life and tastes them, and the Guru beholds him in joy. What Kabir says is hard to understand: the bird is beyond seeking, yet it is most clearly visible. The form-free is in the midst of all forms.

Who has awakened into love and non-attachment is free and never descends to death; who experiences the simple way of awakening that is other than rites or ceremonies reveals the stillness in the midst of all activities.

The Word reveals all, but who knows whence the Word cometh? (*When we have experienced the word symbols: Lila, God, Ananda, Nirvana and Plenum Void, we can be silent and still.* –Sunyata)

You are weaving your bondage of falsehood. Your words are full of deceit. With the load of desires which you hold in your head, how can you be carefree and move lightly?

He whose words are pure and who is free from pride and conceit of agency awakens in *Swadharma*. The Yogi dyes his garments instead of dyeing his mind in the colors of love; I do not 'know' what manner of God is his. The Mullah cries aloud to Him and why? Is your Lord deaf? The subtle sounds of anklets that ring on the feet of an insect when it moves are heard by Him. Take your beads, paint your forehead with the mark of your God and wear matted locks, long and showy, but a deadly weapon is in your heart. So how will you experience God? He has spread his form of love throughout all the world. Where the ring of manifold joys ever dances about Him, there is the sport of Eternal Bliss. When we know this, then all our receiving and renouncing is over. Henceforth, the heat of having shall never scorch us. They call Him 'emptiness' in whom

all truth is stored. There is an endless realm,
my brother, and there is the name-free, home-
free Being of whom naught can be truly said.

They are blind who hope to awaken into unity
by the light of reason, which is the cause of
separation. We can reach the goal without
crossing the road—such is the Eternal *Lila*.

Sunyata and Lama Govinda

18 🌱

Carl G. Jung

Psychology, as pursued in the West, is only mentology, a science of the mind rather than a science of the psyche. It is safe to say that every one of my patients in the second half of life fell ill because he lost that which the living religions of every age have given to their followers. None of them have really healed, who did not regain his religious outlook.

—Carl G. Jung

Jung says, "Our Western air of superiority, in the presence of India's understanding (insight), is a part of our essential barbarism. We occidentals have learnt to tame and subject the 'psyche', but we know nothing about its methodical development and its function. Our civilization is still young, and we therefore require all the devices of the animal trainer to make the defiant barbarism and the savage in us, to some extent, tractable. But when we reach a higher cultural level, we must forgo compulsion and turn to self-development. For this we must have the knowledge (wisdom awareness) of a way or a method and, so far, we know of none.

We plug up the emptiness in our souls with efficiency, and psychology."

This statement is interesting as coming from a leading psychoanalyst of the abstraction we call "The West!" "To tame and subject the psyche" is still ego-conceit of agency, and "self-development" is ego-development, mere evolutionary or becoming consciousness (into supra-mental egos? Wu!). The confusion is in the use of word symbols like "I" and "ego" and "Self," and "soul," "mind," "man" and "psyche." Fancy the chief doctor of psychosis in quest of the psyche, which he is supposed to "doctor," to make integrally whole. He calls himself "barbaric mentologist!" Still it is said that he who knows that he is a fool is not a great fool and that he is wise who knows how little he knows. In Greek, "psyche" is "mind-soul" and in Chinese "mind-heart" is one term symbol and "Wu" is yes and no.

Spiritual scientific psychology (Self-search) has been successfully practiced in India from time immemorial. A Himalayan *rishi* reminded me, "We are ever always aware, Sunyata." Yes, the essential psyche is ever aware in the integral Self. But the swell ego, the ego-ridden mind and the cute mentologists seem to have no joyous ease, no integral grace, no healing gratitude. Wu!

I quote another of Carl G. Jung's advice to the youth, to adolescence or to a particular young man:

> You are so young and at the very beginning of things that I must beg you as earnestly as I can to be patient towards all unsolved problems of your heart and mind. Try to care for the questions themselves as if they were closed chambers or books written in a foreign language. Do not search now for the answers which could not be given to you because you could not live them. The important thing is to

> live everything. At present, live the questions
> and perhaps, little by little, almost uncon-
> sciously, you will, at some distant date, enter
> into and live the answers.

This seems mature advice, but maturity is not in a span of years, nor is death (of ego) in a body's decay. All babies are wise. Some are born mature and retain their pre-ego-consciousness (or prenatal wisdom awareness) co-existing and unclashing in the disease of duality-consciousness and ego fuss. The integral Being awareness remains and suffuses the "be coming" and "be going" ego-consciousness and we have the rare born mystics— the *ananda*ful, ego-free and integral artists in Life. Wu!

In the fifth century A.D., India's celebrated poet Kalidasa experienced and revealed what Western mentologists in their "essential barbarism," even now, comprehend only imperfectly: "That the world was not made for man, that man reaches his full stature only as he experiences the dignity and worth of a life that is more than human."

It is three years since, in France, I happened to glance briefly into Dr. Carl G. Jung's superbly mature autobiographical book and spiritual testament, *Memories, Dreams and Reflections*. Only now has a copy of this Self-revealing book found its way to my Himalayan realm, so that I can really read it at leisure and "go with" in empathy and in "participation mystique."

It is a pilgrimage of the spirit toward psychic wholeness or Self awareness, whose theme is the inner integral Being Consciousness Grace, which is denied by our utilitarian, scientific, artificial society. This copious disclosure of his inner life is perhaps as near as one can get to a literary confession of integral wholeness. It is profuse in subjective materials, dreams and premonitions and conscious guidance and grace, but relatively bare of data about more commonplace, external events, social and family interrelatedness.

While Jung accepted and fulfilled many social responsibilities and duties such as treatment of patients, participation in psychoanalytic conferences and family life, it was the hidden domain of his Life Play that he valued and was impelled to reveal. It was "innerstances" rather than "circumstances" and "personal influences," "psychic wholeness," "intuitive apprehension," "Grace" and "empathy" rather than "analyses," "actualities" and "mere mental understanding." "Insight," "wisdom" and "integral wholeness" is what, in his final backward glance, the erudite doctor of psyches chose mainly to expose and to elucidate. It was guidance rather than willful and conscious choice. The task of communion was imposed on him from within, inspired by his inner "Guru" or integral Self, in the invisible Real, Inner Life.

> A book of mine is always a matter of fate. There is something unpredictable about the process of writing and I cannot prescribe for myself any predetermined course. Thus these autobiographical reflections are now taking a direction quite different from what I had imagined at the beginning. It has now become a necessity for me to write down my early memories. If I neglect to do so for a single day, unpleasant physical symptoms follow. As soon as I set to work they vanish and my head feels perfectly clear.

The chapters move as conversation or spontaneous narration, as beams of intuitive and integral light that only fleetingly illuminate the outward events of Jung's work and life play. They rather transmit the atmosphere of his intellectual, psychic and religious world—and the spiritual experience of a man to whom the psyche was a profound reality. "God" was an experience, a living Grace and the unconscious was bravely investigated—as the undiscovered Self, or as the Christ conscious Emmanuel—within. Only the intuitive, spiritual essence of the psyche's life experience remained in memory as of value and as worth the effort of telling. The sage had regained the childlike, and needed not the technical or psychological jargon or term symbols.

Jung writes:

> In maturity we are drawn back, both from within and from without to memories of youth and childhood, aye, to babyhood and to pre-ego-consciousness. But I know too many autobiographies with their self deceptions and downright lies and I know too much about the impossibility of Self portrayal to want to venture on any such attempt.
>
> This task has proved so difficult and singular that in order to go ahead with it, I have had to promise myself that the result would not be published in my lifetime. Such a promise seemed to me essential in order to assure for myself the necessary detachment and calm. Fate will have it—and this has always been the case with me, that all the 'other' aspects of my life should be accidental. Only what is interior has proved to have substance and determining value. As a result, all memories of outer events have faded and perhaps these outer experiences were never so very essential anyhow, or were so only in that they coincided with phases of my inner development.

19 ❧

Mysticism

Sunyata never considered that he was anything special. He was therefore, quite surprised when Ramana Maharshi remarked that he was a "rare born mystic." At the time he did not know what a mystic was so he promptly obtained a copy of The Oxford Book of English Mystical Verse. *He wanted to learn more about what constitutes a mystic. The folowing article is a result of that investigation.*

*E*velyn Underhill has defined mysticism as the art of union with Reality. A "mystic" is an individual who has attained, or awakened into that union to a greater or lesser degree, or he is the one who has an inkling of that unity and who aims at it. In the unity awareness of a mystic, there is no sense of personal or individual identity—and yet it is a kind of a witnessing and affectionate awareness. In this awareness, there is affectionate detachment, appreciation of rightness, but no analyzing, no mental discrimination or judgment. I, me and mine are not there—nor is there any sense of the past or the future. It is only awareness of Being. The Eternal Now encompasses all that has been and is.

Nothing seems to be unnecessary or out of place to

a mystic. Harmony reigns in the mystic's vision; unbroken perfection is in and over all. It is a perfect blending of all into an indescribable expression of grace, joy, peace, beauty, love, compassion, and wisdom awareness. The One is the non-dual experiencing, the no-thing-ness. To know God is to be God. Being Awareness Grace. *Tat Twam Asi*.

There is a new dimension, a realization that "all is well" now and always, that the power of love, empathy and "participation mystique" absorbs all and transcends all. Self, God, Grace is an ever-present reality that enfolds us always. In *it*, we live and move and have our Being. This is the mystic's experiencing in wholeness and grace awareness. Whether things we attain in the Life play or things we miss, everything is acceptable and right. It is all acceptance; it is in a new but very real sense, loving *it*, awaring and loving our Self in all things, phenomena and happenings.

Love pervades everything. All conflicts and sufferings are like surface waves upon the quiet ocean depth. There is nothing that we habitually call good either, since the truth of all opposites is beyond all seeming contradictions and takes them into the Self. There is something perfect in all created things. Ultimately, they can live by it and nothing else matters. The mind's knowledge is never certain. Intuition alone reveals Reality. Only Self awareness is certain.

The duality of body and soul does not exist for the Self-realized sage. In the bodily, mental and spiritual functions, there is only a difference of degrees, but not in essence. When the mind has become luminous, the body too must partake in this luminous nature. This is the reason for the radiation which emanates from all saints and the Enlightened Ones. The aura which surrounds them is described and depicted in all religions. The radiation is visible only to the intuitive or spiritual eye. In ego surrender, the light of wisdom and the warmth of the heart are united.

Dr. Von Veltheim describes his experience with Ramana Maharshi thus:

> When my eyes were immersed in the golden depth of the Maharshi's eyes, something happened which I dare describe only with the greatest reticence and ego humility. The dark complexion of his body transformed itself slowly into white. The white body became more and more luminous, as if lit up from within and began to radiate. I looked at my watch, my diary and my spectacles, then again I looked at the Maharshi, who had not averted his glance from me. With the same eyes which a moment ago had been able to read some notes in my diary, I saw him sitting on the tiger skin as a luminous form. It was so simple, so natural, so unproblematic. How I would wish to remember it with full clarity in the hour of my death.

A genuine mystic feels intuitively but knows very little mentally. Thought is still duality, whereas intuitive feeling can be ego-free and experiential. A mystic, pure and simple, does not care. He is carefree, age-free and ego-free. All mystics feel the same intuitively, but they express it in different ways.

Grace is not the kind of euphoria hippies talk about. It cannot be ingested chemically. If it could, what would be the merit of saints and ascetics? Spiritual consumatum can be achieved by everyone, "high caste, low caste, dog eaters—nay, even women," as the *Bhagavad Gita* puts it so charmingly.

All mystics are *sadhus*, but very few *sadhus* are mystics. The term "mystic" is derived from "*mystisthai*," the silent one. The sage Bharata acted insane so that people would leave him alone. When the Basrah Sufi awoke Self illumined, he ran about shouting, "*Anur Huk! Anur Huk!*" (I am God, I am God). This proved fatal and his head was chopped off by his pious, orthodox brethren. What the hippies, the neo-mystics and the occultists seek (in contrast to the pious) is something quite different from the goods that the churches promise to deliver. Heaven is not enough and certainly health, wealth, mental well being are not enough. Mystic insight or aware innerstanding is sought, freedom from conditioning, impositions and possessions is sought, the esoteric is sought, the essence is sought and the integral self expressing is sought.

A noble lady asked her husband, a seer in the *Upanishads*, "What is it that one has to find, which, once having found, nothing else remains to be sought?" Sri Wuji says, "It is nothing you find or achieve, attain or become. You simply, naturally and maturely need to wake up in conscious integral awareness of what *is* and what you ever *are*."

In order to aware what transcends the ordinary things of life, one has to turn one's gaze, from outwards to inwards, inside one's Self. Focus the Center—the Core, the Essence. It is one's Real Self you are seeking. You are that already—and not the ego you that has a voice, two arms and a sex. You are divinity, nothing less, not the ever-changing bodies, mind or intellect. Hence, the most important thing is to realize, aware and experience one's own absolute divinity. *Il faut chercher, trouver et "experiencer" cet qui ne passe pas—dans ce qui passe* [Seek, find, and experience that which does not change in all that changes].

In the eclectic, elliptical prose, the modern Swamis are the holymen. They speak English and fly in aeroplanes. They wear watches. They are punctual and they are knowers of *Brahman*. They hardly use the word "mysticism," although their Western disciples use it all the time. The roaming Swamis know the word, of course, but it does not appear to be part of their spoken code. They use the word self-realization for the Zero experience. A Self-realized person is a mystic. A revitalization or reawakening movement into integral Grace Awareness has begun to span the globe. Shankaracharya said nasty things about scriptural knowledge and "learned ignorance," after he himself had that kind of knowledge. Intuitive knowledge is wisdom.

Our Sri Anandamayee Ma gives simple down to-earth answers to ego questions. Their profundities lie in their directness. They are not thought-out answers, but spontaneous and intuitive reactions to common-sense situations. The experientially open find it easier to enjoy the Zero experience without interpretation. The Christian mystics who did not make the interpretational compromise of talking permissible language about the Zero experience were in trouble. Meister Eckhart died a prisoner in his monastery. Giordano Bruno and Joan of Arc mounted the stake and, similarly, the Sufi Al Hallaj was killed by his pious, orthodox brethren for shouting "*Anur Huk!*"

I innerstand intuitively, awarely or unawarely, all the eternal while and my body tools will last as long as they are needed in *prarabdha* play. Distance, divisions and detachments are not real enough. Reality is in and beyond "time" and "thought" and "egojies." "*Notre soleil brille toujours.*" [Our Self-sun always shines.] I do not shout or assert my truths. I live them.

The "Zero experience" comes to those to whom it comes, regardless of what they do. It also comes to those few who strive very hard over a long period, as was the case with Ramakrishna. It is a matter of sincerity, maturity and *prarabdha*. Many people who do not seek or try at all have stumbled upon the "Zero experiencing" and it is this fact which the scholars and the ecclesiastics resent. "I came by a private lane and not by their mapped out way. And their scolding grew louder every day," says Rabindranath Tagore.

The mature mystic has developed his own private meaning as he reads and interprets dogmas and gospel truths. Monolexis is an individual code for absorbing and transmitting doctrines without risking dysfunctional conflict with the surroundings. What distinguishes the mystic's religious doctrinal language from that of the ecclesiastic's is precisely this monolexis. He uses words from the Writ, but he uses them in his own code. In fact, you can recognize the school of the mystic by the way its members use scriptural terms in a non-scriptural sense, through the process of monolexis. "Peace" to Jesus, the mystic, seems to mean "peace with one's own esoteric experiences" in innerstances and in circumstances. The mystic (i.e., the silent one) does not have to assert, express or explain his experience, nor does he have to insist on ontological corollary to his experience. There is no outsider qualified to check and tell whether the mystic's experience is genuine or not.

Schizophrenia, paranoia, hysteria, depression, mania and catatonia are so many emetic terms—part of a jargon of Euro American psychiatrists, who have never had the "Zero experiencing" and would not see any worth or value in it nor any meaning if it was reported calmly and factually.

It is not people qua people whom Wuji appreciates, but people qua Zero experiences, and herein lies his being antisocial. The fundamental idea of mysticism is that the essence of life and of the whole world is an all embracing spiritual substance, which is the Reality in the core of all beings, irrespective of their outer appearance or activities.

When people asked Ramana Maharshi how he came by his powerful experience of Oneness, his answer was, "I did not do anything at all." The newly intuited Reality is not a reality like the law of thermodynamics, but a Reality privately certified by the impact which the Zero experience wields on its subject.

There are hippies and kindred communities in North America now which use ritualistic copulation, with or without ejaculation—as in the Oneida community and as in tantra, as part of their ego discipline (*sadhana*). Ego was the helper. Ego-consciousness is the bar.

Treat mysticism in its own right. It is a phenomenon that can well stand alone, devoid of the artificial or historical accretions which have been attached to it.

Sri Anandamayee Ma used to have conversations with tree friends during her childhood. She says, "As the whole and complete tree is contained in the seed, just so is the divine, in its fullness enthroned, is within you as *you*. Become an explorer of Eternity, not a drifter of mortality. Focus intuitive light on your Self. Your Self is always with you. You need not feel lonely. '*I am*' (is) the very embodiment of Peace. Whatever you think me to be, that I am. '*I am*' is not striving after anything, so there is no question of any exertion. In the infinite 'many' is the sole I—the Self. Let all thy Self be Krishna."

Be your Self in conscious awareness. Krishna resides within everybody. Egojies need not feel lonely or lonesome. The Self is always here—*Sthithaprajna* (established in wisdom). "Beatitude is the only Reality," says Anandamayee Ma and adds, "All else is mirage." She may be prompted by "*Khayala*" to complete withdrawal within her inner Self (depth-consciousness). *Khyala* is an intuitive, psychic emergence, a spontaneous urge. The body is a transient shell or a tool and the Self is far beyond its narrow confines. We may drop our blinkered ego conceit of agency. This body never speaks to "another"—that is why it talks in such a topsy turvy fashion.

20 🌿

Toward the Mysteries

Sunyata read Towards the Mysteries *by Swami Omananda and in response wrote the following*

I have been reading Swami Omananda's recently published book Towards the Mysteries (Neville Spearman, London), and I find the teaching of "The Brothers" therein very ably edited and annotated by Swamiji and in very congenial term symbols. The teaching seems to emanate from a very high, deep or mature Source.

The teaching of the Brothers is a corroborating and confirming light on our natural, intuitive, unconscious and lovely solitary "Yoga," or joyous yogic play in the *anandaful Swalila*. There is a delightful emphasis on Intuition. Cultivate the feeling principle, which is natural to intuitive awareness. The boat of intuition carries you across the ocean of duality to the Source of *all*. The sea of *samsara* is awared through intuition leading to the ocean of graceful *Ananda*. Always build from within, not from without—from intuition, not from instinct.

Intuition has the dissolving element and it dissolves in instincts. It dissolves egoji. Wu! Intuition is the manifestation of pure truth and right desire is born from it. There is a right and a wrong desire. Effort-free desire is right (need), effortful desire is wrong (want). Think it out.

Intuition comes from a cosmic thought. Intuition is the action of the Man HimSelf. It is the direct action. Knowledge is of the world, while intuitive wisdom is of the soul (or Self), of the whole, integral psyche. The real intelligence is the collaboration of the mind and the intuitive psyche. After the opening of the third (intuitive) eye, the mind functions in cooperation with the intuition. With the closing down of the third eye, the mind has "become a mass of facets."

The facets are the movements of the mind under sway of "want." In that state of mind, rather than one clear mirror of intuition, the mind is broken up into many small mirrors. Desire should be for the use of the mind; it should not *drive* the mind. Desire should be born of instinct and intuition. "Need" is simple necessity, being right desire, as distinguished from "want" that is for the unnecessary, being wrong desire.

Man is powerless against his own intuition, whether that intuition functions or whether it does not. Intuition is the action of God, of the unitive Self. Be simple. Be natural, spontaneous and ego-free.

The art of living is living by intuition. You cannot do it because you have not developed your intuition, not awared, trained and tested it. If you had developed your intuition as much as you had developed your mind, you would have found your soul (in Self-experiencing). In developing your mind, you have made your effortful desires a temporary success, but at what cost! Instead of sacrificing your effortful desires—"wants"—to your intuition, you have sacrificed intuition to your wants.

Take away the obstacles and there is always a flow

from the cosmic. Action should proceed from the Source
and be spontaneous action. You people do it the wrong way
around. You must quiet the mind (and the desireful, willful
egoji). Be Still to practice intuitive, whole and direct perception. Spontaneity does not come from the mind.

The mind is always circulating, but intuition feels.
Instinct is for the protection of the animal in man,
whereas intuition, the feeling principle, is for the protection of the psyche, the soul of man. Stop egotism and
you liberate both instinct and intuition. Do away with
choice (effortful desire) and let the intuition decide, i.e.,
let intuition be the guide.

Choose without "want." Be choice-free and your
choice freeness will liberate your intuition, which at present is stifled by your wants. Do not try. Eliminate effort.
Effortful choice has "want" in it and "want," in whatever
high a plane it is, always fetters the soul.

Religion is that which is opposite of the mind. The
mind as such is incapable of spiritual discernment. The
fountain is in the individual spontaneity. Live intuitively
and you *are* religious. A religious man, especially, should
not conform to any standard except that sanctioned by
his intuition.

There is no attachment apart from the mind.
Permit the dissolving to take place. It is so simple to the
intuitional, so difficult to the dissolving mind. Intuition
guides you only along the gentler path, the path of non-
resistance, non-aggression. Mind takes you along the
ways of chaos, aggression and misunderstanding. If you
become mind-free, the chaos ceases.

The mind is like a locust, eating up the finer qualities of the human. The action of that mind should be to
reflect purely that which comes through the intuition.
Intuition is to be felt, not pondered. The mind is the
"slayer of the Real" (it blurs and falsifies). Your intuitional faculty cannot be concentrated. It is already con-

centrated. It is charged from the Cosmic.

Give your Self a chance egoji. It is the Internal Ruler, your own immortal Self. Everything else is mortal, is ever-changing forms and phenomena.

The ultimate Reality cannot be comprehended by thought or described by words. It can be awared—experienced and lived—at joyous ease. The method of "realizing" (or awakening into) the Absolute is known as intuitive wisdom of the heart. One can realize it by direct, immediate experiencing. It needs no special language and knows no boundaries of religious dogma. Some of the term symbols used, such as soul, love, spirituality and God carry a more mystical meaning.

The following statements quoted from Brothers' teachings—lend themselves as aphorisms:

Under the aegis of Reality, there is no beauty, no ugliness, but only true values.

Welcome suffering. Leave your mind alone and the pain will dissolve. Emptied or pure mind reflects fullness. The realm of Grace is within you. Go within or go out to meet Him. (Can the integral experience be a Him? asks Wuji). Merge into *it* and *be it* awarely—in ego-free consciousness.

Religion today is but a crutch. God made man with HimSelf within man, so that man might lean on Him, not on religion.

The ego may and should be lost, but never the Self. Welcome pain. Modern man has forgotten how to absorb pain. You have cut yourself off from your Self. Four fifths of the human race are existing on their nerves—not living fully, wholly and at joyous ease.

Live not in expectancy. Expectancy is an illusion. Spontaneity is the kernel of Intelligence. By true spontaneity, you gain true perception. Be spontaneous. Be your Self. *Be what you are*, integrally, abidingly and consciously *aware*.

Recognition is of the mind but "awareness" is of the whole Being. Be at one with your Self. Be your Real Self. Then only can you be at one with fellow beings and so with God.

To get people to answer their own questions is the only true way of teaching.

Only in the last moments of your lifespan do most of you really live. Those moments are the time when most people really comprehend life and themselves.

So you want to become a Christian? You want to tread the same path as Christ trod! Are you prepared to suffer as he suffered?

Your greatest possession in the whole world is No-thing-ness. Into no-thing-ness you can put everything. Patient acceptance of outer circumstances mitigates and destroys so called evil.

Do not try. Just Be. One man cannot be like another, because all are beautifully different. You can only "try" to do spontaneously what you deem to be right, using intuition to decide.

Be individual—not a "personality." In the place of the personal, build individuality. Preserve the magnetism which is in your eye. Do not fling it about. He who has become indifferent to himself (the ego mask, the personality) will not be affected by others.

For the practice of natural or intuitive Yoga, academic learning is a hindrance. Mere academic learning reduces a person to the status of a reproduction machine. The more the mind is cultivated, the stronger are the barriers between mind and soul.

When you are looking into the Void, *sunyata*, or even into space ether, *akasha*, there is affectionate detachment towards things and fellow beings, human, mortal ego souls. Through right culture, the third eye, the intuitive faculty, should still be functioning. It was for our use, and man himself has clouded it. Many things played a part in the clouding, such as wrong desire. Man repressed his inward impulses, the natural actions of *Sahaja* Yoga, and so prevented them from becoming manifest. You can only put the soul into practice, you can only experience *It*. You cannot aware *It* just by thinking about *It*. You can only aware, recognize and realize the soul, or Self, through experience. Artificiality has dampened the polished film of your perception. Just take life into you without bias and without predilection. You have not found out yet that you *are* the soul (Spirit, Self) and that it is your mind that fights it.

Do not cling to conventional thoughts, religion, concepts and so on. Let go! Drop all artificial conceptions of Life, for it is only then that it can be taken into you, or you into it, in conscious Self awareness.

Be simple. The art of living is living by intuition. Do not cling. When you stop building, the barriers go of their own accord. You will have to accomplish the art of letting go.

We have already planted the seed of "Awakening" by making you aware of your lack of awareness. There is no shortcut, because you don't have to travel to liberation (from delusive bondage to salvation, grace or awakening). It comes to you. No travel at all is required. The travel is within. It is the birth, or conscious awakening of the indwelling Christ Emmanuel.

Each one builds his own bridge and, when he passes over it, he cannot come back. After he passes over, the bridge is broken or it vanishes. "He who sees (or experiences) Jehovah—dies."

Empathy, *Mahakaruna*, Grace and *Prajnana* are term symbols pertaining to the non-dual *Advaita* Experiencing, the wholeness of Self Awareness. If "God is Love," so also Hate. Grace is neither Love nor Hate, but the fine balance between all opposites.

Human love has three aspects: instinctive, mental and intuitional. Instinctive love implies the physical and emotional creative urge. Mind love: Mental affirmities and intellectual urges. The intuitional mode is for "liberation" or "awakening." It is the highest human love—the love that is unattached, affectionate detachment—also called *Mahakaruna*, or Empathy. It cannot be possessive, pitiful, exclusive or jealous. It is ego-free, mind-free and God-free. It does not merely partake of divinity: *It is* Self radiance.

Attachment always means pain. Remember that *Karuna* is not attachment. It breaks attachment and knows no degree of higher–lower, lesser–greater. It partakes of the universal and the cosmic.

When I tell people to become non-intellectual, I mean stop educating your mind to become mechanized. There is no room for want or desire where there is spontaneous whole-heartedness. I mean by "work," be simple. Live from moment to moment, spontaneously, intuitively. Be Individual without being individualistic. Aim at integral wholeness awareness rather than at power, learning and holiness. The spiritual is the natural. Samsara is Nirvana. Integral wholeness is Grace in the Life Play, joyous ease in the Self interplay. Beauty is always alive. No dark power can enter that portal. The "Taj" is a light unto the world. It has not been copied. You cannot copy a Light. You can only make another one.

You do not think only in the brain. Each chakra is a functioning organ of thought. Thought is a microscopic atomic process and growth. Life grows through the vibrations of the atoms, the marriage of cells. Knowledge is a process of nature. Because of your artificialities, the gates of wisdom and *Mahakaruna* are closed to you. There exist in man "sub" and "super" atomic structures.

Experiencing "Being Awareness" is a getting back to the origins. ("Seek, find and experience ye first the Source, the natural realm of Grace.") Unless ye re-become simple and spontaneous as a babe, ye can in no way and in no wise enter and awake into the integral and conscious Self awareness. Wisdom is by identity, by ego-free wholeness awareness. In the process of knowing, the knower enters into and "becomes the thing known." Empathy is a faculty of Yoga, literal at-one-ment. Take away the obstacles and there is always a flow from the Cosmic. Spontaneity does not come from the mind. Let your gratitude be your healer, *Be* "whole."

There can be no integral awareness when you are catering to the personal. The only way is to cater to the

"Impersonal" and to satisfy the essential needs of Life and not the wants. Be desire-free, lust-free, ego-free and so, awarely, death-free. In the freedom of no desire, there is no ego willfulness and no conceit of agency, of doership. You are free in Life. You are the *Lila* Self interplay—The *I am*—Being Awareness Grace.

Because you are ego critical in the wrong way, you cannot experience awareness. To psycho analyze "yourself," in the generally accepted way, is but a barrier to spontaneous action within your Self. Psychoanalysis should proceed from the source of spontaneous action. You people do it the wrong way round. You must quiet the mind and the desireful urges of egoji. *Be Still* to practice the patience, to mature, and to be intuitive and integrally whole in direct, immediate perception. The right thing is that which comes freely to you and goes freely from you. There is no need to desire or to aspire. Be choice free. Choice implies emphasis on the personality, which is God eclipsing.

The erudite Meister Eckhart states, "The smallest creaturely image that ever takes shape in thee is as big as God. How so? It shuts out the whole of God" (Awareness, the sense of wholeness and of at-one-ment). The usurping ego-consciousness bars Self experiencing, the non-dual Awareness. As soon as the image appears, God disappears (from our awareness) and as the image fades, God comes. "Thou shalt find in solitude what thou shalt often lose abroad. As often as I have been among men, I have returned less a Man," says Thomas à Kempis, "The more of the creature, the less of God awareness." The Self is immanent and omnipresent. Awareness is all. If unattached, you are above hate and love. There is no sense of I or personality, external or otherwise.

Spontaneity does not come from the mind. Your higher creative urge has been repressed; the evil, which civilization has built up for ages, cannot be dissolved in a short time. Natural sex is spontaneous at its lowest manifestation. It is only legitimate in this lowest form when it is effort-free and desire-free, a need that is not mental lust. In the ages long ago past, man had a spontaneous sex life. Now mental man stimulates that life. He puts his creative urge into lower things and feels wound up or run down like the spring of a clock. Wu!

A stage can be arrived at, or even be natural, where, although the sex urge is present, there is no need for the lesser manifestation of it at all. There is natural control without discipline. An artist is a constructive creator, not a creator of destruction or of waste. He may not necessarily be a painter, a poet or a musician and not necessarily a creator of forms and symbols, but is an artist in creative and unitive living, in silent vibrational emanation and mutual interpenetration in Empathy. To become a constructive creator, you get into what is an atmosphere of yourself. It is your Real Self that is a wholeness, unity and empathy with the cosmic thought, which wants or needs to express itself through you. Egoji is a channel rather than an actor, and you may drop your blinkered conceit of agency. That atmosphere of the Self is already here and now. You have to change the vibration of the individual, the persona mask, into the cosmic vibration. It is then that you become an artist in life, if not in specialized forms. Drop ego-consciousness. Experience is not vitally fruitful unless the absorbing element comes out of it. Experiences, we all have. Do we learn their lessons, their import and their value in the whole? Let the impersonal absorb the personal.

Remember that it is not what your heart is in, but what is in your heart that matters—and what is in your Heart will remain. It need not occur that you become deadened and lose your individuality in the cosmic-consciousness or in integrally whole Self awareness.

Remember who and what *you are*—and you are free in circumstances, as in innerstances. The wanting to *Be* is effort-free desire. Effortful desire is ignorance, "ignorance" of the state of Self awareness, of unity beyond union and opposites, of integral wholeness, living.

Unless man is lost, he never finds Himself. Develop and practice the "Feeling Principle" and you will aware integrality and grace. The pairs of opposites, the two together, make completeness. They are complementary and constitute a whole. When you have taken the experience out of evil, it becomes comprehension; therefore, why deplore the existence of evil, or of anything? The wise mature *Jnani* comprehends that *Prajnana* consciousness really means the Heart and only apparently the mind. The mortal is aware of the mind only when the Heart has not blossomed, when the thousand-petaled lotus has not unfolded, just as when the moon is seen only when the Sun has not appeared.

Permit the mind to become free of its own entanglement. The basic seeds of the entanglement are memory, on the one side and forgetfulness on the other. Ananda *grace (not mere happiness) is diffusing and suffusing. It denotes the stage of the individual's at-one-ment with Self. Get rid of egotism, attachment and personality, get rid of happiness, and you will get rid of misery.*

21 🌿

Sunyata Ever Is

There is nothing abnormal in the world. There is only lack of comprehension of the normal. Do not try to 'become' this or that—but look and aware what is One does not 'realize' (make real) the Self; Ego only dissolves into it

—Sunyata

Siddhartha Gautama said, "Do not complain or cry or pray, but open your intuitive eye and 'see' (i.e., be the Awareness) for the light is all about you and it is wonderful, so beautiful, so far beyond anything that man has ever dreamt of or prayed for and it is forever and ever."

Do not nourish pity for yourself or for others; that is the play of mind again. Pity is condescending and even compassion can be so. But co-passion or empathy is pity-free, ego-free and so also mind-free. It is the mind that distorts the vision of Reality, Truth or Self Awareness.

Where there is non-attachment, there is no sin. There can be affectionate detachment. Non-attachment does not come until the experiences proper to the individual have been lived through, and their fruit consumed.

The "Will of God" manifests itself quite distinct from the will of man. You cannot interpret God. God interprets man.

The Void happens. *Sunyata*, the full, solid, concrete Plenum Void or No-thing-ness ever *is*. It happens in conscious awareness or in integral experiencing in the due and mature fullness of time or time freeness. The Void is felt intuitively apart from any mental process. Space-time is secondary; the Void, *sunyata*, is primary.

Ordinary individuals are dual natured, personal and impersonal. The complete Individual includes the cosmic experiences we all have, but unless we are mature to live in, and Be the "experiencing," we are but dormant. The complete individual is unified and integrally whole.

You should permit your desires to be dissolved. "You will aware in due course that your grace lies where you permit 'God' or 'Self,' and cease to exist," says Ramana Maharshi. Therefore, become effort-free, desire-free, will-free and permit God to enter. You cannot get "peace of mind"—that is a fallacy. But you can be in joyous ease and grace when the mind is forgotten. You can be free *in* mind (mind-free) as in other tools, thoughts and things. Empathy, *Mahakaruna* or Compassion is Grace in action; it is Love minus attach-ment. Don't "become" non-attached or "try" to Be. Just permit yourself, egoji, to be non-attached. You can only be non-attached and in at-one-ment, when you are out-side the pair of opposites. Transcend ego consciousness and *Ananda* Grace is awared.

A Guru is a bridge—not a prop. The Guru must come from within, not from without. He may be met outside, but he is recognized by the indwelling Self, Christ Emmanuel. "Jove nods to Jove from within all of us." "He, or She, who sees Jehovah dies!" Egojies vanish in the integral "experiencing." I am against discipleship in the sense in which most of you interpret it, but I am for letting go of the individual, the personal, the egoji, and letting the Guru, the Self, take hold.

After the union of *Shakti* and *Purusha*—there is unity—and a branching-out of "radiance" or "sound" from that unity. The force that comes out after the state of *Ananda* Grace is "super sound" or "bliss radiance." It is the state above Bliss, above manifestation. You are all concerned with saving your soul, whereas your soul is already saved. The obstacles you meet are stepping-stones across the waters of *samsara* and ego life to Self awareness or God experiencing.

The Soul, or Self, does not go anywhere after death of the body tools, because there is nowhere to go, because it is there all the time—all the Eternal while. Wu!

But, ducky, you do not attain, achieve or possess *Samadhi*; *Samadhi* takes you. *Samadhi* is not through the mind because the mind is the distorter of true values. Be atoned in at-one-ment. Do not gather knowledge. Be atoned in the cloud of unknowing and you will have *anubhava* [mystical experience] of intuitive wisdom—part of the Source of true existence. "Where is the wisdom we have lost in knowledge—Where is the Life we have lost (awareness of) in ego living?" Where is the *Ananda* Grace we have lost sight of in mere happiness, in mere ego gratification? It is within and around us all the eternal while, says Wuji. "In *it* we live and move and have our Being," whether we aware or ignore *it*.

There is no attachment apart from the mind. Permit the dissolving to take place. It is so easy to the intuitional, so difficult to the dissolving mind. Intuition is to be felt, not to be pondered over. Love is to be experienced, not to be made or fallen into or to wallow and splash in. There can be no love and no hate outside the "personality." Anand is first-hand love and love is second hand grace. You can give love, but you cannot give grace (*ananda* bliss). It is something that flows out of you or through you. It is something in which you live, which is part of you, which is you.

Permit yourself, egoji, to be drawn into the Self. Be unattached, effort-free and wholly spontaneous. Let gratitude be your healing. I cannot bless you. God is within you! Why then ask for blessings? Blessings are often but "spiritual" condescension, false identity, linked with the ego. God would be "selfish" to give Himself blessings. A lie is far less injurious than a half truth.

Do not become like Christ or like some Guru. Do not imitate or be like anyone. Do not emulate or be in imitation of a projection. Be the Guru yourself. Be your Self integrally aware.

Wants accentuate personality. It is only safe to arouse *Kundalini* when the impersonal is dominant. A spiritual cripple is a terrible disease. Our birthright is something far greater than happiness. It is *Ananda* Grace *Mahakaruna*, which can only grow out of wisdom or complete ego surrender. In *Ananda*, the human becomes verdant. The mind largely belongs to the animal instinct. "The ego-ridden mind and the mind-ridden egoji? What is the difference?" asks Sri Chow Chu Wuji. You cannot look for God. God or Self is not lost. God is all—everything minus attachment. Spontaneous discipline, which is unconscious, is the real thing. The other disciplines only hurt. Look at the people who live under it! Wu! By artificial civilization, mankind has diverted the correct flow of cosmic life forces in the human body and the psyche. If these life forces were flowing rightly, the ills of old age, disease and nervous and organic illnesses, and instability of all sorts would be put an end to. It is because the *Rishis'* life forces are flowing rightly that they live long and maintain their strength.

You want God to lean upon? A slavish attitude! While you are spiritually a cripple, how can you be "whole"? Civilized man has forgotten how to absorb pain. He has forgotten how to stand on his own feet or how to be individual without being individualistic in aloneness. Wuji says: "In the world today, if you find a man without personality, that man is unique. In truth, such a man is 'whole' in spiritual health."

22 🌿

A Whole Man

On the spiritual path. "Nothing is me" is the first step.
"Everything is me" is the next. Both hang up on the idea
"There is a world and there is a me." Then this too is given
up. There is no me or egoji as Reality. You remain what you
are—the non-dual Self. You are it here and now....

                                                        —*Sunyata*

In his first conversation with Laura Huxley, J.
Krishnamurti, in answer to her question "But what
do you do?" said, "Nothing. I am only a religious
man—not a Guru, a healer, a psychologist or therapist or
any of these things, but only a religious man." Earlier, he
had made similar statements and Laura asked him,
"What is a religious man?" Krishnaji changed his tone
and spoke now calmly and incisively: "I will tell you what
a religious man is. First of all, a religious man is a man
who is alone—not lonely you understand—but alone—
with no theories, no dogmas, no opinion, no background. He is alone, and loves it. He is free of conditioning and impositions and enjoys it. Second, a religious
man must be both man and woman—I do not mean sex-
ually—but he must know, be able to experience, the dual

nature of everything. A religious man must feel and be both masculine and feminine in Empathy. Third (and now his manner intensified again), to be a religious Man, one must destroy everything, destroy the past, destroy one's convictions, one's interpretations and destroy all ego hypnoses until there is no center, you understand— *No Center.*"

Do ye think Sri Wuji is a religious man? Is he a *Jnani* or a mature, pure Guru or an *Atyashrami* or an "un headaucated" simpleton, the pure Fool, Grace aware? Sri Wuji does not agree with Krishnaji's third formula of "a Religious Man," simply because there was nothing in me to be destroyed or renounced, no sin complex, no swell egoji. Wu!

There is no need to be iconoclastic, when there are no idols, images and no conditioning. There is nothing that hinders "the rare, born mystic" from intuitive, integral, spiritual Self awareness. There is no bumptious egoji. There is no sin complex. Nor are there any inordinate desires, lusts or fears. Mind and the other bodies are good tools, serviceable in the *Swalila* [Self interplay]. They present no hindrance to "Enlightenment'" and "Grace awareness" unless we identify our Self with them or unless we abuse or maim them. Why kill or destroy such tools when we can be free in them, transcend them and let them function in their natural rhythm?

When Ramana Maharshi was asked if the officious official's personal questions had tired him, he said, "No, I did not use my mind. They can ask me any length of time." He spoke spontaneously, intuitively from the core that is Self radiant. Does the Self-radiating Sun or Silence get tired? Looking into Ramanaji's eyes, I awared Eternity.

Already in the 1920s, I used the adages, "Awareness is all" and "Spiritual suffering is a contradiction in term symbols." Ramana Maharshi was an example. When asked to desire his body's healing from malignant cancer, he explained that it was impossible: "There must be something called ego mind to create desire, but there is no such thing." When the clever doctors advised amputation of the diseased arm, Ramana said, "From the very beginning, I told the doctors that I felt no pain, so there is no need for an operation. But nobody (egoji) would listen. Just as you have come here, so the tumor has come. I see no difference. For whose sake should I have desire to cure the tumor? For your sake? Oh, you are among those here. That is all right. Just as you have all come, that also has come to climb up on my arm and sit comfortably. I feel no pain in either case. I identify with whatever is before me. I have no separate identity. I am universal. I communicate these thoughts through my eyes."

This is what Sri Wuji and you are, whether you merely understand or know it or not. Sri Wuji innerstands at joyous ease in the *Maya Lila* Self interplay. It is *Ananda* Grace, he says in a single Wu!

The Self you want to know and understand, is it some second Self? Are you several selves? Surely there is the only Self you are. Remove and abandon your wrong ideas of your Self and there it is in all its glory. It is only your mind that prevents Self awareness. The mind is not Real. It changes and misleads. There are ideas and some of them are wrong. Abandon the wrong ideas for they are false and obstruct your awareness of your Self.

There is no higher or second Self to search for. You are the "highest" Self. You have only to give up the false idea you have about your Self. Both faith and reason tell you that you are neither the body nor its desires and fears, nor are you the mind with its fanciful ideas, nor the role society and *prarabdha* compel you to play, the person you are supposed to be. Give up the false, and the true will come into aware consciousness, or conscious awareness.

You may say you want to know your Self. You *are* your Self, our Self, *The Self*. You cannot be anything but what you are. "To know God is to be God." Is "knowing" separate from "being"? Whatever you can know with your mind is of the mind, not of you, "the spirit." There can be intuitive, spontaneous, spiritual wisdom awareness and integral Grace awareness and *tat twam asi* ("that thou art"). About your Self, you can only truly say: "I *am*, I *am*—Awareness, Life Itself." As a persona, ego and body tool, you are being lived by Life, Self, God.

It is the person you imagine your Self to be that suffers—not you. Dissolve it into awareness; it is merely a bundle of memories and habits. From the awareness of the unreal to the awareness of the Real, there is a chasm, which you will easily cross, once you have mastered the art of pure awareness. Dare the existential leap into the *Turiya* [highest] realm and into the Self radiant, ego-free *Sunya Plenum Void*. Wu!

Your direct, intuitive insight tells you that you "know" your Self first. There is unconscious awareness, inherent wisdom and intuitive consciousness in the pre-ego conscious state. Nothing exists for you without *You* being there to experience its existence. (We always have our Self as company). You imagine you do not know your Self, because you cannot describe the Self. You can always say, "I know that I *am*," and you will refute as untrue the statement, "I am not." But whatever can be described cannot be your Self, and what you are cannot be described. You can only know your Self by being your Self without any attempt at Self identification and Self description, as in Wuji's childhood.

Once you are aware that you are nothing perceivable or conceivable, that whatever appears in the field of consciousness cannot be your Self, you will apply yourself to the eradication of all self identifications as the

only way that can take you to a deeper or fuller realization of your Self, *The Self*. You literally progress in awakening into conscious awareness in your Self by affectionate awareness and affectionate detachment regarding things, events and egojies. You are aware that you are
neither the body nor the mind, though aware of both.

You create disharmony and then complain. When
you desire and fear, and identify your Self with your
feeling and your mind, you create confusion, sorrow,
bondage. When you act and "create" wisdom and
Mahakaruna—in affectionate awareness—and remain
unattached to your creation, the result is harmony and
peace and your Self is graceful, contented at joyous
ease and spontaneity, in Self-radiant Silence, wholly
innerstanding.

But whatever be the creation of your mind, in what
way does it reflect on you? It is only your Self-identifica-
tion with the mind that makes you happy and unhappy
in ego-consciousness. Sri Wuji equates or identifies ego
with mind and asks, "The ego-ridden mind and the mind-
ridden egoji, what is the difference?" *Ananda*-Grace as
intuitively affectionate awareness pertains to your Self,
while mere power and mere happiness pertain to egoji
and mere mind. Wu!

Rebel against your slavery to your mind, aware that
your bonds are ego created, and break the chains of
attachment and of revulsion. Keep in mind your goal of
freedom, until it dawns on you that you are always and
ever free. That freedom is not something in a distant
future to be earned with discipline and painful effort, but
it is perennially one's own, to be used and—lived spontaneously—in Wei Wu Wei.

Liberation, as Enlightenment, is not an acquisition
or a possession, but is rather a matter of courage and
maturity of mind and of egoji. (Is egoji mature enough to
commit suicide?) It is the courage to discern that you are

free already and to act on it. Dare the existential leap into Sunya's no-thing-ness, into spiritual Grace awareness, into Eternity's sunrise in intuitive consciousness!

"Unbroken perfection is in and over all," says Rabindranath Tagore. Awaken to aware and to live in all Rightness. All is well, all is right that seems most wrong and evil, to egojies. "Resist no (seeming) evil." "Sin is behovely (necessary)." Ignorance, blinkers and unawareness play their due role in *swalila*. "Ego was the helper. Ego is the bar." It is the ego that is the great hindrance or obstacle to our awakening into conscious Self awareness. Like egoji, mind and emotional blinkers, evil too has no real existence. They constantly change in forms and moods and appearances. Only the Eternal is Real enough, and "*Tat twam asi*." Thou art truly Being Awareness Grace. Wu!

"Our birth is but a sleep and a forgetting," says the poet seer, Wuji, who remembers his pre-ego-consciousness and says that babes are wise—and that it is not birth itself that creates a kind of sleep. It is only a Christian truth that we are born sinful. It is the surroundings, the impositions, the conditionings in early childhood that make us forget our Self. The primordial sin is the illusion of a separate, personal existence, of duality and divisions, as being Real. "Persona" was the Greek word for a mask, and that is what the person is, a mask for our own reality. The Fall into mere knowledge of good and evil, and pairs of dividing opposites, is repeated constantly. Wu!

There may be billions of universes. They all pulsate with the same energy. *That* is but one. Sages call it by various names: God, Jehovah, Allah, Tao. Is it a He? asks Wuji, a Father, a Ma, or a sexy something, or is it a sex-free no-thing-ness? "I and the Source are One." "The realm of Grace is within." There is the indwelling of Christ—Emman-u-el, our Real unitive and universal

Self. Wu! So let *mahakaruna* guide. Let the intuitive Light reveal *it*. Christ-consciousness dawns: The sun has risen on a new era!

Let's move with the rhythm of the universe. Thinking and trying are still duality. The all pervading Self does not think, nor does *it* try and fuss, as do human, mortal egojies. "Seek, find and experience ye first the inner realm of grace, and all else will be added unto you." Oh ye of little faith! Providence will never forsake one who really, sincerely seeks. Ye need not make plans or progress. Ye are already the Self and ye are being led, and guided, and used according to the Great Plan–your *prarabdha* destiny.

Ramana Maharshi's silent teaching and radiance belong to the realm of Spirit, of Reality, of the Self. Are we not Spirit, time-free, ego-free, sex-free, death-free and name-free? Or are we name and form, body and mind? When revealed in words, the pristine purity of the silent teaching and nonverbal transmission must necessarily be somewhat modified by the limitation of mind conceptions and words. In wordiness and duality play, we forget our Self, the Real Self, Truth, Spirit, God. All these terms are different names for the same, name-free and ineffable Reality.

It is always and everywhere present; hence, *it* is also in our consciousness as Christ Emmanuel, but our ignorance or "ignore-ance," covers *it* with a veil of thought. Yet Ramanaji reminded us "we are always aware." The presence and the Self radiance of the Maharshi makes us remember, recollect, and aware our divinity. In his eyes—and in his look—I could aware Eternity and the grace of *mahakaruna*. He said, "All that is necessary is the removal of the veils and the duality blinkers; then the intuitive light will shine by its Self, and permeate all your being. Then there is no need for seeking and thinking that it is somewhere else. The Realm of Grace is within

us. Christ is our Self, your Self, The Self, but we are
veiled and unaware. We cannot remember, we are
unaware of the spiritual radiance and the nonverbal
presence of one who is pure spirit."

"To the pure all is pure." Rabindranath Tagore,
Ramana Maharshi, Sri Anirvan, Sri Narayana, Ram Das,
Anandamayee Ma, Sri Yashoda Mai and even Bapuji
Gandhi naturally recognized the rare, born mystic in
me—in simple external disguise, the human form!

The West may envy the deep sense of reverence
which makes Indians instinctively and intuitively recognize spiritual greatness and saintliness wherever they
meet it. The West easily recognizes the material power
and fame, diplomas and certificates of learning and the
quality of daring enterprise, but such a phenomenon as
Ramana Maharshi would pass almost unnoticed or
would be put in a lunatic asylum.

That which projects and sustains the universe also
knows how to look after it in the best possible way, without our fussy, well-meaning interference, although we
may be duly used. If one has such firm faith and clear
awareness, then our ambitions and desires to change the
world drop away.

The spiritual current, as in a Quaker meeting, uni-
fies, clarifies and heals. No one interrupts the Silence,
no one is bored by it. Our Western art of conversation is
sparklingly poor. There is now a growing awareness that
the forms are not Real and only That which has no form,
such as Spirit and *sunyata*, has Reality. Only the Eternal
is Real and that which changes is not real enough. The
Word is word-free and form-free and "we" as Spirit are
likewise so. Just aware that you are Spirit, no-thing-ness,
and you are body-free, ego-free, mind-free, time-free
and death-free and free in your body tools. Thinking is
still duality. Unity awareness and intuitive enlightenment
can be thought-free, a state of contemplative witnessing.

Thoughts may come and pass by, but the intuitive Spirit is free in them and can dismiss the thoughts that are trivial and repetitive. Once we are free in the realm of thought, and stop the function of brain mind and ego thought, the new state of consciousness must necessarily dawn. Ego oblivion is Self awareness. Not "*Cogito ergo sum*"—Descartes (I think, therefore I am), but "*I am, therefore aware intuitively.*" Yes, in depth consciousness "I" am the awareness, "I"-free, and ego-free. Thoughts and forms constantly change and time flows on. So they are not real—enough.

Old Heraclitus said, "You cannot step into the same river twice." "God" is in all these changes—yet change-free and "I" can also be ego-free, mind-free, time-free, death-free and carefree. Wu! Heraclitus also states, "Power corrupts. Absolute power corrupts absolutely." So do not aim at power in any form, comments Sri Wuji; "spiritual" energy is your birthright. Awareness is all. Wu!

"I have seen eyes, which told me without words: Grace, Peace and Spiritual Freeness." The Light in the Ramana Maharishi's eyes seemed to convey the Truth that sets us free. In other words, he said, "The Spiritual Being dwelling in you is the Real Bhagavan, as you call me. That is what you have to realize."

Sahaja Samadhi is the natural state, the supreme state. Once realized, we do not identify ourselves anymore with our personalities, as we are above and beyond them. We breathe Freedom, Grace, Wisdom, and *karuna* Love. Spiritual magnetism is the most powerful element which awakens the mature psyche into awareness from its physical and psychical sleep in the Light of the Real. The permanent and eternal that we Are becomes more important than all the seeming, actual "reality" of the visible world. When egojies disappear, all troubles vanish with them. By giving up everything, we find, aware and experience that we are All, the Whole, the Eternal.

A saint can only be recognized if he chooses to reveal himself. Only an intimate contact will reveal his saintship; if a flower has honey, the bee will find it. It is not the flower which seeks the bee. If we are unhappy, it is our own error. Therefore, do not believe that there are circumstances or conditions which are responsible for the darkness in us. It is the ego mind which begets this lie.

Aware your Self by means of *Vichara [the continual asking of yourself, "Who am I" as taught by Ramana Maharshi]*. You will find your Guru within yourself, in your own heart. It is your Self. Unless you give up the idea of the world being Real, your mind will always be seeking it. If you take the illusions to be Real, then you will never aware and experience the Real itSelf, although it is the Real alone that exists. Wu!

Tennyson's "Flowers in the Crannied Wall" was spun from a Goethe couplet. Like Paracelsus and Goethe, Tennyson was convinced that true wisdom was to be gained, or awared, not through man's intellect, but through his intuitive ability to aware and accept the naturally simple truths of life. Everything radiates wave lengths, which can be identified as sound, color, form, movement, perfume, temperature and intelligence. The radiation varies, but the same flower species always gives off the same radiations. It is awared by those whose inner criterion is sufficiently advanced. A few people become ripe enough to tread the new path. Mature awakening into conscious awareness is all.

"In *Sahaja Samadhi*, there is only the feeling of I! I! and no thought," says Ramana Maharshi (and Wuji). There is only the word-free, thought-free, and effort-free Unity awareness, harmony and joyous ease, also called Grace. Such a state is beyond all incarnation, limitations and conditions. There is no subject or object, no duality, no opposing opposites, but unity, wholeness, harmony and grace. The mind is left as an instrument of consciousness. There is the pure peace, the joyous ease, the intuitive light and the *ananda* awareness, which surpasses all human, mental knowing and standing under or over. In the instinctive, mental belief that we are our bodies or our minds lies the cause of our bondage and our blinkers. Ramana referred to all the occult phenomena as being a play of the man's own mind, which has no subjective reality. By "mind," the sage understood all supra-physical manifestations, including Siddhis as occult powers.

Expel all thoughts and remain with your own ultimate core of Being, your Self, our Self, *the* Self. Inner preparation is necessary in every case, unless you belong to those few who come to earth already enlightened in wisdom—having achieved, or awared, the final Light in their glorious past. Some of these beings may prefer not to share the inner treasures, not to write or discourse, but to remain silent in the *Swalila*. They may have no urge to express or to explain. In this way, they can avoid complications with the ego world, which usually attacks the twice born and the forerunners of human evolution—by trying to silence their speech, or to imprison or even to kill their bodies. Within some physical forms, the imperishable, eternal Light is already kindling, and the Life awareness beyond all death and suffering is already realized.

We leave the explanation to your own intuition, for it is intuition which presents the proper instrument for spiritual cognition and enlightenment. There are people who possess the inherent unity wisdom without referring to the memory of former experiences. Intuitional wisdom comes from man's distant past, that is, from earlier incarnations, in which he developed these qualities empirically. They were retained in the Silent sanctuary, in the inner temple in contemplation. Wu!

More and more, maturely developed people do not lose their intelligence and activity in old body age. They remain radiantly wise to the end of their lifespan. Inner development evidently overrules the influence of age in such people. The content prevails over the outer shell. It innerstands at joyous ease. The developed consciousnesses transform their bodies to their needs and aims. Wu!

On one level of ego-consciousness, duality, sex, desires and fears reign supreme, while on another level they cease to matter: we are free in them. In a third mode of awareness, they cease to exist. On this plane, vibrations and intuitions ("the peaks of intelligence") are reflected as consciousness, or acting intelligence. The majority of us cannot imagine existence without the visible world that surrounds us. Innerstand: live your Self in conscious awareness, or aware consciousness. There is also unconscious awareness and affectionate detachment. *Sahaja Samadhi* is just pure Being Awareness Grace, the silent and all embracing wisdom, the Light that is without shadow.

Be in the world and not of it. Be a witness, not participating in all that happens around you, in all conditions. Do not be attached to these conditions but, in affectionate detachment and affectionate awareness, be free in the interplay. It is *Swadharma* in *Swalila*. The one thing that matters is to find, aware and experience the inner silence and not merely talk about it. Rare are those who find, and numerous are those who talk without having had due experience. Silence is the best. It is Self-revealing.

The man who has reached absolute detachment from all illusions and everything relative has no individual will anymore. He wants nothing for himself—and his will is necessarily one with the omnipresent will of the whole. You may call It God. A great teacher tells us, "I and the Source are One. I came from the Source, not to do my own will, but to do the will of the Source that sent me." *Sahaja Samadhi*, in which there are no desires and no fears, is the grace of Eternity, which we awared in the eyes and being of Ramana Maharshi. He said that the biblical formula of God, "I *am* That I *am*," depicts the whole truth, as can be attempted to express it in speech or in words.

The whole secret of attainment or awakening lies in personal, inner experience. *Samadhi* alone can reveal the truth of integral Being. A flash of intuitive wisdom, without thinking, can illuminate the whole. Yet, for awakening into conscious awareness, ripeness is a deciding factor. No visions or other abnormal applications are a guarantee that the state is not a mental delusion or ecstasy. One is simply beyond all expectations, anxieties and strivings. One is sincerely aware that everything is as it should be. Awakened Beings do not care whether or not their actions and wisdom be recognized.

The whole secret of conscious Self awareness lies in inner experience and not in study, learning, standing "under" or "over" or in "mere" happiness. "We inner-stand at joyous ease," says Sri Wuji. Reality does not assert itSelf. It just naturally radiates—like the sun. Its language is Self radiant Silence. We may be utterly unconscious of the fact of invisible assistance and guidance, but our Wujies are "divinely indifferent," whether or not their guidance be mentally recognized by egojies or not. In *Sahaja Samadhi*, man (the persona, the ego mind) as we know him, "does not exist." It is not Real—enough. Your "I" or "me" does not exist even now. Wu!

The primordial sin is belief in being separate, in egoism, the Fall into mere knowledge of good and evil or "pairs of opposites." The central Light is all that really exists, call *it* God, Spirit, the realm of Grace or *Satchit-*

ananda: Tat twam asi. Words are so poor, so powerless to render the true meaning of the consciousness of the future, at the present time. Why make an attempt to convey something which cannot be comprehended by mental, duality egojies? Wu!

23 🌿

Wholeness

At one level of consciousness, ego values, duality play and physical sex reign supreme. In another state of consciousness, these values and divisions cease to matter. In a third mode of conscious Self awareness, they do not exist. There is "wholeness experiencing."

—*Sunyata*

An Indian Baul verse says, "Sometimes naked, sometimes mad, now as a scholar, now as a fool; thus they appear on the earth, the free and whole MAN." Man (Meneske) includes woman.

The time-space is a unity—as inseparable as birth–death, up–down, inside–outside or male–female. The so called opposites are complementary and constitute each other and one another. He who knows the male and yet keeps to the female becomes like the space containing the world of actualities.

Our unitive Self is awared in all things, all moods and in all the changes in the phenomena. *Maya Lila* is Self interplay. Our due *prarabdha karma* can be accepted in the *Titiksa* [endurance of pairs of opposites] mode of approach. It can be played, endured and enjoyed at joyous ease and in Self controlled spontaneity. There is no fear, no sin complex, no ego conceit of agency.

Chuang Tzu says, "When a drunken man falls out of a cart, though his body may suffer, he does not die." If such security may be gotten from wine, how much more it may be found in *Ananda* [bliss] of *sahaja*, ego-free *samadhi* of "wholeness" rather than "holiness."

In the *Gospel of Thomas* we read, "Jesus said, 'Whosoever knows father and mother shall be called son of a harlot. When you make the two one, you shall become sons of man. Whosoever drinks from my mouth (source) shall become as *I am*, and I myself will become he, and the hidden things shall be revealed to him.'

"His disciples said unto him, 'When will the Kingdom (the Realm of Grace) come?' Jesus said, 'It will not come by expectations. They will not say, 'See here or see there,' but the Realm of Grace is spread upon the earth, and within you, and men do not aware it.'"

Mythological images often imply that holiness is hermaphroditic. The whole, complete and integral human being is at once male and female. He is also aware of being spiritual, that is, more than a mere human, mortal ego soul. Wuji defines spirituality as "simple intuitive awareness." The man who has been gifted with it or who has developed his feminine aspect, and the woman who has developed her masculine aspect in harmonious interrelatedness, is the whole *man*.

In Buddhist iconography, the *Bodhisattva* is very frequently a hermaphrodite. One thinks in particular of the Bodhisattva Avalokiteshvara, who, although masculine in name, is always feminine in form, especially in the Far East. There he appears as Kwan Yin or Kannon, the goddess of mercy, grace or *karuna* love, the Yin and the Yang duly coordinated and harmonized.

The traditional thirty-two physical marks of a Buddha include the obviously androgynous symbol of the retractable penis. It is not uncommon to find ardha-nari, or half woman images of Shiva, in which the body is a female on the left and male on the right (*Gauri Shankar*). The ever-transmuting and transforming *Nataraj*, ever dancing the universe into Being, is whole in body, rhythm and Self-radiance.

In Christianity likewise, God, the Son, the second persona mask of the Divine trinity, is Logos, Sophia or Word and Wisdom—the latter referring back to the feminine personification of the divine wisdom. (See Proverbs 8: 1, 9, and 12.) St. Sophia in Rome and Michelangelo's Christ are strikingly feminine. What is the sense of Jesus saying that in the Realm of Grace or state of wholeness we shall be "as the angels, neither marrying nor given in marriage?"

In Christian iconography, the angel is almost invariably feminine in form, though masculine in name. This is a characteristic common to Persian, Hindu and Buddhist angels (Devas). The profane interpretation of this imagery is that holiness is sexless (or sex-free). If holiness is wholeness, or integral awareness, the meaning of androgynous imagery must be plus rather than minus, suggesting that the second innocence is not the absence of the erotic, but the fulfillment. The virtue of the action of those who are "whole ego-free beings" lies in the complete coordination of their beings—body, soul and spirit, yin and yang, the inner and the outer man—all at one, attuned and atoned in natural harmony.

At one state of consciousness, sex and duality awareness reign supreme. At another state, these do not matter and, in a third mode of consciousness or integral Self-awareness, these do not exist.

The hermaphroditic imagery suggests that there is that state of consciousness in which the erotic no longer has to be sought or pursued, because it is always present in its totality. There is sensuous, not sensual, awareness of oneness with the external world, which we (nearly all) have forgotten in our ego conditioning and our learning to adopt our social roles and persona masks.

Love is a vague and ambiguous word symbol. To some ego souls, God is Love and made in their own image. Especially to the extroverted, externalized Western conditioned folks, God's image is a Person, a Father concept male, and external to their identity concept. He that is "impersonal, immanent and omnipresent Source and Urground" is seemingly ignored or not experienced.

In India, we have the Mother image concept and the male gods have their complementary *shaktis*. Comprehended in them all is the impersonal, sex-free *Brahma* or *Param Atman* experienced in the invisible Real. "In the whole world, there is nothing but God. All is good because God is all," says Wuji.

Jesus said, "The foxes have holes and the birds of the air have nests, but the Son of Man has nowhere to lay his head." (No possessions and no fixed abode, like some modern-day hippies.) "Be not anxious for the morrow, what you shall eat, what you shall drink or how you shall be clothed. Sufficient unto the day is the trouble thereof." Live intuitively and spontaneously in the eternal *Now*. "If thine intuitive eye be single and whole, thy whole body (aye, all bodies) will be awared as brimful of Self radiant Light."

This intuitive "White Light" never was on land or sea, as it ever *Is*. It is also in ego darkness and death though "the darkness comprehendeth it not." Nor do human, mortal egojies aware and comprehend it, even though it is "the Light that leadeth and guideth every ego soul that cometh into this world play."

There is sure guidance and inevitability in our *prarabdha karma*. The "whole man," a *Jivan Mukti*, may, to egojies, seem to be insane, because he does not take choice seriously. There is no real choice and no real egoji. Life, God or Self is One Whole with no opposite.

From the *Jnani's* point of view, it is not a matter of becoming whole or being saved or liberated. It is awakening maturely and abidingly into conscious awareness of the whole.

William Wordsworth and Thomas Traherne knew, "Heaven lies about us in our infancy." It is within us, and all around egojies, all the eternal while. Our "second childhood" denotes the second birth or awakening into conscious awareness. Unconscious awareness is there in the pre-ego mode of being, says Wuji. "Our birth is but a sleep and a forgetting." Ramana Maharshi, the Christ conscious sage, would agree. We forget our Self, our real I-dentity in duality consciousness, in ego fuss and ego antics. Wuji did not wholly forget—Grace awareness was there in his infancy, though unconscious of its Self as there were no contrasts.

Meister Eckhart says, "If I love a stone, I am that stone. If I love a man, I am that man. If I love God, nay, I durst say no more. If I said I *am* God, ye might stone me." It is not the kind of love we can make or fall into and make a mess of, but *Maha karuna* (Empathy). That, which recognizes in the light of this pure, ego-free Love, is within our Self. Everything is there. "To the pure all is pure," and "blessed are the poor in Spirit." The realm of Grace is theirs. So many of our loud assertions, judgments and criticisms about fellow beings are blatant ego projections. What Paul says about Peter tells us more about Paul than Peterji. That which recognizes is within us. Egoji protects and betrays itself.

Sri Wuji's ego was not very bumptious. He was ego-free, rather than egoless (Egoji endured several salutary deaths). Unassuming and unassertive, he was hardly noticed. A patient and a kind listener, he had no ambition to be seen, to shine or to be loved. They say they

176 ◆ Dancing with the Void

love, but they do not see, aware or know "me" at all, was sometimes his intuitive feeling—and he did not seek such love. In empathy, he could easily Be—the consciousness of the other egojies or of tree friends and nature's moods.

Jacob Boehme says, "We forget the sensuous language of nature," but Wuji did not. He practiced it and was at home in the natural wholeness and healing grace within and around, in innerstances as well as in circumstances. He needed no "other," no better or worse halves or fragments for his fulfillment. To him, sex did not matter in the light of *Ananda* Grace and wholeness awareness. His body and mind were fairly virginal until his late 30's and, if he then experienced a mature woman, it was not his lust or need for gratification. Rather, it was her felt need to experience sex union and its love fulfillment. Her fiancé had died in the First World War. She had maturity rather than mother complex or *Shakti* business. A woman may need sex experience more than a man.

In his childhood, Wuji was himself integral but he was not yet in conscious awareness of Integrality and Grace. There were no contrasts and no word symbols; there was no urge to assert, express or explain. He was not in search of identity, yogic union or external Guru guidance. He was, as the Christ-conscious Ramana discerned and reminded him, "one of the rare, born mystics" and, in depth-consciousness, "always aware." He was at joyous ease when he was alone in nature, away from the craving, assertive and diseased egojies. Their presence was apt to usurp his awareness of the graceful reality of Silence, of integral Selfhood. There still was, to him, no term symbol for this wholeness experiencing.

Nor was there any temptation or urge in him to dissipate his energies in sex, stimulants such as nicotine, alcohol, or other drugs. There was no ambition to become this or that, no quest of learning, of knowledge or of power. "Knowledge is Power," say egojies. They worship the powerful Bhagavan Sri Dollar but power is apt to corrupt egojies and "absolute power corrupts absolutely." Wuji had no desire for property, family blessings or even for security. He made no plans for the future. He enjoyed the present with gratitude for the past. It was as if he intuitively awared that "The Plan" was there, and he had to fit in willy nilly and better so willy. Nor did his "wholeness" dissipate in wordiness or in ego assertion. He was rather a receptive and kind listener, an observer, and a Father Confessor—unjudging and unenvious.

An individual is almost universally unaware that he (or she) has learned to confuse his identity with an abstract construct built up through years of self dramatization, or of "ego play" between himself and his associates. It is a purely artificial status or role. This is the role which he mistakes for his essential Self and which he fears to lose in body death. Since this role defines him as a separate individual and an independent agent, he is blind to his real union and interdependence with the external world and with the Eternal.

"Whoever would save his ego soul shall lose it." So egoji should not crave to be saved. A grain of corn falls into the ground and dies. It is likewise with egojies.

The Christ-conscious Jesus said, "I *am* the Light that is above *all* and in *all*. The *all* came forth from *me* and the *all* attaineth to *me*." This saying is identical with the Vedantic truth. "Cleave the wood, I am there. Lift a stone and ye will aware *me* there" (Gospel of Thomas).

In most religions, the gospel truth is that God is omnipresent and immanent and graceful. In my intuitive awareness, Self is likewise the same. Let's practice the divine Presence and awaken maturely and abidingly into conscious, integral and graceful Self Awareness—with joyous ease and Self controlled spontaneity in all ego fuss, interplay, interdependence and mutual interpenetration in the *Swalila*.

The universal, cosmic Self is in the ever-changing forms and phenomena. In it, there is no conceit of ego agency, no fear of death, no illusion of seeming duality. Stripped of attachment and sticky possessiveness, accept your *prarabdha karma* in affectionate detachment and *Swadharma* in the *Titiksha* mode.

Wuji needed no initiation into mystic union, nirvana or *sahaja samadhi* this time. The born mystic must have learned his lessons well in previous lifespans or maybe it was just gratuitous Grace. When you have already experienced God, Grace or Selfhood, there is no need of external Guru guidance, or of ego concepts, abstractions or learned lore. All our knowledge, understanding and learned ignorance evaporate in the ego-free "Cloud of Unknowing." Where is the inherent wisdom we have lost in knowledge, information and powerful ego antics? asks Wuji. It is all within our Self. Just awaken maturely to aware, experience and Be It. *Tat twam asi.*

Samadhi denotes a state of ego transcendental consciousness or Self experiencing, in which dualities of subject and object, and of all opposites are dissolved. Anything and anybody can be the Guru awakener at the psychological moment. A burnished pewter dish which reflected the sunshine emitted such splendor to Jacob Boehme that he fell into an inward ecstasy. It seemed that he awared the principle and the deepest foundation of things. At first, he believed it was only a fancy and in order to banish it from his mind, he went outdoors. He remarked that he gazed into the very heart of things. The very herbs and grass and all of nature harmonized with what he had inwardly awared and experienced. He said nothing of this to anyone, but promised and thanked God, or Self, in Silence.

At another time, a knot in a piece of wood produced in him a similar state of Self-awareness and ego freeness. Such experiencing may have nothing to do with previous yogic practices, learning or willful yearning. Remember Ramana Maharshi's Self experiencing at the body age of 16, abiding for 50 years among egojies.

We have Alfred Tennyson's statement regarding his mystic "self hypnosis."

> A kind of waking trance I have frequently had, quite from boyhood, when I have been alone. This has often come upon me through repeating my own name to myself silently. All at once, as it were, out of the intensity of consciousness of individuality, the individuality itself seemed to dissolve and fade away into boundless Being. This is not a confused state, but the clearest of the clearest, the surest of the surest, the weirdest of the weirdest, utterly beyond words, where death was an almost laughable impossibility, the loss of personality was but the only true Life.

Wuji does not remember repeating his own name or any mantra in order to unmask. There was no intensity, no trying, no ecstasy, but there was a natural *Sahaja* unmasking in graceful and grateful Self awareness in ego-free solitude.

As a child, Wuji must have been aware (unconsciously aware, perhaps) of the meaning of his *Sat* Name "Em-man-uel," the indwelling, immanent and innerstanding Self or Christ-consciousness. At seven years of body age, Wuji wondered, "Why do I laugh? Why do I forget?" When, later on, he read Henri Bergson's "Psychology of Laughter," he knew why he had laughed with and at the egojies. Ego laughter and the forgetting were only on the surface and like ego play, they were not very real. They were still due and behovely [necessary] in the interplay of his *prarabdha karma*. Ego crucifixions are also due. Life or Self sends us these ego purifications in the due fullness of time. So Mohammed could cheerfully advise, "Die before you die."

24 ❧

Gautama Buddha

Gautama Buddha was a mystic. He shrank from giving descriptions of ineffable states which can only be felt, realized and lived by intuition. Reason cannot explain them. He remained silent about metaphysical questions relating to God, Soul, etc. His silence is significant; it is an answer rather than an expression of suspended judgment. According to Buddha, the real expression and form of Truth is Silence, the full, solid, word-free, time-free sunyata.

—Sunyata

Rta [Order] and *Satya* [Truth] are the practical and theoretical sides of one Reality. The Real is a realm of perfect rhythm in vibrational form of color and perfume. Disjointedness, separateness, incoherence, lack of rhythmic ease are all marks of the ego life.

Gautama Buddha's key word *Mahakaruna* [literally, great compassion] denotes a realm of awareness, which is "a state of love without an object of love. It is a state without any trace of pity or of otherness." One awakens into the direct immediate realization of the Real here and now. We discern, behold and live the spiritual that is hidden in the outer appearance.

"Right contemplation" to Gautama Buddha is the end and crown of his eight fold path. When the senses, mind and other tools are harmonized, we are free in them. When discursive thought ceases, we enjoy the effort-free, untrammeled bliss of our own nature. In simple awareness, we cease to desire and to regret. We cease to fear and to fuss. We are free in the form and the formless, gay in pain and delight. Likes and dislikes do not blur when we awaken in the realm of Being, as distinct from that of existence.

When we focus the total energy of our consciousness in the innermost center, we experience awareness of integral Unity. The Unity awareness is not to be confused with the changing empirical aggregate. If thy eye be integral, intuitive and simple, thy whole body will be full of light. The realm of grace is within. Look within. Thou art Buddha!

Know ye not that ye are gods! Be still and know that thou art God! The Self is the Lord of egos. Leave nothing of my ego in me! Get rid of attachment to what is not yours: form, feeling, perception, etc., are not yours.

To the question "What is nirvana?," the answer was, "You push your question too far, Visakha: The religious life is plunged in nirvana. Its aim is nirvana, its end is nirvana. The sense of egohood vanishes. He who has awakened into the light knows no fetters of becoming. Whosoever is emancipated by perfect wisdom, to him the thought that anyone is better than I, or equal to me or less than I, does not occur." Nirvana, the fruit of noble path, the freedom *in* passion, the ease that knows no break—it is the life that even the gods are said to covet. This goal of all striving is not "nothingness." It is rather the breaking-down of the barriers that constitute illusory separate existence. It is the change-free life in the time-free all. When the word symbols "death-free," "end- free," "change-free," are applied to it, they refer to the quality of being and not to the duration of existence. No measure can measure him who has awakened into Eternity.

The consciousness experienced in nirvana is so different from the ordinary human consciousness that it should not bear the same name. "Verily, I tell you that you understand not: the Self is Silence! *Upasanto yam atma.*" The tradition of teaching by Silence has been an ancient one in India. "The eye does not go thither, nor speech, nor mind. We do not know. We do not understand! How can we teach it? It is different from the known and it is also above the unknown." Thus we have heard from those of old who had awakened to conscious awareness of innerstanding, "*mauna hi bhagavana— tathagata.*" The highest truth is Silence. We pass beyond theories and facts and awaken to the Real, the Eternal in time. Dionysius dared to call it "a reason that did not reason, a word that could not be uttered, an absolute non-existence that is above all existence!"

Buddha had to contend with the theologians, ritualists and worldlings whose prayers took the character of private communication or ego bargaining with God, seeking for objects of earthly ambition and inflaming the sense of ego, instead of nourishing the glow of Self. Buddha taught that the preparatory stages of student life and married life were not essential. One could awaken at any age and time to simple, conscious awareness of the Eternal in one's Self.

Buddha said, "Do not complain and cry and pray, but open your eyes and see, for the light is all about you. It is so wonderful, so beautiful, so far beyond anything that man has ever dreamt of or prayed for, and it is for ever and ever."

"Be a lamp unto your Self. Be awake and at ease.

Be not artful or artificial. Be your simple Self in the light of Buddha *dharma*. Your bondage is delusive, not real. If only they awaken to realize they are already in the *tathagata* or nirvana, for all things are in nirvana from the very beginning." (*Lankavatara Sutra*). In *Mahakaruna*, we simply see and be our Self as we are. Our inherent wisdom, grace and equipoise are uncovered.

The ego veils dissolve. We innerstand and are ever free in the Buddha *dharma*. To hold is to shut; to try is to falsify; to let freely pass (like a mirror or a medium) is to be free and beautifully useless. In the ego-self that clings and tries, there is birth and death. But in the Self which is unclouded is life and all life is one in the all comprehending *sunyata*.

Behind the persona mask is hidden the happy wisdom. It is safely hidden and is yet ever self-revealed to the eye that is simple and intuitive. We are further hidden by our wordiness, assertion and trying, but still "God nods to God within each of us."

In the unitive wisdom beyond knowledge, all things are divine. There is no real difference between the outer Sun and the inner Light. All is Holy Being. The essence is bliss and grace and ease of Being. The real Presence is joyous moment to moment unfolding. In Eternity, here and now, we can live our Unity Awareness in joyous ease. Our Sun awareness is awake in empirical ego woes and in phenomenal shadow play.

25 🌿

Dhammapada

The Dhammapada states, "Possessing nothing. Wanting nothing. He is full of power. He has come to the end of the path. Over the river of his many lives, his many deaths, he has come to the end of the path and merged in the Tao way. All that he had to do, he has done. And now he is one." These are the last golden sutras of Dhammapada, which reminded me of a poetic phrase which fascinated me in Denmark when my body was 15 years young. "Inlet at eje, intet at onsek, intet at ville"—to possess nothing, to desire nothing, to will nothing, as a desirable, mature state of being and of being aware, rather than being powerful, clever or knowledgeable.

There was a simple, sane peasant culture around me, as was contentment, harmony, acceptance and, one may say, a simple grace awareness and unity of what *is*. I had no ambition to be full of power or willfulness, no lust to go in Viking raid for conquest and vain glory and no religiosity.

It must have been innerstances from the past memories which made the child familiar with the fragrance and the radiance of such phrases as the above, of Ibsen's

"*Sejrens sejr er alt at miste*," the victory of victories is to lose all, and also later on, to recognize Beethoven's last four quartets as kindred and Ramana Maharshi as Self-realized.

Meister Eckhart uses phrases similar to "The Dhammapada" to clarify and illuminate the rather obtuse beatitude. "Blessed are the poor in spirit"—to possess nothing and to be awarely a No-body, a no-thing-ness. "Fool that I was to call anything mine." To will nothing; the Will is ever being done—let God happen. All things happen providentially by themselves. Kailash (meaning desire freeness) is within, as is the realm of Grace. Don't gad about, but be simply and awarely at home in *swalila*, swa darshan and *swadharma*.

Man wants to possess, to aggress and to shine. This is because he is unaware of who or what he is. He is unaware of his being, his wholeness and his allness. This ignorance (*ajnana*) kindles his desire, craving and lust for possessions, power and pleasure. Babes become egojies as they grow up. They imitate their parents and the folks around them, aiming at possessions, power, prestige, respectability, name, fame, security, influence and admiration. They feel that knowledge, cleverness, grade and competence must be attained. Egojies feel they must be able to compete, to excel, to achieve, to control, to aggress and to have something to sell, to assert, to give and to share.

"Possessing nothing, wanting nothing," says Buddha. Be aware that thou art no thing and no body, no mind, no egoji. Wu! That's where sincere meditation in intuitive light can reveal Reality, Selfhood, Grace awareness.

I am no more interested in possessing and progressing. I do not lust after anything nor do I renounce anything—not even egoji. The real *sannyasin* [renunciate of worldly things] never renounces anything. I simply innerstand everything—the inner realm of no-thing-ness, its beauty, its benediction, its grace.

In affectionate awareness, I feel an affectionate detachment with things, events and egojies. Your chronological age may be 70, 80 or 90 but you, yourself, are age-free, childlike, yet not interested in any more toys. In inner contemplation, in solitude and graceful Silence, the childishness of the clever grown-ups disappears. Ego oblivion is Self awareness. In maturity, you again become childlike but on a different plane. Not childish but absolutely childlike—the same purity and innocence, the same wonder, awe and joyous unity awareness. "Possessing nothing. Wanting nothing. Full of grace."

A Buddha—a Christ conscious being—is unaffected by others' opinions, likes and dislikes. He is Self aware. He has an intuitive, ego-free sense of his own being. He awares through intuition and not through mind. He needs no "other" for fulfillment—no better or worse half—or a fragment for wholeness, authenticity or integrity.

Sunyata with unkown people

26 🌿

Suffering

The following letter from Daniel to Sunyata, was written while Daniel was a patient in the mental ward of an army hospital. Sunyata's reply reveals how sufering can be put away by right innerstanding.

Daniel's Letter:

Dear Sunyata,

I am in a state of anxiety—my anguish seems unbearable. It is not mental depression, but just anxiety, fearful and blinkered, perhaps. Breath is choked, a heavy weight lies on the heart, the pain is both physical and mental. What is the meaning of this overwhelming pain? Why? Wherefore? How to escape it? How to live through it?

At first sight, the cause is obvious. I had been kept in the army hospital for six weeks. I was considered a schizophrenic, suffering from depersonalization and treated as such for two weeks. I was even isolated in a cell with an iron door. I was administered pills which I managed not to swallow. Nobody told me anything. I could just hear the shouting of other isolated fellows. "Maman! Maman!" or "What have I done? Why do you give me pricking? Why are you keeping me here? I swear I am innocent! Just tell me what I have done?" Silence answered these shoutings. When the hospital attendants had enough of the noise and the banging against the doors, they just administered a new pricking by force in order to have peace and quiet.

The horror was long. I did not know how long I would be kept there—one month? two years? This was perhaps the worst. But I had courage and unfailing faith. After two weeks, I was sent back to France and put in a free room among people suffering from mental depression and anxiety. I did my best to comfort them. I had courage, and it is only when I returned here that I found myself in this state.

Certainly, the nervous strain has been enormous. There I saw and experienced the horror of suffering. Surely, suffering is the characteristic of human life. But in a hospital, in a prison and in a mental home, this suffering is starkly uncovered and undisguised and strikes one right in the face.

Suffering can be helpful towards God. But suffering can also numb, deaden and kill the soul completely. A great amount of suffering for a prolonged period can sometimes leave an unhealable scar. Life seems utterly hopeless after such a blow. It is like an earthworm half trodden on the ground or a butterfly pinned while alive. Many things can be said about suffering. Many explanations can be given. It is because of sin, say some Christians. It is karma, say some Hindus. It is God's *Lila*, playing as the Sufferer, say some others. It is the way God takes us to him, etc., etc. But really—suffering has no satisfactory explanations. The story of Job shows us that even a just faithful and orthodox right believer can suffer and can be overwhelmed by it. Even the greatest sage can be overwlelmed by it, even Jesus the Christ before crucifixion begged and besought the dharmic source to remove the cup of suffering from him. On his cross, he groaned "Father! Father! Why didst thou abandon (forsake) me?"

There is an apparent abyss of horror, which is perhaps the cause of our aforementioned anxiety. I am living some kind of death. Words and mental concepts may help me to verbalize away my experience of suffering, explain it away. I do not innerstand or realize or suffer through and beyond it. I am apt to hug my blinkers, to brood in my ego pain and to lick my sores noisily and mentally. I am slightly hurt and I cry Murder! Murder! As you say, all our ego-wriggling is duality fuss; spiritual suffering is a contradiction in terms. Wu!

It is always a joy for me to receive your letter, your *ananda* play in word symbols. They come by chance—or is there any chance? I had with me two of your scribbles while isolated in the hospital cell (treated as a schizophrenic) and each time I read them, I felt Himalayan grace and peace descending upon me. You have truly found the way to express the "inexpressible." Each word, each sentence, is true and full of spirit. It is the very breath of what *is*. Nothing can be altered or changed. It is full by itself.

Art is Being, you say. And not only you say, but you are. You are truly a real artist. Your writings are poems full of light, and word symbols are as good as anything— if properly and even strangely used.

Daniel

Sunyata's Reply:

Dear Daniel,

Thou hast been in the Lion's den! Wu! Rejoice that you escaped alive and whole and unembittered. I rejoice with you that you avoided the pills, the pricks and the iron traps and came through and—beyond. The psychic bleeding is a natural reaction. The anxiety and fear will heal, will cease by and by in the due fullness of time.

In suffering together, we suffer one another and vicariously, victoriously "I" in you will win and get to the integral grace. "I love you beyond mind and meaning and measure," chants the *sahaja*, mind-free Wuji in one purpose-free, Himalayan Wu!

Empathy is more than sympathy, more than love and hate and union in duality play. No space for "I" and "Me" and "Mine"—(naughty word symbols), says the fastidious Wuji. It is non-dual, conscious awareness, intuitive innerstanding, in feeling, in passion, and in suffering. Such emphatic, concrete Empathy—so free, so new—like nothing else on earth, in hell or in heaven! Wuji is eternity wallah and, so, at home everywhere. He kens that El Porte del Paradise is always open.

The state of anxiety is a due reaction, necessary to a successful death of ego. Bear it patiently. It has come upon you in dharmic dueness. Accept it serenely. Let it overwhelm you, if it can; let it splash and purify; let it cleanse the kinks and the sediments, without your trying to expel, hide, escape or forget it. Do not will to think it away—or explain it away in perennial philosophizing and claptrap truisms. Live the problem, the suffering, live through it, suffer through it. It is not only bearable (except to blinkered egojies), but can turn into a crown of glory rather than one of thorns.

There is a Zen answer to the question "How to escape this damned heat (anxiety and suffering)?" Face it. Then go right into its center and experience it fully, integrally, essentially, and ye are done with it. You gasp and frizzle and all your bodies are numbed or sore by the pain, the burden and the bewilderment. The pain is both physical, mental and in the emotional feeling body, as all the bodies are actually interfused in mutual interdependence. The cause is in psyche as the unconscious dharmic integrality is duly impaired. It will come clear by and by.

Spiritual suffering is a contradiction in term symbols! Hard on egojies to accept but a cosmic truth nevertheless. A death is also a birth. Opposites are complementary, not opposed. So rejoice, dignified in and by suffering, the crucial crucible. It may turn into "Hallelujas" of ego humble gratitude.

Never mind the mental whys and hows, the whither and the whence. In the eternal now of suffering, you are the "know-how-wallah (one who knows)." Sufferings, like egojies are necessary passing shadows, inevitable, beautiful and, like sin, behovely. "Is not She who created misery wiser than thou and Job?" asks Wuji, and who was there to overhear Joshua ben Joseph in his Gethsemane beseeching the source, "May this cup of agony and ego crucifixion be withheld. May this experience pass me by (if it be thy cosmic Will!)."

Our whimpering is human and, as ye say, we cry murder over ego important trifles, for instance, when Wuji happens to step on tender corns on our lotus feet— or to tilt our halo askew. The supreme identity and integral truth is that we are more than human, more than mortal ego souls. Ye must transcend your humanity and be free in it. The circus, the shadow puppet play and our swell ego antics are really divine *Swalila*. Enjoy the Self radiant, all suffusing *Ananda*!

I am being divinely playful and bouncing harm-freely. My utterly uneducated, uncivilized peasant touch is gentle, even kind, even healing on the naked psyche, though ego wounds may bleed. It is sediments and poison that bleed away and vanish into pure *akasha.* Inwardly, you innerstand that the inherent integral grace along with your natural freedom is always there, in spite of tantric tricks, clever antics and analytical know-hows.

Bondage, like lovable egojies, is delusive, but sin is behovely. The veils of ignorance or unawareness are unavoidable. Accept them also and abide in patience and divine indifference till integral awareness dawns in Himalayan consciousness.

You took body and birth this time in a certain family setting, race, circumstances and conditioning, all due and right in *Swadharma.* There is no real choice, renunciation, death or ego, but there is karmic interplay and dharmic interdependence and ji-ji muge, natural, perfect, unimpeded and mutual interpenetration. And All Is Well!

The supposed or alleged cry of the human Joshua on his ego cross, "Why has the Awareness of the Source forsaken me?" is apparently a mistranslation of the original Aramaic, a wrong hearing, a false recording by egos. The dark night of the soul is also a due experience, though "notre Soleil brille toujours." Our weeping and passive suffering turns into "Hallelujahs" of grace and gratitude. We have seen several other translations of Joshua's duality statement and the most plausible is, "Ah! What glorification! Consummatum est!"

Weep and cry—Dan, accept and dissolve. Let the due suffering overwhelm ego and the ego-ridden mind. You will emerge. You are invincible. Sin, Karma, Self, God, etc., are all words, words, words, concepts and abstractions, until they happen to us and often painfully. The sin is ignorance, unawareness, blinkers and ego blindness, so don't harbor, develop or nourish a sin-complex or guilt complex.

Karma, prenatal, pre-ego and ego-made, must be accepted as a fact in living. It can be atoned—and we need not accumulate any more *prarabdha*. By our attitude and integral awareness, it is accepted, atoned and transcended. So let's drop our cumbersome conceit of agency, says Wuji.

Karma only partly explains our futile whys? Our chief concern, task and "busyness" is our very own *Swadharma*—in the cosmic Play. Who or what are ye? For what reason and experience did ye take body and birth and many deaths? Find out—Awake, Arjuna! Court experience but do not rush giddily into trouble. Give temptation a chance and, maybe, lend the devil a little finger, but don't let Her grasp the whole hand or tender lotus feet. Let Her have egoji instead. If egoji did not suffer agonies and crucifixions, it would be swell and bumptious. It would strut and assert: "*Anur Huk* (I am God)!" says Wuji. It must mature to say "yes" or "Wu" to this ego annihilation. "Ripeness is all. Readiness is all." Conscious self-awareness in mature, inherent grace and integral wisdom is all. Ego oblivion is Self awareness. Wu!

We feel that if your bodies were here in the Himalayas—our nearness would heal, harmonize and wholify them, especially the ego-ridden mind, which is your chief troublemaker, refusing to coalesce and integrate. *Karuna* would heal you. Sri Himalaya would soothe you like a swell soothsayer and the pure, krishna blue *akasha* would cleanse all. All this is within your Self.

The singing Silence, the Source, the Self effulgent radiance of *Prajna* Light, all is there, as here. But, of course, here is the Himalayan Wuji in the Invisible Real—to keep you awake and consciously aware of It—with a swell Wu! *Aum!*

Old newspaper clipping found in the attic of Sunyata's cabin after his death (Sunyata is seated far right)

27 ❧

Awakening

The following description of an "ego death" is both authen-
tic and revealing. "A" may be referring to Albert, Sunyata's
friend of many years, currently residing somewhere in
Europe.

His sweet humility and tenderness could only be a prey of death. His mien, his gaze, did not seem to belong to him. In his speech, in his voice and, above all, in his eyes, one could read plainly that detachment from what we call life. His psyche was lifting its wings out of the ken of the living. His body was sinking, shrinking, and parting. But he was indifferent to our important trifles because something else, something supreme, was being borne in upon his consciousness. His emotions were dying by degrees. The fowls of the air sow not, nor do they reap. Yet the eternal source feedeth them. It also clotheth the so called wild lilies of the jungle so that they may not toil or worry or fuss in agitation, fear or assertive insecurity.

A. grew silent. Words would but blur. No, they were useless. The kind, sympathetic friends would take his meaning differently. The living egos cannot understand that the feelings, beliefs, and opinions, which look so dear to them, and all these thoughts, concepts and abstractions, which seem so important, really do not matter. A. knew that it was death alone that matters. He was half-dead already by this conscious detachment from all earthly interest and by the strength and radiant beatitude that filled, suffused and healed his integral Being. He lay waiting for the inevitable and the ineffable, without impatience or trepidation. The great, eternal Truth, unknown and seemingly distant, which all his life had dwelt in the background of his thought, was near now, close at hand. He could feel it, almost touch it. Is death the secret of life and not its opposite? Do we die to live?

Formerly, he dreaded death. Twice he passed near the fearful gulf of death in agonies. Now he no longer feared it. His eyes that had been facing the beauty of the woods, the mountains, the deep blue sky, now saw death rushing at him. But when he regained ordinary ego-consciousness, the flower of Grace and of vast, intimate empathy had blossomed in his conscious awareness. He was freed for a while from the care of earthly surface life. The fear of death had vanished. The barrier between life and death had lost its terror. In the absence of any attachment, bondage gradually gave way. There was no real detachment, no real divisions and no real death.

"What is the meaning," he wondered, "of loving all mankind and of ego dedication or of crucifixion through love, unless it is loving no one in particular—and being consciously in touch with the Source of all, the Eternal, in 'time' and 'ego play'? Aware of the Real in and beyond love and hate and all opposites?"

He beheld the end with real, divine indifference. No revolt of flesh or of ego against the unknown. "Love," he thought again, "what is love?" It is the recognition and negation of death. It is Life itself. Death is the secret of life—the awakening into death-freeness. All that I have experienced, I have innerstood by love, empathy or Self identity alone. "I" comprehends and suffuses everything. Love is God, and Death is the re-absorption of the atom of life that is myself. "To die—to awaken." The idea, the intuition, flashed in his consciousness like a lightning gleam. Death is the awakening. A corner of the veil which still parted him from the unknown had been lifted from his psyche. His Being was releasing him from the illusory bond that still held it to earthly phenomena and ego values. A mysterious beatitude came over him, which henceforth did not desert him. In integral Self-experiencing there is inherent Grace.

A. was silent. These loving solicitudes and discussions of personal relations and predilections made him feel uncomfortable. They threatened his solitude, in which now alone, his Being could breathe in comfort. Alone he felt free, "whole in unity" and fully alive without blur or restraint or compulsion. Its discipline was inherent, ontological and spontaneous. He took this inward solitude for granted as one accepts the weather or the atmosphere in which one lives. But when it was managed or menaced, he became only too painfully aware of its importance to him. He fought for it as a choking man fights for air. It was usually a fight without violence, in a mode of passive positivity or negative capability, or retirement and deference. He instinctively entrenched himself in Silence—in the calm, intuitive awareness, or experiencing, in the unitive life, that is behind, beyond and within all things, all phenomena and ego noises.

A. felt as if he were melting into green and golden tranquility, sinking and being absorbed into living unity. Stillness flowed into stillness. The Silence without became one with the Silence within him. The turbid liquor of existence grew gradually calm. All that had made it opaque, all the noise and uproar of the world, all the personal anxieties, desires and feelings began to settle like sediments. They fell slowly, noiselessly out of sight. The turbid liquor became clearer and clearer, more and more translucid. In and behind the gradually vanishing mist of actuality was Reality, was God. It was a slow progressive revelation—an awakening from duality and ego shadows to integral Self-awareness. He breathed softly and the last faint ripple died away from surface life. The opacities churned up by the agitation of living dropped away through the utter calm of Being. There was perfect ease. He had no desires, no more preoccupations. The liquor, which had been turbid, was now quite clear, clearer than crystal, more diaphanous than air. The ego mist had vanished and the unveiled Reality was Silence—a positive No-thing-ness, a living grace. The gradual revelations were now complete. "A" had died or awakened into self-radiant, joyous ease, integral grace and ego-free *Ananda*.

Were any of the deaths you have endured or witnessed like this? It rings true also of many psychological deaths or integral awakening. We can have many deaths in one body without giving it up entirely. There is always the letting-go of identity and of attachment, the letting-go of worry and of duality values, of reason, mind, thought and time. There is always the inner solitude, the healing Silence and the creative contemplation until we *be* the contemplation, the silent empathy, the integral grace. It is a matter of maturity for egoji to die in stark sincerity—and of patience to mature, says the mind-free Himalayan Wuji.

"Die before ye die!" Life is a constant dying and becoming—projection and withdrawal—involution, evolution and revolution. Wu! We think we understand and know, while really, all the eternal while, we innerstand ego-freely and death-freely, and "we are always aware,

Sunya!" says Wuji. Aye, we Are the awareness, the Grace, the Wu!

Oh those words! One is thankful to have escaped from them—from sticky, ideal concepts and from the bondage of thought and time and body consciousness. It is like getting out of a prison that is artful, artistic and artificial, full of frescoes, tapestries, abstractions and what-not. Wu! One prefers the genuine, natural country-side and the pure Silence that is real, spontaneous inter-relatedness, empathy and natural interpenetration, rid of craving, willing and word symbols. Such Unity Awareness is healing and immediate. It is unassertive, inherent wisdom and joyous ease.

28 ❦

All is Divine Play

A *Jnani* accepts and rejoices in everything that happens as the "Divine Play." Nothing is rejected because he knows that essentially "All is Well." "A sure sign of self-enlightenment, self awareness or salvation from ego-consciousness," says Wuji, "is a calm, joyous and serene radiance in *sat-chit-ananda*, or Being Awareness Grace."

When you are whole, you are also holy—in essential harmony with all Life and all manifestations. All that lives is holy, says the graceful mystic.

"All is alive, all is energy," said the scientist Einstein when leaving his body. "Energy is indestructible—and I *am* energy."

Ramana Maharshi could say, "You are perturbed and desolate that Bhagavan is leaving you. Where can he go to? He is always here." You are free *in* life when you aware that essentially you *are* Life. It is You, Life, God that happens all the eternal while. So let God happen, dear egojies.

All happens wisely, providentially. Accept, discern, rejoice—and radiate peace at joyous ease in *Swalila*. All is divine Self interplay. All is right that seems most

wrong to busy *egojies*. Deep is woe, but joy, ah *ananda*,
is deeper still. *Ananda* is a sequence, a consequence, of
being Aware. A wise *Jnani* who has awakened into conscious Being-Awareness-Grace rejoices in letting God
happen.

The Will is ever being done on earth as in heaven—
all the time—yes, in, around and through. One needs to
be aware that it is so. Why fuss or worry or pray that it
may be done? It is ever being done. Forgive egojies.
They do not know what they do or what they are and so
may be forgiven.

In ego conceit of agency, we think that we push
and pull, conquer and control, whereas all the while it is
we who are being pushed and pulled, used and led in
swadharmic Self interplay, in due *jijimuge*—perfect,
mutual, unimpeded interpenetration.

When a confused and bewildered soul sought
advice from Ramana Maharshi, he was told, "Do not
fuss or fret or worry. What has to be done through you
as work will be done, whether you like it or not.
"*Prarabdha karma* has to happen but we can change
our attitude to events, to pain, to death and to calamities. Aware in the *titiksha* mode of acceptance, like
Ramana Maharshi in terminal cancer. "If there is pain,
let it be. It is also the Self and the Self is *purnam* [ful-
filled, perfect]."

What is being done and what can be done in
dharmic interplay is fulfillment and grace. *Swadharma* is
our chief concern, not egojies' play. As egojies, we play
such fantastic tricks before high Heaven as make the
Angels weep. Or is it laugh? asks Wuji. He suggests
"smile" in grace awareness. After awaring the Greek
tragedies, Shakespeare's beyond-comedy-and-tragedy
"The Tempest," or after seeing a Chekhov play or read-

ing his short stories, one can have the feeling that all is forgiven. There is nothing to forgive. It would be strange not to forgive and not to rejoice in Grace Awareness.

Let God happen in divine All Rightness.

The S. S. Vallejo, Allan Watts' old houseboat in Sausalito,
California, where Sunyata gave weekly satsangs

29 🌿

Eternal Silence

We may name Silence "Shunya," "Turiya," "Brahma," "Eternity," or "God." It is essentially a mode of sahaj samadhi, a state of mahakaruna, or pure, integral awareness. It implies far more than the word-free mouna. It is actually ego-free stillness.

—Sunyata

Silence is the one, eternal Reality, which suffuses and sustains all the actual and temporary manifestations in the divine Self interplay or *Swa lila*. In his *Gita*, Sri Krishna sings, "Of the mountains, I am the Himalaya and of the men of mystic wisdom, I am their Silence. Out from the eternal Silence issues the Word made Flesh and Phenomena, and into Silence it all returns.... With one fragment of myself, I projected all these universes: I remain."

Sunya Silence is all-comprehending. It innerstands all forms and functions in the divine *Maya Lila*. It is a poor term symbol for the "ineffable experiencing." It is the cessation of desires and of false identity with ego. "I", "me" and "mine" are naughty word symbols in the *Advaita* mode of experiencing. In the light of Self-controlled spontaneity, we are naturally fear-free, ego-free and death-free.

I was four times in the darshan of Sri Ramana Maharshi at *Arunachala*. His dynamic and integral radiance is our living beacon of actual *sahaja samadhi*. I asked no question and stated no problem in his presence. Like Dakshinmurti in earlier times, Sri Ramanaji taught us and his fellow *rishis*, chiefly in mature Silence, in natural, ego-free Self-radiance. Integral grace and inherent freeness radiated from the Maharshi's pure consciousness. It is transmitted or awakened into, silently and effort-freely in a kind of empathy, according to our receptivity and our maturity. That which recognizes itself is within. The initiation into intuitive and conscious Self-awareness is often conveyed by a look, rarely by touch, and usually in pure Silence. It is for us to be ego still and to attune to receive it.

This Shunya Silence, or *advaita* Self-experiencing, is essentially name-free and ineffable. Intuition for the experience can be trained and purified, but assertion or trying to share or to explain is futile. Words are metaphors and they falsify the Real. Names and labels hide the name-free, the invisible Reality. Even our beliefs and ideals, concepts and abstractions, are hindrances to the authentic, integral Self-experiencing in non-dual awareness. Can we be inwardly still to reflect purely? Can we, in graceful empathy recognize and *be* our Self in the Silence of fellow pilgrims? Can we experience our Self at joyous ease and in the anandful grace of natural spirituality?

In the light of Self-controlled spontaneity, all our questions and our quest ceases, or ceases to matter. Ego oblivion is Self awareness. In ego transcendence, we experience that we are more than human, more than fussy, fearful and mortal egojies. We experience that there is no death of the Real—that we ever are.

Resuming our dharmic interplay in actualities after such *advaita* experiencing, we are naturally fear-free and ego-free in tune with our unitive Self—everywhere. In Shunya Silence, we can meet and merge time-freely and ego-freely. This is empathy and *karuna* grace and gratitude. All is well!

30 🔥

The One Remains

L ila, an orthodox nun from Greece, who had come to my abode in Almora, India, in the 1950s, wrote to me in America after a gap of 30 years:

> Dear Sunyata,
> Time passes, friendship remains. This is a gift of God and I am grateful for it. I have some nice photos—so real—so the same throughout these 30 years. Marvelously so. More and more, I realize the body does not exist (as a reality) and therefore I do all that people need to be done. My real Self is else-where. Wonderful. Wonderful! Bliss, joy, Grace, Grace awareness, love, joy
> —Always in His Love,
> His Lila.

It was always the same during 30 years, aye, dur-ing 90 graceful years. I nearly called the first cottage sanctuary in Himalaya "Samata"—until Ramana Maharshi called me Sunyata and I fastened that label on my shelter.

Regarding this *samata* [sameness], I find confirma-
tion with Nisargadatta Maharaj. This "Beri Baba," who
remained unknown during 40 years of Christ-consciousness, said, "I am now 84 years old and yet I am the infant
of 84 years ago. I feel clearly that, in spite of all the
changes, I am still that child. My guru told me, 'That
child which is you even now is your real Self (*swarupa*).
Go back to that state of pure being, where the 'I am' is
still in its purity, before it gets contaminated with 'this I
am' or 'that I am.' Your burden is of false self identification. Abandon them all. Trust me. I tell you, you are
Divine. Take it as absolute truth. Your joy is divine. Your
suffering is divine too. All comes from God. Your will
alone is done. Remember it always—You are God. Your
will alone is done.' I did trust him. Soon I realized how
true and accurate were his words. I did not condition my
mind by thinking 'I am God, I am wonderful, I am
beyond.' I simply followed his instruction, which was to
focus the mind on pure being—*I am*—and stay in it. I
used to sit for hours together with nothing but *I am* in
my mind—and soon the peace and joy and deep, all-
embracing love became my normal state. In it, all disap-
peared—my ego mind, my guru, the life I lived, the world
around me. Only peace, joy and Grace remained, and
unfathomable Silence."

Behnji [meaning respected sister] Anandamayee
too feels this sameness. When devotees asked her,"Who
are you, Ma? A reincarnation of which goddess, or an
avatar of Vishnu or of Shiva?" She simply said unto them,
"What I am to you, that I am." When a learned *avadhuta*
asked her, "Mataji, what is the nature of your *samadhi*?"
her answer was, "It is really for you, Pitaji, to give names
to the various stages of *samadhi*. This mad girl can only
say that, throughout, and in spite of all the changes of
forms, conditions and circumstances in the Life play, I
feel that I am the same as in childhood's infancy."

Yogananda Paramahansa asked Anandamayee Ma, "Please, Ma, tell us something of your life." The reply was, "Pitaji knows all about it. Why repeat it?" She evidently felt that the factual history of one short reincarnation was beneath notice. When Yogananda repeated his request gently, he was told, "Pitaji, there is little to tell." She spread her graceful hands in a deprecating gesture and said, "My consciousness has never associated itself with this temporary body. Before I came on this earth, Pitaji, it was the same. As a little girl, it was the same. When the family into which I was born made arrangements to have this body married, I was the same and, Pitaji, in front of you now, I am the same. Even after the dance of creation changes in the Hall of Eternity, I shall be the same.

Sunyata in America shortly before his passing

31 ✤

There is Only the One

A Christian missionary asked a Zen Master, "Is not the end point of man's journey the union with God?" The Master replied, "No, the end point of man's journey is not union, because there was never any separation." The Source and I are a non-dual One. Awakening into Christ-consciousness, we aware the oceanic existence and, awarely be the non-dual experiencing in Grace. It is "Self-experiencing," dear egoji. Thou art thy Self, the object of thy search, says Wuji. Wu!

All that is needed is an intuitive flash within you, which reveals Reality—Grace Awareness, the Vastness, the Wholeness and the All Rightness. Wake up from your duality dream and aware that All is one, a non-dual One. The Source and I are One. "We are always aware, Sunyata." We have always been one with Existence, Love, Light, God, Self, Truth and Reality.

Synchronicity happens. All happens by itself, spontaneously and providentially. The ultimate prayer is a monologue, not a dialogue between Thou and I. Judaism and Christianity got stuck there. The Source and I are a non-dual One. In the intuitive Light, all your distinctions, fragmentations and divisions disappear. The "thou" and the "me" also vanish. The enlightened person is no longer there. Egoji has vanished like a shadow in the Self Sun; *Samsara* is Nirvana. You cannot know your Self, God, Reality. You can only *be*. Beauty is always of the beyond. It is in the eye and the consciousness of the beholder, who is open and clear to aware and to reflect it purely. Wu!

To know God is to be God. To aware a Buddha, a Christ or a Christ conscious Being, there is That within you which reflects purely, which re-cognizes its Self. There is Self radiance in the oceanic Existence. Distinctions of Time and Death disappear in the intuitive light of wholeness and Grace awareness.

God is happening all the eternal while, yet no-thing is happening. God is not a thing and not even a sexy She or Ma. It is divine no-thing-ness, no ego, no mind— "*anatta* [non-self]." God happens ego-freely, cause-freely, providentially and Self radiantly. Wu! Dear egoji, let God happen and *be* at joyous, graceful and grateful ease. That is my advice in the invisible Real, in plenum void, in *sunyata*, in wu-ness.

Desiring a state of freedom from desire will not set you free. Nothing can set you free, because you are free. Aware your Self with desire-free clarity—that's all. Delve within and aware what is Real in you. Even if I tell you that you are the witness, the silent watcher, it will mean nothing to you unless you aware the way to your true being. Give up all questions except one, "What or who am I?" After all, the only fact you are sure of is, that you Are. The "I am" is certain; the "I am this" is not. Seek, find, aware and experience what you are in Reality. The "I am" itself is God. Seeking Self is to seek God.

32 🌿

That Thou Art

This article elaborates on the non-dual teaching that in the ultimate reality there is no duality between the individual Soul and the Absolute, "That Thou Art" ("Tat Twam Asi" in Sanskrit).

A Himalayan *Jnani* said unto me, "Here and now, through all your bodies, shines Awareness, the pure Light of Chit." The Sanskrit word "Chit" I would translate as pure intuitive intelligence, pure cognition, or unconscious, unmental and impersonal awareness. It is the awareness we have or are, when we appear in a body and also when we leave it. This is rather difficult for egojies to understand and overstand, but it was there in my ego-free consciousness in my seven years of early childhood. It was unmental awareness, ego-free intelligence.

Our *Jnani* continues, "Without *Chit* Awareness, the body would not last a second. There is, in the body, a current of energy, affection and intelligence which maintains and energizes the body. Discover that current and stay with it." Yes, affectionate awareness, intuitive Light and pure energy. Wu!

We hear now about "energy crisis." The mystic scientist, Albert Einstein, could say when he was going to leave his body, "Energy is indestructible and I *am* Energy." So Energy can be another name for Self, God or the I awareness. Of course, all these words are a manner of speaking. Words are as much a barrier as a bridge.

The only words Sri Ramana Maharshi said unto me were, "We are always aware, Sunyata." Yes, we are *that*, intuitive awareness. Seek, aware, intuit, recognize and experience the spark of Life that weaves the tissues of your body. Be it awarely. It is the only Reality the body has. It is beyond time. Life weaves eternally its many webs. The weaving is in time, but Life Itself is time-free and time-less. It is also name-free, whatever name and shape you give its expressions. It is like the ocean, never changing, ever changing. The waves, the ripples and the billows are all close to the sea, so near that there is no room for a Way. We are the Tao Way, says Wuji. We are the oceanic Experiencing. The Source and I are a non-dual One.

Seek, find and experience ye first the inner realm of Grace and all things, all you need, will be added unto you. Aware, intuit and *be* (consciously) the Grace awareness, the non-dual Experiencing: "I"-free, you-free, ego-free and death-free. Unless we admit and accept the Reality of *Chit*, of pure cognition, ego-free, mind-free, will-free and choice-free, we will not aware, recognize and *be* our unitive Self. You assert your self to be what you are not and deny your self to be what you are! The body and the mind are only symptoms of ignorance. Behave as if you are pure awareness (*Chit*), body-free, mind-free, space-free and time-free—beyond "where" and "when" and "how." Dwell on it, think of it, learn to accept its Reality. Experience *Chit* and *be* the experiencing in *Sat-chit-ananda*. Being Awareness Grace; *Tat twam asi*—that thou art. It is *Swalila*. Sri Wuji, in the invisible

Real, can play in words.

In Grace awareness, questions and problems resolve themselves. There is no planning, no striving, no worry, no fear, no inordinate desire, no dis-ease, but there is joyous ease. Spontaneity becomes a way of Life. Mere happiness turns into abiding *Ananda* Grace. If you awarely innerstand in Selfhood, you will aware your Self everywhere as *the self*. Wu!

All things and all egojies change and pass. *The Self* is not a thing and does not change. It innerstands and contains all things and all phenomena. You, your Self innerstands ego-freely whether you are consciously aware or not. Wu!

In my childhood, there seemed to be unconscious awareness, unmental, intuitive intelligence, inherent wisdom and unconscious Grace. Neither mind nor ego obtruded there as contrasts. There was no sin complex, no sense of guilt, no bondage. And so, there was no search of freedom, salvation, enlightenment or Wholeness, no quest of God, Guru or I-dentity. Thou art thy Self, the object of thy search. The Tao, the Source, the Self is a non-dual One and *Tat twam asi*.

Sunyata in Greece with unkown person

33 ✦

Awareness is All

Forgive me, Oh Shiva, my three great sins:
I come on pilgrimage to Kashi,
Forgetting that you are omnipresent and immanent.
In thinking about you,
I forget that you are beyond thought.
In praying to you, I forget that you are beyond words.
　　　　　　　　　　　—Author Unknown

S o sin is but ignore-ance, forgetfulness, or
unawareness of our Self, the Word, the indwelling
Emmanuel, Christ within. We are much more
than human, mortal egojies. Wu!

Speech divides and diffuses, words can stain and
wound the Word but Silence unites and strengthens,
cleanses and refreshes. In word silence, or Shunya mode,
are health and wholeness, insight and clarity unto the
deepest depth, the Ur ground, the eternal Source of all
phenomena, the invisible Real in all actualities, the
Essence and the Integral Whole. Wu!

Our blinkers, our sins, our immaturity, our ego-
consciousness, all must be accepted as due and behovely in our *Swadharmic* Life play, yet we can court ego

death and have the experience in Beyondness, in Self-Awareness, of our unitive Self in all forms and phenomena, all fellow pilgrims, all life. To the mature mystic, "all that lives is holy" (one unitive Whole), and all is alive. Life (Self, Truth, God, Grace and Consciousness) is one integral Whole with many aspects, arbitrary divisions, levels, and awareness in insight and outsight, innerstanding or mere mental understanding, or standing under.

Mere knowledge is not wisdom, and much less *Prajna* or *Mahakaruna*, Empathy, or Shunya. No-thing-ness. Intellect is not intuitive intelligence. Power corrupts egojies and is not the integral strength of Being Awareness Grace.

Knowledge is not mental. In the Biblical sense it, like Theoria and Philosophia, was much nearer experience, or Darshan awareness. Miriam said to Sri Gabriel, "Having not experienced a man (the male in me), how can I conceive (the holy, the Whole)?" The simple Jewish maiden did not aware that we are all immaculate conceptions, and that only through Christ-consciousness do we aware and experience Emmanuel, the Self, the indwelling Christ and the eternal Source, the Godhead beyond Gods and gods and ego-consciousness. Forgetfulness of Self is the cause of all our troubles, conflicts, problems, and ego woes. The non-dual experiencing implies the loss, or letting-go, of ego-consciousness and duality values.

Perhaps we cannot know (mentally) our own *Swadharma*, but we can divine and aware it intuitively in direct perception, in immediate, integral awareness, and thus cooperate with and accept destiny...simply, naturally and gratefully in *Titiksha* mode. Yes, clucky egoji, you must lose your life to live integrally, fear-freely and ego-freely. "I live, yet not I, but Christ in me." Well said and well experienced, Saul, yet "I," "me," and "mine" are merely word symbols in Unity-awareness, or Christ-experiencing. "Fool that I was to call anything mine." Eternity (God, Grace and Self) is all around us and within, but egojies are not consciously aware or integrally conscious.

Ego oblivion is Self-awareness and Self-controlled spontaneity. So practice the art and craft of dying, of *sahaja samadhi*, of ego transcendence. The Spiritual is the natural, and only the Eternal is real. "Aware your natural fa :e that was yours (or You) before your parents were born." Let ego-consciousness die, and you aware and experience that there is no real death, no death of the Real, the Eternal, which we ever, ever *are*. "Before Abraham was, I *am*...the light that never was on land or sea," because it always *is*. Such death or integral awakening can become a habit (like sex and drugs, alcohol, *japa*, yoga, and other methods of change or extension of consciousness) or be temporary; and such experience, or non-dual experiencing, can be valuable. But it is rarely abiding, nor maturely lasting.

There are the few rare, born mystics, who seem intuitively aware from babyhood, and whose pre-ego-consciousness can be co-existing and unclashing with the usurping and ever-shadowing ego-consciousness playing in duality values. These few are rarely very vocal, but keep wisely mum. There is nothing to assert, or to teach, no ego to aggress or lust in *Shakti* business, no ambition in power antics, name and fame and ego-fuss. Yet there is all acceptance and response to egojies and a *karuna* Love which cannot be possessive, exclusive, pitiful, or jealous, and which needs no recognition, requital, or reciprocity.

Our Ramana Maharshi, at 17 years of body age, unsoliciting and unknowingly, was sincere and mature enough to experience a lasting ego-death, or the abiding *Sahaja Samadhi*, and thus *be* Christ-consciousness, ego-free and consciously death-free, during his 50 years of vital play among us egojies. Our maturity we cannot help. Our *Swadharma* destiny must be accepted, but we can practice ego stillness.

> Ask thy lone soul what truths are true
>   to thee,
> Thee and no other. Stand or fall by them.
> The Cross on Golgotha thou lookest to
>   in vain,
> If not within thy Self, it be set up again.
> If Christ a thousand times in Bethlehem
>   were born,
> And not within thy Self, it were forlorn.

When a man has reached old age and has fulfilled his mission, *Swadharma*, he has a right to confront the idea of body death in peace. He has no need of other men. He knows them and knows enough about them. What he needs is solitude and peace. It is not good to visit this man or to talk to him, to make him suffer the banalities. One must give a wide berth to the door of his house, as if nobody lived there in Shunya No-thing-ness. Wu!

34 🌿

Beethoven's Four Quartets

It was in the late 1920s that I became familiar with Ludwig van Beethoven's four quartets. Called 'the impossible quartets' in academic circles, at one time, these were not accepted as technically well crafted. They were rarely performed until a hundred years after their composition (at Beethoven's death centenary), when they were actually recorded on gramophone and eventually became quite popular as chamber music and in radio broadcasts. —*Sunyata*

While these word symbols are bubbling up, I am actually also playing Beethoven's last quartets. They are ever playing themselves in the Himalayan Silence, in the *akasha* vastness of Advaita *Sunya*. "Heard melodies are sweet, but those unheard are sweeter." At present, they are also actually playing themselves by my side on the verandah, to the snowy deva peaks around us, yes, through a gramophone record.

Thus it was my habit in the late '20's, when I first heard these melodies, that I would let them play them-

225

selves while I was writing or doing things. When I am ego-freely alone, there are no clashes in the seeming dual consciousness. The music goes on and is responded to— aye, merged into, by the deeper Ground of consciousness, while the surface play, activities and thoughts, go on co-existingly. There is full conscious awareness and the deeper aware unconsciousness. Wu!

Do ye ken these four last quartets of Ludwig van Beethoven? He was at that time almost tone deaf. Perhaps he could, therefore, better hear these harmonies of the spheres and let them come forth through him. In the stress of trials, tragedies and ego crucifixion, he had perfected the technique; yet even at a deeper level, he had come to full acceptance, the ripe maturity, the joyous ease. He had lived what his tone poems express and reveal—or if you like, he had died into *it*. No, not completely, for then there would have been nothing (but *Sunya*) to assert and no urge to express the ever Self radiant, his integral Whole. There is still his immature floundering in regard to nephew Carl and other fellow pilgrims, but essentially and integrally, in his deepest and most real Awareness, there was grand acceptance, the supreme Affirmation.

These last four or five quartets reveal it. If you can ego-freely "go with" in stillness and *be* them, you will aware. They play you into freedom, into full acceptance and so, into the "essence" and "beyondness," "immanence" and "transcendence," that is joyous ease. These four quartets are as if *sotto voce* intimate statements, a simple and natural contemplation bodied forth to Himself, rather than for public appreciation and sharing. In his earlier, violently storm swayed and powerfully discordant compositions, Ludwig is asserting and sharing his subjective truths, agonies, and pain-joys. In these quartets, the *Ananda* and the *Advaita* modes prevail. The Ninth Symphony may express the same Victory, but now loudly, now stridently aggressive, it breaks into the human voice in gladness, in *Freude*, in *Freiheit* and in the "Millionen umslungen" acceptance.

The quartets are a kind of pure contemplation. The problems and discords, as in the F Major, are solved in the very statement of them. There is a freeness, a joyousness in the very assertion that they exist. Ludwig is free *in* them; he has been beyond Ludwig, and he can play freely in sound, as in the more important pauses of silence in and beyond.

In a friend's home, I became aware of Beethoven's four quartets in the late 1920's. "A" is a teacher of music and revealer of composers and their compositions. She is a self-made, "uneducated" woman, holding her university classes by her sheer and natural insight into meaningful music and her sheer ability to get it across to fellow pilgrims. She studied and lived with the composers, with their human problems, their pain-joy and success-defeats in their work. And she could communicate and transmit it, not easily, but creatively, evocatively, and joyfully.

A. said unto me, "I have found you in music!" It was the B flat, opus 130, Beethoven quartet, and she seemed right. Her medium was piano, not especially congenial to or favored by me and, really, as a peasant boy and menial, manual worker, I had no musical education whatsoever—and had happily escaped all academic and classical "headucation" altogether. Wu! Music was to me a rather meaning-free noise, pleasant or otherwise jarring or congenial, to "go with" in contemplation. It usually jarred the real Silence—and it was in no way a language of experience or of integrality. I had no artistic insight into music. It was only A.'s insight that had made me aware.

When presented with these four last quartets of Ludwig van Beethoven, I was startled in glad wonder.

It seemed they were intimately familiar to me as something as kindred as my own, silent contemplation. It was a new word-free language, stating and revealing the same mode of awareness—the same thing—as "No-Thing-ness." Yes, the B flat in particular, but also the C sharp, the A minor, and the most concise F major. They all say or reveal the same Awareness—beautifully, purely and rightly different.

The C-sharp is now going on, playing itself to Sri Himalaya in the *Sunya*. Are ye familiar with it? We especially associate it with Con, our artist friend, an artist in woodcarving, in architecture and in various other forms, who, by now, is perhaps a form-free artist in Life—in Florida Yankeestan of all places. When I played the C-sharp to Noah for the first time, he exclaimed, "It takes us at once into Heaven!" It is true. Daringly, yet maturely, it begins with the slow movement, a brooding, clear and gracious contemplation, as in the prenatal and pre-ego conscious awareness. The rest of the Quartet is rather diffused in many statements (as in ego life), yet with exquisite loveliness and integral beauty, interwoven and broken out in pure joy, in all suffusing *Ananda*, yes, rather like artist Con. But the finale approaches the beginning, and as "heaven lies about us in babyhood," when we trail "clouds of glory from our Home," so also in death we approach and come Home. Our pilgrimage is a homeward journey unto ego death, and even now we are ever free in the Eternity here. Mature reawakening into conscious awareness is all. Ignore-ance is simply unawareness.

Meanwhile, I play on in *Swalila*. Shall I play you the A minor for healing a psychic illness, or after a salutary ego crucifixion? There is profound gratitude, the grace of profound acceptance. There is also the pain of crucifixion that endures and still lingers in memory. It is finally all transcended and all forgiven, aye, accepted as right, inevitable and beautiful. The slow movement in all the four quartets always seems the most movingly lovely, and not least so in A minor. At the end of Aldous Huxley's *Point Counterpoint* is a moving description of the A minor quartet, as a counterpoint to the vulgarity and *asuric* antics and death of Strickland. There is all acceptance.

Then the B flat. Yes, I recognize it as my Self, as integral Consciousness. In the very beginning, there is the brooding acceptance, then the browsing assimilation and finally the emerging in mystic clarity. Above all, the Cavatena was utterly familiar, but also the stately andante, the gay alla danza tedesca, the pure joy of a folk dance—such light, playful *Lila*. Wu! All were accepted and right, except that awful finale (which I hardly ever play, not even by itself). But, as you may know, it is not the real and original finale. The true one is the Grosse Fugue, which later on got its separate opus (133). It was impossible for the egos to accept, and they utterly rejected it. It seems that, for once, Beethoven played down to his audience and substituted in its place any odd thing he had written. Yes, it is Beethovenish, but it is not the finale of the B flat quartet. It is true, the Grosse Fugue is impossible for egos to accept as experience. I was perfectly contented and fulfilled with the Cavatena's finale, playing me out into kindred life. Yes, even after my salutary "death" in Devonshire.

I remember sharing the quartet with Rabindranath Tagore in the "Solar" of Dartington Hall, sharing it in the sense of playing it to him and afterwards giving him the album of records, as he loved the music. What we really love is ours in a sense far deeper than possession, legality and exclusiveness. But the Fugue had not then been recorded and so the Cavatena served as the finale. How like the gracious curves of the Devon hills and the woods in springtime it is! The Grosse Fugue was "accepted," but not liked and not really lived until I came to Himalaya and had died (in ego) more integrally. Here it is, grandly working itself up to the climax of crucial crucifixion and final transfiguration. The immanence is in that transcendence. The Within is also the Beyond. You "go with" the music up and beyond, into silence. You soar and soar on intuitive, uncloyed wings of Light and then find your Self, in *karuna* rhythm and in *Sunya Turiya* Silence, the Self at joyous ease in the All.

The final quartet in F major is the shortest and the most perfectly concentrated. The first statement implies the solution, the solving of all quests and questions. The statement is evolved, revolved and resolved, and then worked through into the marvelously moving slow movement. Then the brief, but vivid and poignant crucifixion, the acceptance of "It must be! *Es musg sein!*" Finally, the transcendence, the simple transfiguration into natural Freedom and Grace, *Mukta Ananda*. How lovely, like Ludvig van Beethoven, to dance finally into Life (or into death) in such gay insouciance, *sans peur et sans souci. Such dolce far niente!* Let's do likewise at joyous ease.

Thus I have played the four quartets to you. Wu!

35 🌿

Who is Wuji?

Sunyata often called himself "Wuji," a reference to his "Self in the invisible Real." It was also the name of his dog whom he originally named Wuti. He explains the meaning of Wuji in the following questions and answers recorded on tape during one of the Friday meetings at Dr. Arwind Vasavada's residence in May, 1980, in Chicago.

Question: *Who is Wuji?*
Sunyata: For 10 years, Sri Wuji was a Himalayan dog (originally named Wuti) and now seems to be a spirit-wu-al or spirited no-thing-ness in the invisible Real—our alter ego, a *Sat* presence, our playmate.

Q: *What is Wuji really like?*
S: Wuji is like no-thing on earth or in heaven. One of his name tags is Sri No-thing-ness.

Q: *Why is there a Wuji?*
S: If God did not exist, he would have to be invented. Likewise, Sri Wuji.

Q: *Where does Wuji live?*
S: Here and now in space-time rhythm.

Q: *When is Wuji going to happen next?*
S: Sri Wuji may not happen as a phenomenon in *Swa lila*. He apperceives Eternity.

Q: *How is Wuji doing?*
S: Sri No-thing-ness Wuji is not a doer. He is an august Presence, simply and purely awake to aware, intuit and apperceive.

Q: *Is Wuji a kind of connection, a process, an event?*
S: Yes.

Q: *Is Wuji a consciousness?*
S: Yes, a playful, impish, sex-free and God-free consciousness, or conscious awareness.

Q: *Is Wuji an angel or a god?*
S: Yes. Both and neither. Wu!

Q: *Does everybody have a Wuji? (or does Wuji have everybody?)*
S: Sri Wuji, Mr. No-thing-ness, is not possessive, nor a possession. "He" innerstands at joyous ease and awarely. He intuits and appreciates, apperceives and is really sex-free, body-free, birth-free and death-free. Wuji is ego-free in non-dual Oneness or Wuness. Wu!

Q: *Is the meaning beyond meaning?*
S: Yes.

Q: *Is Wuji all a big joke?*
S: A Himalayan joke, for in noumena, there is no Wuji.

Q: *Is Wuji something to sell? Can it be purchased? In what marketplace?*
S: No and Wu!

Q: *Is Wuji uncatchable, always just a step ahead or behind?*
S: Yes. He innerstands and also outerstands. He is the beyond that is also within. He is a mirrorization (as we all are).

Q: *Please tell me how to catch the uncatchable, eff the ineffable, seek the unseekable, be the unthinkable. Please tell me why I'm Wuji. I forgot.*
S: Ye are That, Truth is *Sat* already. Wake up in pure awareness. Intuit, apperceive and *be* in Selfhood, Wu-hood. Be Grace-aware, and there will be no questions, no quest and no questioner. Apperceive. "To the pure all is pure." The Self and its shadow are a unity; ego shadow in Sun-Self. Wholify, apperceive, and rejoice in Divine gratitude, says Wuji. Our wordy and worthy play fellow, our impish guardian is one single wordish sound radiating, "*I am that I am.*"

So Wuji is a "no-thing-ness", a silence in and around all manifestations, all phenomena and is also the "I" in the I Ching, the "I" in all phenomena, the "*Swa*" in the cosmic *Lila*. Apperceive *it*—Him—Her as the Androgyne, the Presence.

36

The Wisdom of Sunyata

The following short passages have been extracted from Sunyata's notes and writings.

In deep dream-free sleep, we touch the Source and wake refreshed for the due task in the life play. It is a short death. Body death may be a longer sleep. In deep, dream-free sleep, there is no memory, no sense of ego. We can court this kind of death experiencing à la Ramana Maharshi.

From deep, dream-free sleep, we can awake refreshed for each day's task in the play. The Real is also in the actualities. Eternity is in time. The whole is in the part play; the sea is in the dewdrop and the microcosm (or Christ) is within. It is *Swalila*, a divine Self play.

I happened to be in the body presence of Ramana Maharshi four times, a fortnight each time. I was silent and asked no questions. In fact, I had none worthwhile uttering. I had no inner or outer problems. I asked nothing and craved nothing from the Sage. It was just ego-free sharing in "participation mystique." At the first darshan in 1936, he asked me briefly about mutual friends and about my *sadhana*. At a later darshan, his radiance was focused especially on me when, unexpectedly, his five words stunned me in Silence. "We are always aware, Sunyata!" In all humility, I accepted Maharshi's words as a blessing, recognition, initiation, mantra and name.

Ramana Maharshi called himself no Guru. He was chela-free and did not initiate in the orthodox Hindu mode or fashion. He transmitted spiritual energy by a look, rarely by a touch. The transmission was chiefly in eloquent silence. Pilgrims came to *Arunachala* with innumerable questions, problems, cravings, ambitions and lusts, but in Maharshi's presence, all these were either subdued into Silence or were felt too trivial and petty to be worth uttering. Often, the answers came from within the individual questioner himself. Such was the powerful effect of Maharshi's *Sunya* silence.

With one fragment of my Self, I projected all these universes—I remain! Sri Silence, *Brahman* or *Sunya*. Maturity is all. Awareness is all. We must endure our coming hither and our going hence: Ripeness is all. Be sincere, utterly self honest and stark, as is undressed wood, with no disguise, mask or fancy dress.

Contemplate *Sunya* or *akasha* or your Self until ye become the contemplation, the Awareness, the graceful experiencing—and ye will not be attracted by drugs, tantric tricks, sex lusts or Yogic *tapas* [austerities]. Beyond Yoga and union, there is unity, the unity of all things, that is beyond raptures, coitus, ecstasy and words. Beyond God is the silent Godhead.

Before Abraham was, "I AM!" Be still to aware it in *Karuna* Love and Empathy. Eternity is also in time play and a treasure in the *Invisible Real*. It is all within your Self.

I had a passion for solitude and was not lonely when alone. Actually I was all one in unity and was most fully myself. In this life play I have not been in quest of Guru, God, Truth, Grace, Salvation, nirvana, or power lust, nor I had any guilt complex. I had no ambition to be different from what I *am*. Blessedly, I had escaped headucation, and I was free of any imposed knowledge. I had no property. I did not marry. I did not belong to any clique or creed. I was not attracted by their magnetism. I felt all is within our Self. I had nothing to assert or to resent. Nor I had anything to boast about or to regret. I was fully contented. I had joy in "that which is." Whatever happened was accepted by me in positive passivity, negative capability and intuitive sensibility. It was a "participation mystique" in effort-free empathy. It was this attitude which made me accept the various cults and creeds kindly. I did not condemn them nor did I feel any enthusiasm towards them. I saw many beautiful differences among them. They were different approaches to the goal of one unifying Self.

Silence is the language of the ineffable Real. Sometimes it seems that power and knowledge and efforts to teach are the greatest hindrances to integral wisdom and *Mahakaruna.* "Where is the wisdom we have lost in knowledge? Where is the life we have lost in living?" asks T.S. Eliot. I would say, it is safely within our Self. It is the ego that loses sight of it in its cravings and unholy fuss. The mystics may stutter in all manner of languages. An immature one may even shout an *"Anur Huk"*—I am God, Reality, Truth, the eternal Self—and have his godly head chopped off by the respectable, orthodox brethren.

It is the immature who shout, assert or even try to awaken other fellow pilgrims in consciousness. It is all Bhagwan's business. As Ramana Maharshi states, "There are no others." It is necessary to drop the conceit of agency or ego. Place trust in your destiny. Guidance will come in self-controlled spontaneity.

If anyone says, "I have realized! I am a Mahatmaji," do not trust him. It cannot be truly said in ego terms. We are all Mahatmajis when "we" are not; but only a few are aware of this death and live it. "We are such stuff as dreams are made on, and our brief life is rounded by a sleep." (Shakespeare)

Mere mental beliefs are a hindrance to integral awakening and they must go. "Reason was the helper. Reason is the bar." The helpers are always the intuitive light, *karuna* Love and Empathy. The meaning and aim of Yoga

is union—awareness in the unity of all things—
Satchitananda.

What we are, really are, cannot be expressed and
explained in mental or verbal terms. It is always *neti neti*
[not this–not that]. Even thinking is duality while feeling
awareness can be intuitive, integral.

At one level of consciousness, the ego mind, sex and
duality—with their desires, lusts and fears—reign
supreme. At another level of awareness, they appear
unimportant and cease to matter. In a third mode of
"Being awareness," they cease to exist.

The majority of us cannot imagine existence without the
visible world that surrounds us. In our thinking and feeling, the physical activities are real. Aware and experience
that you are Spirit and that Spirit is time-free, space-
free, sex-free, ego-free and death-free.

When Ramana Maharshi was asked what ashram [which
of the Hindu four stages of life] he belonged to, he said,
"*atyashrami.*" It is beyond the four commonly known
ashrams. There is no restriction for *atyashramis*. They
may do what they please. All depends on *prarabdha*.
Their conduct is not regulated according to any rules or
codes. *Atyashrami* may be called the Fifth Ashram,
though it is really beyond ashram.

Ramana Maharshi was asked how to recognize a Real Guru, *Jnani* or *Maha Rishi*. He stated, "It is not what he teaches or does that can be the real test. It is rather in his being's silent radiance and in the peace, ease and contentment that you feel in his presence."

Ramana Maharshi could say, "I bow down to them first." When asked how he felt regarding the constant stream of devotees who entered the hall and prostrated their bodies, he replied, "How can the partial mind and blinkered egos aware and comprehend the pure, pain-free and ego-free consciousness of a Self-enlightened, Self-radiant Sage who awares and greets him Self in all that happens, in all manifestations? I am equal with the lowest. There is my strength."

If people were to comprehend the real meaning of what they repeat in mantras, rituals and *japa*, they would not need to do all this. How often do you see mantras repeated here? If people were to find out the real meaning and put it into practice, it would be good, but who will do it?

A Christ oriented friend asked Ramana Maharshi, whether, in his present life period, there had been any well-marked stages corresponding to what in Christianity is called "Purgation" and "Unity." Spontaneously and without the least hesitation came the reply. "I know of no such period. I never performed any pranayam [yogic breathing] or *japa*. I knew no mantras.

I had no idea of meditation or concentration. Even when I came to hear of such things later, I was never attracted by them. Even now my mind refuses to pay any attention to them. *Sadhana* implies an object to be gained and a means of gaining it. What is there to be gained which we do not already have or are?"

We all teach best by being what we are. Let us be true to our integral Self in *Swadharma*. As we are being used and led by the Divine, it may well be good to drop our conceit of agency and the swelled ego lust of doership.

Life forms are works of art. It is our task as artists in life to fulfill our individual Dharma and to realize our Universal Self. Our tools and our urges first go outwards. By nourishing the inner seed of immortality, we can open our intuitive eye and see aware where and what we are.

"What is sin?" Nisargadatta Maharaj says, "All that hinders (our awakening into conscious Self awareness)." Wuji answers, "Ignorance, Unawareness and ego blinkers."

Ramana Maharshi was crucified in a cancered body, yet we cannot imagine him resenting this, much less crying out, "My God! Why hast thou forsaken me?" There was no "Me."

By being aware of the perfection of the Spiritual "I," all we will ever need is attracted to us, without any interference on our part. This is the miracle of Life. We do not have to reason or to plan when we are in conscious oneness with the infinite we call nature. We learn to rely on the invisible perfection of Being Awareness Grace, That thou art.

Maturity is in the fullness of time. It is like the rosebud, the baby chick and the butterfly. They cannot be forced to sprout before their time. It happens spontaneously and naturally.

When we pray, "Thy Will Be Done", do we comprehend that this implies an act of total surrender? Truth is utterly simple, but our minds complicate things endlessly. Live spontaneously. Light is, but until we aware and remember to press the switch, we shall remain in darkness. Through awareness, we press the switch, "Let there be Light." We do not make the Light. The Light is already there.

We, as humans, are merely inhabitants of this dream world, this realm of illusions. And we gradually awaken to the truth of our Being. Awareness is all. The spiritual "I" of you, Infinite Wisdom, already knows. All a Guru can do is to help you to become awake and aware.

Human love is a product of the mind and is transitory, as is everything in duality. It relates to ego. However, human love has its place, as does everything else, in the illusion world—and all experiences are for the growth and eventual awakening. Because the finite mind cannot comprehend the infinite, sometimes it can be helpful to have a "master," a Guru teacher, to guide and direct one along the way..

Although a Guru is perhaps more enlightened and more mature, he or she is, nevertheless, a personality as you and I. When we aware the infinite wisdom, then we no longer need a mediator. The Real Guru is ever within ourselves. It is our Self.

What we think of as power in the world of duality is part of the illusion and, in truth, does not exist. The only power there is is God's.

The Patriarch Hue Neng truly said that as far as Buddha nature (or Christ consciousness) is concerned, there is no difference between an enlightened man and an ignorant one. What makes the seeming differential to egos is that the one is awake to aware the light, while the other is not.

The intuitive *Prajna* wisdom-light guides every human, mortal ego soul that comes into this world of weal and suffering. Accept and enjoy all, one's suffering and trials, as privileges. It is not the outer travels or doings that matter most, but rather our integral Being, richly awake in the inner realms of conscious awareness.

We can aware the meaning of existence "without looking out of a window, without going out of the door." It is insight and aware innerstanding that matters.

The didactic and erudite St. Thomas Aquinas did not complete his voluminous *Summa*. After his mystic experience in the ineffable, he declined to comply with beseechings, prayers and desires of his dear ones. He refused to add any more word symbols, in intellectual or emotional verbosity, to the edification and salvation of the poor egos. "Blessed are the Poor in spirit."

Plato and Mencius contend that all wisdom is Self-recollection. It is inherent, while mere knowledge is acquired; it is derived mentally and is imposed.

Jacob Boehme, the simple German cobbler, could write, "When thou canst throw thy ego into *That*, where no creature dwelleth, though it be but for a moment, then the inherent, integral and silent wisdom will discover, or uncover, its Self in Self-radiant, conscious awareness." We are that Awareness—Spirit, full, concrete No-thingness, the integral experiencing, says Wuji. God to him is not an object or a vision or even an experience outside the Self. It is in Thee. Seek and find ye first this inherent and integral realm of Grace within. Then ye will aware it everywhere for the within is also the beyond.

St. Augustine tells us, "I went wandering like a distracted sheep seeking Thee with anxious reasoning without, whilst Thou wast within me. I went round the streets and squares of the city of the world seeking Thee and found Thee not, because in vain, I sought without that which is within. "

Let ego-consciousness, duality awareness and the sense of identity go. Just be free *in* It. All the becoming, evolution and powerful *shakti* business pertain to ego-conscious, mental or emotional "I" fuss. Be still and clear to transcend it and aware intuitively the omnipresent integral Self everywhere.

Hate is as binding as is possessive love. "Love your enemies" and "Resist no evil." Our attitude towards seeming evil must be free from hatred. A continual denunciation of evil and its agents merely encourages its power in the world and in our consciousness. Ego is the enemy to be accepted and loved and used graciously, so that we may be free in it.

Blessed are the Poor in Spirit; they aware God. Meister Eckhart says, "As long as ye desire to fulfill the will of

God and have any desires besides Eternity and God, so long are ye not truly poor. He alone has true spiritual poverty who wills nothing, knows nothing and desires nothing." Such poverty is a blessed freedom from the blinkered ego conceit of agency. The Will is ever being done, so Sri Wuji does not pray like "May it be done." He also "awares" that Eternity, God, Grace or Self-hood is here and now. Awareness is all.

The historical accuracy of Joshua ben Joseph, or ben Miriam, or how many angels can balance on a pinpoint, are not very important truths. The Holy Ghost, or ghostly whole, rarely overshadows our Gurujis, Pandits, Pharisees and Masterjis. There are so many petty squabbles among learned and erudite egos—over immaculate conceptions, abstractions and other important trifles! "Imaginary geese in imaginary bottles" and "learned ignorance," says Wuji. Just experience your God, Christ, ego death, Integrality or Eternity, and ye will fuss less, talk less and perhaps *be* more. In integral awareness, there is no conceit of agency and nothing to criticize, argue about or dispute. Egoji is the enemy to be acepted, loved and transcended, in affectionate detachment and Self-controlled spontaneity.

Yes, Guru Wuji is queer and original, or so he seems to ordinary respectable ego souls. He does not indulge in *tapas*, in *asanas* or in *samadhis*. There is no sin complex or superiority complex in his play. His *sahaja* contemplation is a natural spirituality and it suffices. He does not meditate nor does he concentrate on his navel, his solar plexus or his Shiva eye, and he has no use for ritual, prayers, *shakti* business or any other ego power antics. In Nature and in Solitude, there is easy ego-freeness. Aloneness to him can be All-one-ness. In *Advaita* awareness, ego vanishes and I *am* the contemplation, the inherent, integral grace, so who is there to pray to? And what for? Who can be grateful enough—for Grace? he asks, and his answer is "Wu Wei Wu!"

We may learn from the terrible chaos of modern civilization. Huxley calls it "original insanity."

Learning is not insight. Knowledge is not wisdom. Sages never quarrel or argue but rejoice in the inner self-revealing silence.

The love of Jesus for the fellow human beings made him suffer and die for them (three years—and three agonizing hours). The *mahakaruna* compassion of Buddha made him live for the world forty years after his self illumination. That is the price one has to pay in ego life. Pure love and compassion invite vicarious suffering and Atonement. It is still better to perform one's own *dharma*, though the doing be devoid of excellence, than to perform the duty of another well. Be and let others be. Since there are no others essentially, it would be better to leave off trying to save others and not to fuss about their wrongdoing.

Give not way to prattling speech, but remain in silence. The holy chosen teachings are polluted by impiety, so seek ye solitude.

Appearances external and the mind are one. Shatter then your theory of duality and plurality. Since birth and death are themselves pairs of natural illusory opposites, mere phenomenal appearances—becoming and "be-going" cast upon the screen of time—they too are the voidness, 'sunyata'.

"Oh child of Eternity," sings Milarepa, "waste not thy time in vain talk with the multitude, who seek only to attain the aims and ends of *samsaric* existence, but at once, dedicate all thy bodies and activities to serve thy Unitive Self harmoniously."

"He who sees Jehovah dies" means, in Self-awareness, ego vanishes. Unless a grain of corn falleth into the ground, its fulfillment is not attained.

Eternity was manifest in the light of day. Life is a pure flame, and we live by an invisible Sun within us.

Thomas Traherne was one of the rare psyches or born mystics. God to him was the word (the word made flesh) but he was also beyond. His poem "Silence" reveals his mystic effort-free contemplation.

"A quiet, silent person may possess all that is great and high in blessedness. The inward work is the supreme, for all the other is occasioned by the fall. A man that seemeth idle to the view of others may the greatest business do." This is the mystic, strife-free, effort-free, contemplation, the real action in inaction and the awareness of inaction in activities. Traherne is no escapist but he knows the higher, fuller acceptance.

Mystics do not study mysticism: They live it. They experience God and if they explain it, it is by the way. The mystic's experience is intuitive and reason cannot explain it.

External authority becomes stiffened, institutional and traditional. Rationalism becomes exaggerated and overemphasized. Emotion becomes sentimental, swollen and misused. Love becomes sticky or descends into pity. Religion becomes a thought system or a perennial philosophy. Realize that the wisdom of God is in thy heart. It is there as a speaking word of God in thy soul. As soon as thou art ready to hear, this eternal speaking word will speak wisdom and love!

The average human being, whose soul is scarcely awake, operates from the ego. The ego is a powerful center built up through many lifespans. He calls it "I." Beliefs and thoughts are of the mind and of duality, while trust, faith and intuition is of the heart. Faith does not rely on the mind's belief but uses the heart's intuitive feelings as its guide. The intuitive Light reveals Reality. "Though he slays me, yet I will trust him. The Lord gives, the Lord takes, the Lord's name be praised." So said old Job, who had boils, sores and calamities galore. Whatever happens is Dharmic Law and All Rightness.

Through these three centuries, countless Englishmen have shown us courage, honor and justice. But hardly one missionary or official has shown us the grace of their Jesus Christ. Until you can show me your peace, I will not believe in your victory. It is not energy or power that proves wholeness or grace. Your padres pray that the grace of their Lord Jesus Christ may rest upon them and their devotees. But that Grace does not rest upon them in their Life Play among us.

A man, who had fulfilled the Jewish Law, asked the Master Jesus (or at that time Joshua ben Joseph), "What is my next step?" And he was told, "Sell all that thou hast, and give to the poor, not for their sake, but for your own." The rich man went away sadly. He had many possessions and much attachment to them. Another man, who wanted to go and bury his father was told by Joshua, "Let the dead bury their dead." Come and be among the living, the awakened ones.

Krishna Prem, in my presence, answered someone who asked, "Shall I renounce the ego world?" "If there is any doubt about it, don't." Similarly, a rich man came to Siddhartha Gautama Buddha saying, "Would it not be better if I got rid of my possessions?" Seeing that he was perfectly sincere, Buddha said unto him, "He that is attached to wealth had better cast it away than allow his heart to be possessed by it. But he who does not cleave to wealth and who, possessing riches, uses them rightly, will be a blessing to his fellow men. I say to thee, remain in thy station in life and give thyself with diligence to thy enterprises. It is not life and wealth and power that enslaves men but their attachment to life, wealth and power."

We can be clearly aware that non-attachment is not the same as indifference. Affectionate detachment includes appreciation and love and co-passion. Christ showed appreciation of nature and of people around him. He appreciated the simplicity and beauty of life, the birds, the air, the grass, the fields, the ordinary task of the sower, the reaper and homely housewife. He was, however, not attached.

Christ went into contemplation and is reported to have prayed, "If it is the cosmic will, let the cup of suffering pass by," but who heard him pray thus in solitude? The three disciples were asleep. Who heard his cry from the ego cross, "My God! My God! Why has thou forsaken me?" Was there still a "me"? It is Joshua, the body mind, that is crucified, not Christ. Spiritual suffering is a contradiction in term symbols.

A new dimension in consciousness is needed for an integral experiencing far beyond that of reasoning. "Reason was the helper. Reason is the bar," a hindrance to the zero experience, the non-dual awareness.

"Silence is the language of the Real," say Wuji and Ramana Maharshi. The mature mystic is not impressed by overt or covert terms of abuse or praise.

Around us is a mist encompassing ages of thought. We call it knowledge, civilization, progress and educated learning. But "Life" is hidden to us in that mist. The simple is made complex. The easy is made difficult. The mystery is mocked or ignored. What is Self-revealed is explained away.

Wonders are blurred in the dust of common fuss, in the mist of wordiness and in the ego muddles of fellow pilgrims. How few of the fellow pilgrims we meet are thought-free, carefree and consciously aware in integral unity beyond the domain of mere thought!

In the intuitive wisdom beyond knowledge, all things are alive and divine. There is no difference between the outer sun and the inner light. All is holy Being. The essence is bliss and grace and the ease of Being. The Real Presence is joyous; it is a moment to moment unfolding.

God nods to God from within each of us. In all moments of time, I am aware of the Eternal. I am also aware of the Eternal in fellow pilgrims and can know everything by identity with it.

Yes, queer things happen in the touch of the integral, the eternal, the living Godhead. Only very mature egos dare the existential leap into the unknowable.

Aware the Self that you ever Are, in All (forms), and you'll not be attached to the forms and the changing play. You will not cling to your body and the conceit of agency. "Fool that I was to call anything Mine, Me or I."

Lao Tzu begins his *Tao Teh* with the statement, "The Tao, which can be told or asserted, expressed or explained, is not the real Tao." Gautama Buddha, freshly awakened from ego values and from what ye call life, into conscious Buddhahood, begins his discourse thus, "O Amitaya! Measure not in words what is immeasurable. Sink not the string of thoughts into the fathomless. Who asks doth err. Who answers errs too. Say naught." Sage Dakshinmurti and Maharshi Ramana taught and transmitted to the pandits, peasants and the fellow *rishis* in mature, self-radiant, eloquent Silence that "*Sunya* Silence is our real Nature." Any ego assertion or willful effort mars and blurs, veils and hides our Self awareness, our living integrality.

Thomas Traherne wrote: "Those pure and virgin apprehensions, I had from the womb, and that divine light
wherewith I was born are the best unto this day. In
grace, they attended me into the world and by grace I
remember them till now. All things abided eternally as
they were in their proper places and due interrelatedness. Eternity was manifest in the light of the day. The
streets, temples, people, skies were mine, and so were
the moon and the stars, all the world was mine. I knew
no churlish proprieties, nor bounds, nor divisions, but all
treasures and the possessors of them! But after much
ado, I was corrupted and made to learn the dirty devices
of this world, which now I unlearn and become as it
were, a little child again, that I may re-enter consciously
the 'realm of grace'."

He was one of the rare, born mystics in whom
infancy seemed a most blessed state because it was freed
from all impediments of the senses that had not yet
awakened. Infancy was, to him, face to face with the
world's beauty, rightness, perfection and eternity.

Not "Thy Will be done," but the awareness that *it* is ever
being done, whether egos will it or not. This is the state
of prayer in the unitive life in and beyond Yoga and
Union.

My term symbols such as innerstanding and mind-free-
ness are not scholarly, but a simple carefree fool can play
in words and can step immunely where angels and erudition fear to tread.

Seek ye first, foremost and essentially, the inner integral realm of Grace. Experience it maturely and abidingly in conscious awareness and all the other things (or *dharmas*) will naturally be added unto you.

The word symbol "Father" to me seems half and incomplete without the better half, "Ma." I prefer to substitute it with the word Source, Ground, *Alaya* [God], *Sunya*, as more integral.

Maharshi Ramana lived and died in public with no privacy in forty years of ministry among egos. There was no assertive egoji in him to obtrude or intrude or usurp. The ego in him had duly died in the 17 year young body, and vanished in the young years of *mouna* [silence] in the cave of Siva's heart *Arunachala*. All the same, Ramanaji did function in the bodies—free of them as in egojies. He died from them in public, and during the last few years he endured the parasitic vampire called sarcoma, malignant bouncing cancer, but did he ever whimper or falter or falsely identify the supreme self awareness with his bodies and their due pains?

Suffering like God, Death and Self is a mystery to egojies, but suffering is an open secret in integral life experiencing state of consciousness. Fyodor Dostoevesky makes quite a cult of suffering, as Freudians do of sex. I remember a scene in Paris, where old serene Father Zosima suddenly plunged prostrate before the flighty and body vigorous Dmitri saying, *"Je salute ta grande suf-*

ferance a venir." [I salute the great suffering which is coming to you.] We cannot successfully court suffering or our deaths, but we can greet them and accept them calmly and politely when they duly come upon us. Perhaps we can divine and intuit, sniff and smell, when they are due in us, as also when they are due in our fellow pilgrims. T.S. Eliot's "Journey of the Magi" ends not with a whimper but with a calm, "I should be glad of another death."

In ego stillness, there is the *advaita* Be-ness; the freedom of no desire, no conceit of doership. The "I," the "Me," and the "Mine" simply vanish in wonder and glad gratitude.

It is not knowledge but Silence that is the mode of wisdom. We get as much from reading the *Rig Vedic* "Hymn to Creation" and find verbosity and intellectual spinning utterly tiresome. In the 1930s when Krishna Prem was writing his excellent comments on the *Katha Upanishad*, I remember asking him, "Why do we write?" and his answer was, "We write to our Self—and then we have to clear up the mess." Yes, we write to our Self—to clarify our self to our Self—and we often make a mess and semantic muddle of our attempts. The Self may prefer Silence to our verbosity. Words often falsify the word.

"With one fragment of My Self, I projected all these universes and multiverses. I remain," says Sri Silence. The word became flesh and wordiness and only in poetry paradoxes and *Sunya* Silence do we get nearest to the word-free Word. "In the beginning was the Word and the Word was with God and the Word was God." And beyond God is the Godhead.

We are neither the body nor the mind, but we are pure consciousness. Mature awakening into abiding conscious awareness is all. So do not control the mind (who is the controller?) but transcend it thought-freely. Thinking is always a duality while intuitive feelings can be of unity and grace awareness. Meister Eckhart and Angelus Selenius often speak of the birth or awakening of Emmanuel, the in-dwelling Christ-consciousness. "If Christ a thousand times in Bethlehem were born and not within thyself, it is forlorn."

A *Jnani* [an enlightened being] is beyond the perceptual and conceptual, beyond the so called "pairs of opposites"; beyond the categories of time and space, names and shapes. He is neither the perceived nor the perceiver, but the simple and universal factor that makes perceiving possible.

Just as an unborn child cannot know life after birth for there is no mind to form a valid picture, so is the mind unable to think of the Real in terms of the unreal except by negation—not this, not that, *neti neti*. The acceptance of the unreal as the Real is the obstacle. To see the false as false and abandon the obstacle brings Reality into Being Awareness; it is a state of utter clarity, immense love and absolute fearlessness.

Every grain of sand is God, is the Self in that form. To awaken, to aware and to experience it, is important.

Nothing can happen to us that does not intrinsically belong to us. Do I not choose myself all my destinies since Eternity?

Eternity is here and now within and around us. It is time-free and thought-free and immeasurable. In it we live and move and have our being in affectionate awareness, grace and joyous ease.

Silence is the self-radiant language of the Real.

Self, being the root of Being-Consciousness-Grace, imparts reality to whatever one perceives. This imparting of Reality takes place invariably in the *now* because the past and the future are only in the mind. Being appears to the *now* only. Time is a mental concept. A *Jnani* is time-free, age-free, ego-free and, of course, death-free and carefree. The world that one thinks of is in one's mind.

When the mind has become pure and luminous, the body too must partake in this luminous nature. This is the reason for the radiation which emanates from all saints and the enlightened ones, the aura which surrounds them and which has been perceived, described and depicted in all religions. The radiation is visible only to the intuitive clairvoyant or spiritual eye. In ego surrender, the lights of wisdom and *karuna* are united.

Christianity is one way of putting words together and Hinduism is another. The Real is behind and beyond words—incommunicable direct experience—explosive in its effect on the mind. It is easily awared when nothing else is wanted. The unreal is created by imagination and perpetuated by desires. Remove the verbiage, and what remains? Truth, Reality and Self remain. Our real home is in the unchangeable, which appears to be a state of constant reconciliation of and integration of opposites.

When "God" on Mt Sinai was importuned by Moses regarding *Sat* name (the Truth), the answer came thundering forth, "Je-ho-vah." "*I am that I am.*"

Christ is our Self, the in-dwelling unitive Em-manu-el. Be aware of the intuitive light that leadeth and guideth every human mortal ego soul that cometh into the Maya *Lila* Self interplay. It is divine, graceful *Swalila*. Be divinely selfish and aware your Self—the Self—everywhere.

Cultivate love, trust, and ego humility. You live that you may learn to love; you love that you may learn to live.

Behind our persona mask or the personal self or ego lies another Self. The world sees only a superficial mask we show. The real Self lives in the depths of our hearts. An ancient seer in the *Upanishads* descibes it as "unseen but seeing, unheard but hearing, unperceived but perceiving, unknown but knowing." This is thy Self, the ruler within, the immortal.

Things are as they are. It is all *swalila*. We only fit in. Our part is to live spontaneously in the *now* without judgment, without concern for our destiny, without looking for compassion, rewards, answers or recognition. We should let the cosmic will be done in and through us.

We may think we pull and push, but the reality is otherwise. It is we, as persons, who are being pushed and pulled, used and guided—constantly. We may well drop our ego conceit of agency and will. All is in perfect harmony.

What we call yesterday is but a memory and what we call tomorrow is but a dream. Neither exists in truth. There is only *now*, the eternal now which forever is. Start *now*, right here where you are, letting go the burden of the so called past and the anxieties of the so called future. Only by living totally in the present can we be in harmony. When we are living in the *now*, we are letting God (Self) live through us, we are being lived. We need not strive for anything to plan our lives. The past and the future are but illusions.

By letting go of the personal will and, in its place, allowing the Divine will to live its life through us, everything we need will present itself at the proper time. When we pray "Thy will be done," do we comprehend that this implies an act of total surrender?

It is the mode of Tao, the rhythm of *karuna* love, the intuitive *Prajna* light that reveals our spirituality. Likewise, Maharshi Ramana's ego search for the Source and healing integrality "Who am I?" and Anandamayee Behn's "There is but the non-dual one," Ramdas' "childlike joy and *japa* yoga"—all are the *sahaja* directness, the unlearned, inherent wisdom of grace in integrality. It is the song of the self-radiant Silence—that is our simple, mystic, cosmic and integral Self.

Whether things we attain in the life play or things we miss—everything is acceptable to a mystic. For him, everything is right. It is all acceptance to the life play. He is, in a real sense, loving it, awaring and loving Self in all things, phenomena and happenings.

"The 'One' remains. The 'Many' change and pass. Heaven's light forever shines. Earth shadows fly. Ego life, like a dome of many colored stars, stains the white light of Eternity."

A noble lady asked her husband, who was a seer in the *Upanishads*, "What is it that one has to find, and once having found nothing else remains to be sought?" Sunyata says, "It is nothing you find or achieve, attain or become. You simply, naturally and maturely wake up in conscious integral awareness of what *is* and what you ever *are*."

Love pervades everything. All conflicts and sufferings are like surface waves upon the quiet ocean depth.

Glossary

Acharya—Teacher

Advaita—Non-dualism; the doctrine of monism in Vedanta. Reality is the One that appears as the Many. The One alone is real. The Many or the phenomenal existence is an illusion, like mistaking rope for a snake at night.

Agni—God of Fire

Ahamkara—Ego; the individuating principle responsible for the limitation, division and variety in the manifest world. Egoself appears and disappears and is transitory, whereas the real Self is permanent. Though one is actually the true Self, one wrongly identifies the real Self with the ego self.

Ahimsa—The principle of nonviolence

Ajnana—Absence of spiritual knowledge; ignorance

Akas(h)a—Ether as an element of space. Akasa is the intangible material substance that pervades the whole universe

Alaya—Source of Being; God

Amma—Mother

Ananda—Bliss; one of the three attributes of the Ultimate Principle: *Sat-chit-ananda*

Anatta—A term in Buddhism meaning non self; self in Buddhism is the empirical self (equivalent to ego), which is unreal and is an essential obstacle to the realization of Nirvana

Anubhava—Direct inner experience; any degree of mystical experience

Anur Huk—I am God

Ardhnari—Half woman image of Shiva

Arunachala—Holy mountain located in Tiruvanamalai in the state of Tamil Nadu, India; seat of Ramana Maharshi's Ashram.

Asana—Seat or posture

Ashram(a)—A place where hermits and sages live. Also one of the four stages of Hindu life: Brahamcharya (celibacy), Griharstha (married life), Vanaprastha (wandering life), Sannyasa (life of total renunciation).

Asuric—Term used to refer to the "dark forces", equivalent to the Devil or evil in Western culture.

Atman—The supreme Self. The ultimate identity of the Self with the universal Self, established by the great utterances "I Am That."

Atmavichar—The "who am I" technique of inquiry into the Self

Atyashrami—Beyond the four commonly known *ashrams*; not bound by any rules or restrictions

Avadhuta—An enlightened person

Avatar—Descent of a deity in human form

Behnji—Respected sister

Behovely—Necessary

Bhagavad Gita—A Hindu scripture said to embody the essence of Hindu teachings

Bhagwan, Bhagvan, Bhagavan—Literally, "holy, the exalted one"; epithet for God

Bodhi—Enlightenment

Bodhisattva—An enlightened being in Buddhism

Bodhisattva Avalokiteshwara—Embodies two fundamental components of Buddhism, compassion and wisdom

Brahma—Creator of the universe

Brahmacharya—A celibate; a student

Brihadarnayaka Upanishad—A work that teaches absolute identity between atman and *Brahman*.

Brahman—The Absolute; Supreme Being; also priestly caste in India

Brindavan—A place near Mathura where Krishna spent his youth and played with the gopis, the cowherding maidens; symbolic of divine play of the soul with the Lord; also spelled Vrindavan

Chakra—System of energy centers in the human body

Chela—Disciple

Chit or Cit—Consciousness. Pure consciousness has no subjects or objects; it is only the awareness of Being.

Consumatum—Fulfillment

Consumatum est—It is fulfilled

Darshan—Vision, sight. The guru or any realized man gives darshan and the devotee or the audience receives it.

Devas—Celestial beings

Dharma—Righteousness: totality of duties enjoined by religion

Dhyana—Meditation; contemplation

Dhyana Buddhism—Pertains to schools of Buddhism including Zen, which have their main emphasis on meditation to realize enlightenment

Diksha—Initiation from a Guru by look, word or touch.

Egoji—Sunyata uses this word when referring to those of us who identify as individual selves in the phenomenal world. Ji is added as a term of respect.

Ganga(s)—Holy river in India

Gauri Shankar—Half woman images of Shiva in which the body is female of the left and male on the right.

Ghee—Clarified butter

Gita—See Bhagavad Gita

Griharstha—Householder

Gur—Sticky brown sugar

Guru—A spiritual master

Haimavati—Descended from the Himalayas

Havan—A Vedic ritual ceremony

Innerstand—Intuitive understanding, as opposed to the purely mental 'understanding'. Sunyata's term symbol as a substitute for understanding.

Ishwara—God; the Supreme Being in His aspect of Lord of the world

Japa—Repetition of the name of God or any form of mantra

Jijimuge—Unimpeded mutual interpenetration; from the Japanese, meaning ji (thing) and muge (interdiffusion)

Jiva—The individual soul;

Jiva Yatra—The soul's journey

Jivan Mukti—A state of liberation while still in the body

Jnana—Knowledge of the Self; Intuitive perception of the absolute Reality

Jnani—An enlightened Being

Kailash—Desire freeness

Kala—Time

Karma—There are three kinds of karmas: (i) *prarabdha* (fixed), part of one's karma to be worked out in this life; (ii) sancita (accumulated karmas of all the previous lives); (iii) Agami (karma that is being created now to bear fruit in future births).

Karma yogi—The spiritual path of action; non-identification as the doer of the action

Karuna—Compassion

Khayala—An intuitive, psychic emrgence; a spontaneous urge

Koran—The Holy Book of Islam

Krishna—An incarnation of Vishnu who reveals the great teachings of the Vedas and Upanishads embodied in the Bhagavad Gita

Kumbha Mela —Biggest religious fair of *sadhus* in India, celebrated every 12 years at Allahabad, Hardwar, Nasik, Ujjain

Kundalini—Dormant spiritual energy in every human being

Kwan Yin or *Kannon*—Godess of Mercy

Lakshmi—Consort of Vishnu, goddess of fortune

Laya—Merging, dissolution. A trance like state in which the mind is held in abeyance

Lila or *Swalila*—Divine Play of God in the Cosmos

Mahakaruna—Divine love and pity-free, possessive free compassion

Mahant—Head Priest of a Hindu Temple

Maha Rishi—A variant spelling of *Maharshi*

Mahatma—A great soul

Maharshi—A great sage; a seer of Truth

Mandala—A diagram constructed of squares and circles, symbolic representation of cosmic forces

Mantra—Sacred words of powers memorized for meditation; often bestowed by the Guru at the time of initiation

Mathura—Birthplace of Krishna near Delhi

Maya—Illusive power that veils Reality. It is a term of Vedanta philosophy denoting ignorance obscuring the vision of Reality. It is a cosmic illusion in which the One appears as the Many, the Absolute as the relative

Maya Lila—The Divine Play

272 ◆ *Dancing with the Void*

Moksa—Liberation from worldly existence through knowledge of ultimate reality; the sole aim of the spiritual aspirant

Mouna—Silence; a thought free state of undisturbed peace and total stillness

Mudra—A position of the hand; the index finger is covered by the thumb and the other three fingers are extended

Muni—A liberated being

Muni—Saint; ascetic; sage

Nama—names of God

Nataraj—Shiva as cosmic dancer. His cosmic dance depicts destruction, creation and maintenance.

Neti-Neti—Not this, not that

Nirgun—Without attributes

Nirvana—Dissolution of ego in the supreme void; the Goal of Life, according to Buddhism; synonym for *moksa*

Nirvakalpa—The highest state of concentration in which the soul loses all sense of being different from the universal Self; but temporary state from which there is a return to ego-consciousness

Om—The most sacred word of the Vedas; symbol of the personal God and the Absolute

Paramahansa—A *sannyasin* who has attained self-realization

Paramatma (Param Atman)—Supreme Self

Plenum Void—The full emptiness

Prajna—Wisdom; mystic insight

Prajnana—Full consciousness

Prana—The vital breath in a physical body which sustains life is its manifestation

Pranayam—Technique of breath control; part of Yoga system of Patanjali

Pranam—salutation

Prarabdha—Part of one's past deeds, the fruit of which is being reaped in this life. The *prarabdha* cannot be avoided

Puja—Ceremonial worship with flowers, water, and camphor

Purana—Hindu holy book; contains stories of the gods

Purnam—Perfect

Purusha—Original Eternal Person

Radha—Playmate of Krishna, the best known gopi of Vrindavan

Ramanashraman—The *ashram* in Tiruvanamalai, South India, that grew up around Ramana Maharshi

Rishi—A seer or sage

Sabda—Word

Sadhaka—A spiritual seeker

Sadhana—Spiritual practices

Sadhu—Ascetic; spiritual seeker

Sahaja—Natural

Sahasrara—The higest chakra, located at the top of the skull

Shakti—Power, strength

Samadhi—Profound meditation; the final stage in Yoga in which a state of superconsciousness is attained by direct experience of the Self

Samagri—incense powder

Samata—Sameness

Sangam—Outdoor temple

Samsara—The unenlightened world of relativity one encounters in day to day life, responsible for the cycle of birth, death and rebirth

Samsaric—wordly

Samskars—Innate tendencies; the effects of karma

Shankar—A celebrated teacher of the 8th century, who advocated the doctrine of nondualism—*advaita*. He founded four monastries in India: Sringeri in the south, Badrinath in the north, Puri in the east, and Dwarka in the West

Sannyasin—A spiritual adept who has completely renounced worldly desires and duties

Sarasvati—Goddess, patron of art and learning, who became Brahma's consort

Sat—Being or Truth

Sat-chit-ananda—Being Awareness Grace was how it was translated by Sunyata, but generally translated as Being Consciousness Bliss

Satsang—True speech; meeting of spiritual aspirants for the purpose of 'awaring' Truth

Satvic—Pure Shakti energy or force

Satya—Truth

Shakti—Power, energy or force

Shakti business—Term often used by Sunyata to denote power play by individuals or religious sects supposedly teaching spirituality but actually lacking spiritual qualities

Shastras—Scriptures; sacred books or compositions of divine authority

Shivoham—Mantra of Shiva meaning "I am Shiva"

Shraddha—Faith

Siddhis or *siddhic*—Occult powers

Sivaratri—A day of celebration of Shiva's Light

Srutis—Revealed texts of Hindus. The Vedas and the Upanishads constitute the srutis

Sthithaprajna—Established in Wisdom

Suddha Manas—Pure stillness; no thoughts.

Sufi—A saintly person with no worldly desires, primarily in the Islamic faith.

Sunyata—Void; full solid emptiness; No-thing-ness

Sutras—Scriptures

Svabhava—Behavior

Swa—Self directed, automatic

Swadharma—God's will; carrying of one's own assigned duties in life

Swalila—The divine Play that moves on by itself in accordance with the law of karma

Swarupa—Nature; real form

Tantra—Tantras are known as revelations in conformity with the revelations of the Vedas. They are divided

Wei Wu Wei—Sunyata's own way of referring to God, usually as an exclaimation.

Wu—Both yes and no simultaneously

Wuji—Sunyata often speaks of himself as "Wuji," referring to his "Self." It is also the name of Sunyata's dog, whose original name was Wuti

Wu Ha Da!—Sunyata's term symbol while making a lighthearted, witty point in his writings

Yab-yum—Refers to the statue of the male and female joined together

Yin yang—Two polar energies, the cause of continuous change in the universe

Yoga—Union with the Supreme Being

Yoga Sutras—classical text of Patanjali on Yoga

Yogi—practioner of Yoga

M-21

THE PATH OF THE MOTHER — *Savitri L. Bess*
The Path of the Mother introduces us to a divinity who is at once masculine and feminine, creator and transformer, the all-loving Mother and the true, realized human Self. This inspiring book traces her myriad faces—compassionate, fierce, challenging—in male and female deities of many religions.

ISBN: 81-7822-136-5

CAN YOU LISTEN TO A WOMAN — *David Forsee*
In Can You Listen to a Woman, the author interweaves his life with Swami Radha's, inviting you to be present in their most intimate moments of joy, support and challenge. A remarkable story of a spiritual journey along with one of the West's foremost women yogis, Swami Sivananda Radha, whose wisdom and freedom flows like a clear mountain stream throughout the book.

ISBN: 81-7822-112-8

COLLISION WITH THE INFINITE— *Suzanne Segal*
This is an autobiography of a young Jewish woman from the Midwest coming to terms with the powerful transformation despite the mind's relentless attempts to pathologize it, the experience ultimately blossoming into a full Self Realization. This book provides a context and a companion for those whose destiny it is to experience the emptiness of personal self thrusting itself to the foreground in unimaginable ways.

ISBN: 81-7822-113-6

MOTHER OF ALL — *Richard Schiffman*
It is the compelling story of a great mystic. Mother Anasuya Devi of Jillellamudi revered by millions in southern India powerfully challenged traditional patriarchal views and rejected the common Hindu belief that the world is an illusion.
A magnificent portrayal of a very great human, contemporary and timeless, a unique expression of God's being in the world.

ISBN: 81-7822-114-4